DISCARD

	DATE DUE		

PEOPLE
BEFORE
PROFIT

ALSO BY CHARLES DERBER

The Pursuit of Attention

Power in the Highest Degree

What's Left?

The Nuclear Seduction (with William Schwartz)

Professionals As Workers

The Wilding of America

Corporation Nation

PEOPLE

THE NEW GLOBALIZATION IN AN AGE OF

BEFORE

TERROR, BIG MONEY, AND ECONOMIC CRISIS

PROFIT

CHARLES DERBER

ST. MARTIN'S PRESS ♒ NEW YORK

To my mother, Zelda T. Derber,
who taught me that love ages beautifully

www.stmartins.com

Library of Congress Cataloging-in-Publication Data

Derber, Charles.
    People before profit : the new globalization in the age of terror, big
money, and economic crisis / Charles Derber.—1st ed.
        p. cm.
    ISBN 0-312-30669-5
    1. International economic integration—Political aspects. 2.
Globalization—Political aspects. 3. Democracy. I. Title.
    HF1418.5 .D47 2002
    337—dc21
                                                    2002008065

First Edition: December 2002

10   9   8   7   6   5   4   3   2   1

R 0178557111

CONTENTS

ACKNOWLEDGMENTS   vii

INTRODUCTION: 911 GLOBE   1

1   GLOBALIZATION'S GHOSTS   23

2   THREE MYTHS   35

3   ONE WORLD UNDER BUSINESS   59

4   THE AMERICAN UMPIRE   80

5   THE WTO AND THE CONSTITUTION   105

6   THE UN, THE BARBERSHOP,   127
    AND GLOBAL DEMOCRACY

7   A GLOBAL NEW DEAL   143

8   PEOPLE POWER   170

9   SLEEPLESS IN SEATTLE   199

10 GLOBAL DEMOCRACY AS ANTITERRORISM   234

EPILOGUE: WHAT TO DO RIGHT NOW   271

NOTES   285

INDEX   308

ACKNOWLEDGMENTS

I ACKNOWLEDGE WITH GRATITUDE AND APPRECIATION THE MANY PEOPLE who contributed to this book. I offer special thanks to Ralph Nader and Noam Chomsky for their extraordinary intellectual inspiration and support. Many thanks also to David Korten, who generously helped me develop and refine my vision in the final draft of the manuscript. I want also to thank Naomi Klein, Walden Bello, Lori Wallach, Tim Costello, Chuck Collins, and Mike Prokosch, all of whom have helped inspire me. My special, fond appreciation, also, to Charles Kernaghan and Barbara Briggs of the National Labor Center for their leadership of the anti-sweatshop movement, for giving me the opportunity to meet some of the workers discussed in the book, and for their friendship. I thank also Jeff Ballinger, David Lewit, Ginny Straus, Karen Nardella, Ruth Caplan, Bob Stubbs, and others in the Unitarian Universalist congregations, and Lynn Gargill, Kati Winchell, Nick Penniman, Ronnie Dugger, and the entire Northbridge Chapter of the Alliance for Democracy.

At Boston College, my colleagues in both the sociology department and the Leadership for Change program, including Severyn Bruyn, Bill Gamson, Paul Gray, Stephen Pfohl, Charlotte Ryan, Julie Schor, Eve Spangler, Steve Waddell, Judy Clair, Bill Joiner, Robert Leaver, Ken Mirvis, Joe Raelin, Rebecca Rowley,

Neil Smith, Sandra Waddock, and Bill Torbert, contributed to my thinking. I also received valuable feedback from undergraduates and graduate students who were captive audiences for drafts of the manuscript. Alex Cheney played an important role in catalyzing my thinking, collecting data, and providing feedback. Priscilla Huang also collected valuable data and gave me new insights. And Deb Piatelli was a wonderful source of ideas and support throughout the whole project. The students active in the Boston College Global Justice Project have been an inspiration, and while there are too many to name, they have helped this work move forward.

Outside the BC community, I want to thank especially Steve Piersanti, the president and publisher of Berrett-Koehler Publishers. Steve's contributions have been crucial and I want to publicly express my great appreciation to him. I also want to thank Jeevan Sivasubramaniam, who has been most generous, and Kathleen Epperson, Jeff Kulick, Sandy Chase, Charlie Dorris, and Gena Estes Zolatar for their comments.

I want to express enormous gratitude to Julia Pastore, my editor at St. Martin's. She has made the book possible and strengthened it through her gifted editing. She has graciously attended to all the large and little concerns that I have raised and brought her enthusiasm and dedication to every aspect of the project. No author familiar with the workings of today's publishing industry expects such a committed partnership, and I am deeply appreciative for all Julia has done.

I cannot thank enough my closest friends and colleagues, David Karp and John Williamson, who are copartners in this enterprise in every possible sense of the term. David and John have offered detailed feedback to every successive draft, enduring endless discussions about the argument and style while always offering the enthusiasm and support to keep going. David has never flagged in his willingness to rehash every idea, obsess with me about titles and phrases, or pick me up when I needed his warmth and comfort. John has helped me laugh when I most needed it, listened with his astonishing patience to my ideas and laments, and helped me make key strategic decisions. This book simply could not have been completed without their keen intellects, emotional generosity, and friendship.

Finally, I want to thank Elena for being there with patience and love through another several years of obsession. This has been a particularly intense project, and she has endured the price of it more than anyone else. She has been a source of intellectual guidance, editorial judgment, and unflagging patience and support. I have relied on her far more than can be said here. Thank you, my dear Elena.

PEOPLE
BEFORE
PROFIT

INTRODUCTION

911 GLOBE

All great truths begin as blasphemies.

GEORGE BERNARD SHAW

S ECONDS BEFORE THE EVENTS THAT CHANGED THE WORLD, ONE HUN-
dred people were eating breakfast at the World Trade Center
Club on the 107th floor of Tower One. At the same time a hundred and thirty-five people were meeting on the 106th floor at
a conference on risks in global finance and technology. On floors
105 and below, workers at Morgan Stanley, Merrill Lynch, Fuji
Bank, and hundreds of the world's largest financial companies
were just beginning the trading activity that keeps the global
economy humming.

At 8:48 A.M. on September 11, 2001, a hijacked American
Airlines Flight 11 smashed into Tower One. The 107th-floor restaurant blew up instantly, and the conversation one floor below
was silenced forever. On the lower floors, as terrified workers
struggled to escape, computers at the workstations of the world's
financial heartland exploded and burned as the temperature rose
to over two thousand degrees.[1]

When the Twin Towers crashed to the ground, the idea of a
globalized world knit together by commerce and trade came under crushing attack too. The threat to globalization was more
than symbolic. Cantor Fitzgerald, the global bond-trading company, lost 700 of its 1,000 workers, Fuji Bank reported 62 missing
out of 625, and Euro Brokers/Maxcor Financial Group lost

60 of its 285 employees. Merrill Lynch, the Bank of America, Lehman Brothers, and other financial giants were all hit hard. With the terrible image of the collapse of the Twin Towers seared on our brains, we could easily believe that the global economy itself was falling.[2]

But while the suicide bombers could kill people and harm major global companies, they could not destroy the idea of globalization itself. This was the message of President George Bush to Asian leaders a month after the attacks; he said that the terrorists were seeking to "shatter confidence in the world economic system" and destroy globalization but would never succeed. The companies would revive themselves, and new buildings would arise where the Twin Towers fell. The heroic resilience of New Yorkers pulling together after the attack symbolized the courage and resolve of all the world's survivors to rebuild.

A new debate about *how* to rebuild, though, symbolized a permanent change in the world and the future of globalization. Architects mused whether skyscrapers like the Twin Towers were still viable, and financial companies wondered whether they should relocate around Wall Street or disperse into smaller offices around the nation and the world. Some argued that Ground Zero should become a shrine, while others proposed building reinforced giant towers, smaller buildings, or a totally redesigned urban landscape. After September 11, the architects would have to question basic assumptions and reinvent basic principles of urban planning and of architecture itself.

So too, basic principles of global business and globalization that had seemed settled forever—a reflection of what Francis Fukuyama famously called "the end of history"—suddenly lost their certitude. Few questioned that trade and the global economy could survive, just as few architects doubted that urban towers and cities themselves could be rebuilt. But the architects of globalization—and that ultimately includes all of us—now have to rethink basic assumptions. My argument in *People Before Profit* is that just as we may have to reinvent the skyscraper, so too we now urgently need to reinvent globalization to create a safe, democratic, and economically secure world.

Three radically new circumstances—the World Trade Center attacks being only the most shocking—have crashed upon us at a surprising moment with surprising force, blowing away many of our most cherished assumptions about the world. Each has different causes, is independent from each other in many ways, and will require unique approaches as well as some shared solutions. But they all dramatize a crisis in globalization and alert us to the urgent need to redesign it in a globally democratic spirit.

Chronologically, the first of these new circumstances was the rise of antiglobalization movements on every continent as the globalization process intensified. About six months before September 11, thousands of native Mexican Indians in bedraggled army fatigues and sandals walked from Chiapas, Mexico, to Mexico City. At each new village, they were mobbed both by CNN camera crews and by adoring villagers who hugged and fed them and wept from the excitement of being in their presence. The marchers kept going under the sunbaked skies until they walked right into the Parliament in Mexico City. There, under the protection of Mexican president Vicente Fox, they spoke passionately of the rights of indigenous communities to protect their land against global mining companies and to defend their language and values against the juggernaut of globalization itself.

These were the legendary Zapatistas, heroes to native peoples everywhere for their courageous defense of indigenous communities. A surreal photo in *The New York Times* on March 29, 2001, shows Indians whose faces are covered by wool masks seated in the front rows of the great Parliament hall. A leader known only as Commander Esther, dressed not in a business suit but in an embroidered blouse and sandals, demanded autonomy and a bill of indigenous rights for her community. This would be the only way to protect the sacred rights of Indians under threat of the global property-rights rules of the World Trade Organi-

zation requiring that all natural resources be treated as commodities in the world market. The renowned Zapatista leader,
the pipe-smoking philosopher Subcomandante Marcos, said, "All
we want is a new kind of world. All we want is a world big
enough to include all the different worlds the world needs to
really be the world."

From this colorful Zapatista peasant movement in Mexico to
Muslim female sweatshop organizers in Bangladesh to IMF protesters in Bolivia, Argentina, and Pakistan, popular movements in
poor nations have long challenged globalization as economically
and morally unjust. The movements well up from all different
countries and with so many different faces and visions that it is
hard to give them a name. Labels such as "antiglobalization" do
not fit the bill because the dissenting forces, while vehemently
opposed to globalization, speak passionately of global justice and
the making of a global community.

The global justice movements captured the attention of Americans in the raucous 1999 battle of Seattle. More than fifty thousand protestors, marching in a grand coalition dubbed "Teamsters
and Turtles," protested the policies of the World Trade Organization that they viewed as antilabor, antienvironment, and antidemocratic. Then, as the new century opened, political and
financial elites accustomed to luxury hotel suites, chauffeured
automobiles, and the finest wines suddenly found themselves
besieged by protesters at trade summits and financial meetings.
In Washington, D.C., just four months after Seattle, at the April
2000 meetings of the International Monetary Fund and World
Bank, thousands marched down Constitution Avenue on a brilliant sunlit afternoon to protest the emergence of these secretive
institutions as handmaidens to an unjust, shadow global government. And every few months thereafter—at trade meetings from
Davos, Switzerland, to Melbourne, Australia, from Prague to
Quebec—another colorful, noisy, and occasionally bloody protest
spooked the financial planners of the world.

The antiglobalization movements proclaim globalization a
"race to the bottom," creating environmental degradation, ex-

ploitation of mostly female sweatshop workers, and a polarized world where 458 billionaires possess more wealth than do half of humanity. As shown in Chapter 4, the gap between rich and poor has increased during the last two decades of accelerated globalization (1980 to 2000), as has the sheer number of those living in poverty. Two billion people now live on less than $2 a day. More than three billion people live on less than $3 a day. The enormous power of the rich countries, especially the United States, in setting the trade rules, reinforces the view of globalization as a new velvet brand of colonialism. All of these arguments have not in the least persuaded most people that trade or foreign investment should be curbed. But protesters have helped stir up a new impassioned debate about whether we need a new kind of global economy better serving the poor. And they have helped spark a new struggle for global democracy that involves a radical vision of public participation and transnational corporate accountability.[3]

The second new circumstance of our times is defined by September 11, 2001. A debate rages about whether terrorists targeted the Twin Towers as a symbol of their hatred not only for the United States but for globalization and its seductive culture of modernity and consumerism. Did Osama bin Ladin or other perpetrators deliberately kill hundreds of financial executives to signal a jihad against American-led international business? I do not mean that globalization was the cause of the attacks or that the perpetrators were attacking globalization. Terrorism takes many forms and has many roots—religious, ethnic, and political as well as economic—many with no connections to globalization. But the attack on the United States has changed the conditions that made globalization possible and could dramatically alter its future.

Former president Bill Clinton, speaking a few weeks after the September 11 attacks, described terrorism as "the dark side of our new interdependence." Globalization created a new integrated world that erased national boundaries as if they were dusty chalk lines. But what globalization integrated, terror threatens to divide—and what it has opened, both terror and the war could shut. What Americans did not fully realize before September 11 was that globalization inevitably meant the globalizing of vulnerability. Globalization demands a world of open borders, where goods and services, people, and money are easily and safely exchanged. Closed borders, anthrax anxiety, and fear of flying or foreigners signal the end of globalization as we know it.[4]

American fear of terrorism could lead us to seal our borders, cocoon in gated communities, and bunker down against the world. The war against terrorism could inflame anger against the United States and lead others to shut their borders and brand global trade in ideas and commodities as the work of Satan. But globalization is not destined to collapse in an age of terror. Almost certainly it will survive, but in a dramatically new form. Like the Seattle movements challenging globalization, the lesson of September 11 is that we need to rethink our global vision—both to heal the wounds of globalization and to help attack the roots of terrorism and other forms of international violence.

The same can be said of the third drama currently changing our world, the global economic downturn. Following two decades of a magical "new economy" boom that many thought would last forever, world economies have sunk into recession. Even before September 11 and the Enron crisis, U.S. companies laid off millions—including more than a million workers in manufacturing alone in the year before September 11—while U.S. markets nosedived 25 percent, wiping out the "wealth effect" of the nineties boom, the high-tech revolution, and profits of the world's high-flying global corporations. The New York terrorist attacks and the 2002 post–Enron market collapse were a follow-on double whammy, severely harming prospects for U.S. and global recovery. Investors, workers, and ordinary citizens in the United States faced the scariest economic conditions in decades, with millions losing their jobs, retirement nest eggs, or both, while American capitalism, after Enron, lost its luster as a model for the world.[5]

The downturn in the U.S. economy, compounded by the war on terrorism, created devastating shock waves across the world. Within two months of the September 11 attacks, as the war in Afghanistan heated up, apparel giants such as Wal-Mart shut down a thousand plants in Bangladesh, laying off hundreds of thousands of workers. As corporations fled the extended war region, severe economic shocks also ricocheted through Pakistan and Indonesia. Even before Enron and the 2002 U.S. market collapse, as the U.S. economy slowed and American imports shrunk dramatically, Mexico, Argentina, and other nations in Latin America suffered their own economic quakes. In December 2001, Argentina suspended payments on its huge debt and fell off the cliff.

I was in Mexico in early 2002 when Argentina collapsed. The desk staff and the Mayan women who cleaned our hotel room all knew about the Argentine catastrophe and were eager to talk about it. They saw in it a glimpse of their own future. They were already working for less than a dollar an hour—and they were the fortunate ones with jobs. After September 11, the Mexican tourist trade was way down, and this was only making a bad situation worse. One cabdriver told me his wife had been working at a foreign factory at the minimum wage of thirty pesos a day, roughly thirty cents an hour. But he said that German and U.S. firms were either leaving for cheaper countries or going into the Mexican interior to hire workers at lower rates. And people were rushing to take these miserable jobs because there was no other work.

By late 2001, the IMF was revising global economic forecasts downward, with prospects of zero or negative growth throughout much of the Third World. UN officials worried that hundreds of thousands of refugees would starve in war-ravaged Afghanistan, but hundreds of millions of people in sub-Saharan Africa, Central America, and Asia already faced joblessness, hunger, and homelessness. Deepening poverty, slowing growth rates, and roller-coaster instability combined to create the possibility of a new global depression.

The world has entered a dark era, one that globlization was supposed to prevent. Global recession is a dry term, but it means that half of humanity—those 3 billion people already subsisting on less than three dollars a day—are jobless, ill, homeless, or starving. These are not the people who never got on the globalization train; they are its newest passengers. The train is taking them in the opposite direction from the one they were promised when they bought their tickets. The tracks laid down in their countries have wiped out their old way of life. These ticket holders—like the laid-off Bangladeshis—cannot just jump off the train. They are going to demand that the tracks are rebuilt to take them to the better life advertised at the station.

The debates about globalization—swirling around the problems of sweatshops and labor rights, justice for the global poor, and the creation of democratic governments—have taken on a new urgency. Reinventing globalization has shifted from a passion of protesters to a survival guide in a world of violence and economic turbulence. I argue in *People before Profit* that a democratic cure for the ills of globalization is the most important challenge in the world today. In the rest of this book, I lay out in detail what I mean by global democracy, how it is beginning to be conceived and practiced by social movements and ordinary people all over the world, and why I think it is both realistic and essential.

Antiglobalization movements, international terrorism, and global depression seem a brew for a huge backlash against globalization. But the democratic cure for this crisis requires resisting the romanticism of returning to a preglobalization era and instead working for a future that harnesses globalization's own most powerful rhetoric and energies in new, more positive ways. By transforming globalization through the very forces that it has unleashed, challengers to the existing order are already beginning to create a more democratic world. There are reformist and more radical versions of global democracy, and it should be viewed as a long-term evolving process rather than a magic bullet. But reorienting ourselves toward the democratic path, already commencing in small and moderate steps, is the great challenge and adventure of our age.

Much of the world is weary of idealism and skeptical of any idea that we have the power to remake globalization, a rudderless system that seems to run by itself. Thomas Friedman tells us that "Globalization isn't a choice, it's a reality. . . . No one is in charge. . . . If you want to call up and complain, there is no one on the other end of the phone." Friedman is saying that nobody runs the global financial markets that are the system's nerve center, and thus nobody can change it.[6]

Let us acknowledge the kernel of truth in this argument, one easily misunderstood. The financial and commercial forces at the heart of globalization are enormously powerful and cannot be controlled by any individual or nation. They don't answer to anyone. No cabal of plutocrats in a smoke-filled room and no imperial nation can fire off orders telling the global markets what to do. When they try, they inevitably fail or get badly burned in the process.

The misconception that might follow is that because no suit in a suite and no president of a state dictates to the markets, power has disappeared in the age of globalization. And the more dangerous corollary is that because nobody is in charge, globalization is a system that nobody can change, let alone reinvent. The truth is quite the opposite. Globalization, rather than eliminating human power, is concentrating it on a grander scale than did any revolution in history. Yes, globalization is changing the nature and agents of sovereign power, in some ways redefining power itself. But it is also increasingly creating the possibility of new forms of worldwide collective and democratic power by globally linked citizens, with the capacity to change the world as never before. Some democracy activists who see the possibilities now chant, "No globalization without representation." Global democracy will be the handiwork of dissenting popular movements of workers, environmentalists, human rights activists, women, and people of color all over the world already committed to the idea. They will be joined by growing numbers in the main-

who realize that they cannot be physically safe or eco-
lly secure otherwise.

...hout a shift toward global democracy, globalization will
survive but will move toward a "fortress" model. We see many
signs of the fortress already, a militarized world that puts security
and surveillance over liberty in order to contain the potential for
terrorism and other violence. It will keep the channels of commerce and finance tenuously open while maintaining a fragile
sense of safety in the world. But it will be a world of chronic and
growing violence that could undermine our core values and
much of the prosperity we cherish. A fortress globalization would
weaken the democracies in the West as well as crush the democratic potential in the developing world.

The world needs to give billions of poor and working people
a democratic voice as an alternative to more violence. The solution is not to shut down globalization or to go the route of
the fortress. Instead, it is to make globalization's own democratic
rhetoric real for even the poorest of the poor.

People Before Profit challenges a seductive and entrenched new
common sense that I call the "globalization mystique." The mystique treats globalization as new, inevitable, technologically
driven, and self-propelling. Its economic common sense is that
globalization is a win-win proposition for rich and poor nations.
Its political common sense is that globalization is democratizing
the world. The cultural myth is that consumerism creates meaning for all on the planet.

I reexamine each of these new commonsense ideas using history, stories, and statistics. I show that globalization has been
invented and reinvented throughout history and that we must
reinvent it again because the new common sense is so flawed.
This means not stopping globalization but rewriting its rules to
narrow the gap between rich and poor and put into practice the
democratic rhetoric of globalizations leaders. I show that this will
take a new kind of global grassroots politics that is already sur-

facing—and I outline its basic vision and principles. In the context of our new era of terrorism and economic crisis, we must urgently press forward to make the new vision a reality. You need a roadmap to travel through most books, and mine is simple. In the first five chapters, I dissect the globalization mystique, offer a new view of globalization, and show why we need change. In Chapters 6 to 9, I discuss the vision of global democracy that is already becoming the agenda of popular movements and ordinary people around the world. In Chapter 10, I show how global democracy is powerful medicine, not just for globalization's ills, but for ending terrorism and building our collective security.

In the first five chapters, I show how globalization is not reducing global poverty and inequality and why it is not fulfilling its democratic promise. In the Chapters 1 and 2, I delve into the history of earlier globalizations to help explain the failure. In Chapters 3 to 5, I look sequentially at how business, the United States, and the World Trade Organization and International Monetary Fund interact to create globalization as a new global power system that does not serve poor nations or poor people in either First or Third World countries.

All of the first part is a reflection on global power and how the new mystique has obscured it. Globalization is globalizing not only sneakers and Walkmans but sovereignty as well—taking power and constitutional authority away from nations and giving it to global markets and international bodies like the World Trade Organization. It is shifting the world's balance of power toward a new global oligarchy.

Globalization is anarchistic and oligarchic, but it also lays the foundation for the world's first global constitutional system, a world based on law rather than brute force. As such, globalization *could* become a catalyst for global democracy. Unhappily, though, globalization today not only sustains many undemocratic countries, such as Pakistan and to Saudi Arabia, but it also increasingly concentrates power in the mysteries of global financial markets and new global political elites led from the White House. National governments across the planet remain influential but increasingly disconnected from the local aspirations of their own peoples. National leaders increasingly speak the new global rhetoric of democracy, but they line their own pockets and serve global business interests at odds with the needs of the majority middle classes and poor who elect them. The nation-state—as we have seen in Argentina—is the site where ordinary people's frustrations about their ability to govern themselves explode into mayhem on the streets.

People in many countries seem to feel globalization not as new freedom in the ballot box but as a huge *loss* of choice. Tens of thousands of laid-off Argentine workers revolted on the streets as their government led them into the brave new global order and created an economic meltdown. Hungry people in Pakistan, Indonesia, Brazil, and South Africa rioted against their own governments as corrupt puppets of the global financial markets, the IMF, or the United States, the widely perceived power behind the new global throne. In Europe, French farmer and antiglobalization activist Jose Bove gained national acclaim by helping to block a new McDonald's franchise, and a hundred thousand protesters in Genoa, Italy, protested on the streets, denouncing globalization as a form of foreign conquest shredding their culture, welfare states, and traditions of social democracy. Many see their own democratic governments as abandoning them and becoming servants of an American-backed corporate leviathan. From Paris to Jakarta to Buenos Aires, the rumbling of popular discontent tells us that something has gone deeply wrong and that we'd better start putting the globalization train on the democratic track.

To make any sense of this, you have to understand what I mean by *global democracy*, the subject of the second part of the book. It involves five essentials: (1) limited democratic "world governments," (2) citizen-controlled national governments, (3) publicly accountable global business, (4) local community reinvigorated with citizen participation, and (5) a new international community that limits the unilateral power of even the strongest nation by creating collective security. Global democracy can happen only as ordinary people everywhere take seriously the ideals of democratic participation that leaders of globalization have themselves rhetorically proclaimed. As mentioned previously, global democracy is a path rather than an endpoint. It will not eliminate economic inequalities or give everyone equal political influence. It is fraught with new risks and doesn't promise a global rose garden of peace and prosperity. But it is the only way to create a world serving people as well as profits.

But how do you take this path in a world economy that allots more wealth to a few hundred of the world's richest people than to billions of poor people? Thomas Jefferson was one of the first Americans to warn that massive economic inequality meant the death of democracy. Can a world economy dominated by a few hundred megacorporations be subject to the control of the majority? And can a world in which nation-states are themselves increasingly polarized between rich and poor—and cast as puppets whiplashed by vast financial markets and footloose companies—be truly organized on the basis of citizenship rather than money?

Democracy requires deep and difficult changes in the system wiring of globalization to shrink the gap between rich and poor, between rulers and ruled. This will require a new politics that shifts the power and wealth of global marketeers and CEOs toward peasants, global workers, and the struggling middle classes. This new politics is in its earliest stages of development, but it has already created shock waves among the world's elite and brought new hope for change. In an age of cynicism about democracy, it is emerging from a new global generation passionate to participate in fashioning its own collective destiny.

While global democracy can sound like unvarnished idealism, mainstream leaders, especially after September 11, have been sounding new concerns about the dangers of the current order. U.S. secretary of state Colin Powell told the World Economic Forum on February 1, 2002, that the war on terrorism could only be won by a new commitment to empowering the world's poor. "We have to go after poverty," Powell proclaimed. "We have to go after despair. We have to go after hopelessness." Those potentially attracted to terrorism need to be shown that "there is a better way."[7]

Prime Minister Tony Blair has called global equity not only a moral imperative but in the interests of business and the powerful as well as the poor. He said after the attacks on the United States, "If globalization works only for the benefit of the few, then it will fail . . . the test of any decent society is not the contentment of the wealthy and strong but the commitment to the poor and weak." Blair went on to say that "if the world as a community focused on it [i.e., global poverty], we could heal it." He emphasized that global business itself—which has a big responsibility here—will survive and prosper only if we "make industrial progress without the factory conditions of the nineteenth century."[8]

I recently met with twenty-two-year-old Nisran Ganoor and two other Bangladeshi garment workers who described nineteen hour shifts, at eight cents an hour, making caps and garments for U.S. universities and companies. They have fourteen-year-old helpers who are paid just three to five cents an hour. One worker said, "Sir, I do not have the words to express to you how they treat us." Supervisors use their shoes to beat the workers on their heads and force them to stay in the factories and sleep on the floor between shifts. If these aren't Blair's "nineteenth-century [working] conditions," I don't know what are. Jenrain Maod, twenty, says she needs to keep her job but desperately wants her government to enforce its "own labor laws and improve their condition." Listening to the voice of such workers—who are trying to organize a union and get basic rights to go to the bathroom and speak up about physical abuse—seems a first step on the long global democratic path in front of us.[9]

Thomas Friedman writes understandably, if bluntly: "I feel about globalization a lot like I feel about the dawn. . . . I can't stop it . . . and I'm not going to waste time trying."[10] I explain in *People Before Profit* why I think we should feel differently, but let's acknowledge right away this truth: globalization is the most powerful force in the world today and will not easily be transformed, partly because it offers a cornucopia of real and imaginary blessings. It undermines some traditional regimes run by bloated, horribly corrupt state bureaucracies, and it can threaten leaders who have bloodied and impoverished their own populations for centuries. It brings the possibility of growth and prosperity to many people around the world who have never had enough food to fill their bellies.

Saying "I can't stop it" or "I can't change it" misses, though, the crucial fact that globalization is a historical reinvention of earlier global economies. If we have already reinvented globalization once this century, then it is not as God-given as the dawn, and we *can* create something new. Globalization is unique, but its creation mirrors an eternal, civilizational drama. The history of the world can be understood as a chronic struggle to reinvent earlier collapsing forms of world order.

I share Friedman's view that globalization needs to be treated as a system. He defines it as the world system supplanting the Cold War, marked most of all by a rapidly integrating world economy. But globalization needs to be understood not just as a system of global economic integration, but as one guided by a specific set of economic, political, and cultural principles. I define *globalization* as a system of economic integration (1) driven more than any prior global order by the priorities of profit, (2) managed politically largely by the United States and an allied set of new global institutions such as the WTO, and (3) legitimated culturally by the values of consumerism. In this book, I focus less on the issue of economic integration per se, which has been proceeding for centuries, and more on the distinctive economic models, political powers, and cultural visions that are the essence of today's globalization system. These are what are new and most in need of change.

My optimism about change reflects a view that the rules are

still in flux and are ripe for debate and change. But before saying any more about change, let me elaborate some important caveats to my general argument. One has to do with the term *globalization*, which has become a buzzword for anything related to trade and economic integration and everything new in a technologically dynamic and market-driven world. The term as commonly used tends to obscure the strong continuities with earlier world economies and to disguise forms of power that have existed through much of history. It overemphasizes the fact of integration rather than the specific rules and political forces governing the process. And it is suggestive of a world marching to a common drummer that dramatically understates the persistent differences and divisions among nations—especially between what some have called "the West and the rest."

My own definition makes clear that to be "antiglobalization" is not necessarily to be against trade or global economic integration, nor is it to dismiss all gains that even the current forms of globalization have provided. Many global justice activists *do* oppose integration, but many others instead want to redirect it in a more democratic spirit. I am closer to the second camp. Global integration has brought positive benefits as well as harm, and my argument is that a new set of rules and power arrangements can enhance the gains while reducing the human costs.

Another caveat has to do with my critique of the current business system. I am severely critical of transnational corporations that wield enormous power in the new order. But while I call for major system change, I recognize that large global corporations deliver essential and often magical goods and services, and that millions of people around the world depend on them for jobs. Critics of the corporation have often lost credibility by demonizing companies or failing to acknowledge the contributions that corporations have made to our lives. Even when they exploit exceptionally vulnerable people, global companies sometimes help them escape from even worse conditions. And while I am critical of core elements of the corporate system, I am firmly persuaded that many in the business world would like to help create a more humane order. My intention here is to help both corporate insiders and outsiders to identify the systemic failures and find ways to create a more democratic and accountable form of business.

The third caveat is that I am fully aware of how my own identity as an American citizen creates biases and limitations, particularly regarding the changes we need. Although I am a critic of U.S. economic and foreign policy, I inevitably see the world through American lenses, and so my vision of the future is colored by the political ideologies and cultural traditions in which I have grown up. I have tried to counter these limitations by learning as much as possible about non-Western experiences and traditions, and especially by listening closely to the voices of Third World peoples who have been engaged for years in global economics and politics, and who are now leading voices for global democracy. But I recognize that my proposals for change, which draw on the visions of non-Westerners, remain Western-centric. Ideas about equality, democracy, and human rights that I highlight will not be viable foundations for a new world until they are reformulated by non-Westerners consistent with their own experience and philosophies.

A fourth caution relates to my discussion of terrorism. Because the attacks on the Trade Towers happened while I was writing this book, I pay a good deal of attention to the implications of these events for the globalization system. But the reader should not take this to mean, as noted earlier, that I believe globalization caused the attacks or that global democracy is the exclusive remedy. Neither globalization nor terrorism is new, and the core problems of globalization that I discuss here would be overwhelmingly important even if the attacks had not occurred or if there were no terrorism in the world. We are still much too close to the events of September 11 to assess fully their historical importance and consequences, and too much of the contemporary focus on terrorism in the United States has ignored other long-standing forms of terrorism that have caused so much suffering in other nations. The Center attacks helped call attention to the need for reforms in the global order including major changes in U.S. foreign policy, but it would take a different book to define and address systematically the nature and causes of global terrorism.

A fifth caveat concerns the deep and often confusing contradictions in the globalization system. For example, I stress both the overwhelming power of the U.S. in today's globalization system and the contradictory tendency of the new system to weaken all national power, including that of the United States itself. I also discuss the United States as an "umpire," while indicating that American power has many parallels with that of earlier empires. Globalization is a system suspended between different logics of sovereignty, committed rhetorically to "free markets" that do not exist in practice, and marked by other contradictions that require recognition of the world as steeped in what one colleague of mine calls the "tension of opposites."

I highlight the emerging rules of the globalization system, but also stress that the current world order is scarily anarchistic and profoundly resistant to international law. Globalization may be defined by new global rules, but those managing the system bend the rules to their own purposes and follow their own prescriptions only as long as it is in their interest to do so. For example, the United States and other leading Western powers preach free trade but are protectionist in key sectors such as agriculture and textiles; they celebrate "free market" rules but rely on state subsidies and other major government intervention to increase corporate profitability. My discussion about the emerging constitutional character of the global order can easily create misunderstanding about the central fact that elites in the system play by very different rules than everyone else.

I need to acknowledge here my own role in the global justice movements that I describe in the second part of the book. My sympathies with many of their aims and my close relations with many activists obviously color my perspectives on change. Nonetheless, I have many criticisms of tendencies within the movements, to which I give full expression here. In particular, as noted, I do not regard myself as "antiglobalization," in the sense of wanting to shut down trade or global investment. And my concern here is to speak not just to the activists but to the far larger community of people who are not active in social movements but who are nevertheless concerned about the troubled state of the world and want to understand it and help make it better. I hope my critique of the movements will strengthen the movements themselves and persuade others that it is worth getting involved and adding new perspectives. The movements are still in their infancy, and there is no assurance they will succeed. They will do so only by connecting with the huge numbers of ordinary people who are skeptical about globalization but also about the movements themselves.

Finally, I want to acknowledge the many topics that are not addressed in any detail here despite their great importance. These range from issues of global energy, sustainable resources, and population problems to the role of the mass media and issues of religion and ethnicity. Globalization is such a large topic that it is inevitable that many key issues are neglected, and that there is often not enough space for even many issues central to the problem. And because nobody can be expert on all the issues raised by globalization, inevitably much remains in the realm of informed speculation.

I am optimistic about reinventing globalization today because we are at the dawn of a new Constitutional Moment, a special period in which the rules of the game are up for grabs. Constitutional Moments are rich with opportunity, periods in which the world is fluid rather than frozen. There is the hope of fundamentally changing the way things are rather than living as we always have.

Globalization's project—to create and write the rules of a single integrated world economy—has created this moment of opportunity. The very effort to invent one world and write an informal constitution for the world economy means that the rules are in play and that the sale of globalization to the people has not been closed. This helps to explain the surprising early successes of the globalization activists in the streets and in community organizations, unions, and other organizations dedicated to change. While they do not have all the answers, they have seen that it is the right time to ask basic questions about the fairness and sustainability of the new system—and to start a new kind of global democratic politics.

Sociologist Richard Flacks has distinguished between "making life" and "making history," the former being the struggle to craft a personal life and the latter the effort to join with others and reconstruct the world. Both, he argues, are necessary, but only small numbers of people typically move beyond the struggles and gratification of their personal lives to "make history." Just making a personal life is challenging and saps the energy of most of us. Yet in Constitutional Moments, making history is a realistic prospect for large numbers of people, as they find themselves caught up in seismic struggles over the basic rules of the world they inhabit. Living in a Constitutional Moment should be understood as a privilege because it offers the rare opportunity to make a difference in the lives of future generations.[11]

Can we make a difference? I recently met Craig Kielburger, the Canadian boy who at age twelve read about children in Asia forced to work in factories and denied the right to attend school. He pleaded with his parents to let him go and see for himself. They did, and nothing has been the same since. Craig, who is eighteen at this writing, founded a global organization of children called Free the Children. It now has 120,000 members across the world—all under eighteen. In the past five years, Free the Children has educated people on every continent about the evils of child labor and raised millions of dollars to buy kids out of bonded work so that they could go to school. And because schools often didn't exist, FTC members have built hundreds with their own hands. Free the Children has also lobbied hard and with some success for major changes in the policies of schools, national governments, and global institutions such as the World Bank and the UN. They have helped spark the new debate about sweatshops and global labor rights for young, mostly women workers everywhere.

Craig, who was nominated for the Nobel Peace Prize four times before finishing his own high-school education, believes that if kids can create this kind of change, the beginning of a reinvention of globalization, adults can too. Maybe as we look more closely at what the kids are doing—and at the forces of globalization and violence that are stirring them—we might find that it is time for us adults to follow the children.

CHAPTER 1

GLOBALIZATION'S GHOSTS

Hegel was right when he said that man can never learn anything from history.
GEORGE BERNARD SHAW

History teaches us the mistakes we are going to make.
UNKNOWN

IF I ASKED YOU TO NAME THE PERSON WHO BEST SYMBOLIZES GLOBAL-ization, what would you answer? I bet you'd say, "Bill Gates." As the founder of Microsoft, the leader in the information revolution, Gates is the towering business figure of the age. Do you know of any country in the world that hasn't joined the Microsoft revolution? When I walked through the poorest streets of Bangkok, I saw Internet shops where kids paid pennies for a few precious moments of time on a PC. And now we know that terrorists hiding in hovels in Afghanistan, Egypt, and Pakistan rely heavily on Microsoft software, just as you and I do, to communicate.

If you ask what person symbolizes globalization to me, I think of someone very different. She is Nisran, the Muslim Bangladeshi apparel worker I mentioned in the introduction. She is a hauntingly beautiful and fragile young woman, very thin with large dark eyes. While bombs were falling in a nearby country to kill terrorists, she and millions of workers like her started the engines of the global economy in the early morning and kept them running all day long and late into the evening. Listen to a little of her story:

> *I am Nisran. I am twenty-two years old. When I started working, I was twelve. I had to go to work because my family was*

very poor. So I had to leave school after the fourth grade. For the last ten years, even as a child worker, I have had to work twelve to fourteen hours a day and sometimes up to twenty hours. I have been working for ten years, but I still have no savings. If I die today, my family would have no money to bury me.

Now I work for Actor Garments where I produce caps for many universities in the United States. I am a sewing operator; I do the stitching on the visors of the caps.

When shipments have to go out to the United States, we have to work nineteen or twenty hours until 3 or 4 A.M. There is no space to sleep, so I have to curl up next to the machine to sleep for three or four hours. Then I go home at 6 to wash and eat breakfast, and I have to be back working by 8 A.M. Because I earn so little money, I have to share a tiny room with three coworkers. We have two beds, and two of us share each bed. We have nothing else—no chairs, no table, no cooking equipment, no radio or TV or clock. Five families with a total of thirty people in the row of rooms where I live share one bathroom and one kitchen and one stove. So in the morning I have to stand in line to use the bathroom and to use the stove. Sometimes I have to go to the factory without having breakfast.[1]

We will hear more from Nisran and other global workers because their stories remind us why globalization has become dangerous and could turn millions of people against the United States and the West. Such stories help us understand why changing these conditions may prove the best long-term strategy for reducing violence in the world.

I want you to meet two ghosts. One I will call Cecil, an arrogant and adventurous phantom, the apparition of colonialism. The second is J.D., a Scrooge-like ghost if ever there was one, the specter of the late nineteenth-century U.S. Gilded Age. Cecil, the ghost of European colonialism, and J.D., the ghost of the Gilded

Age, linger to remind us that we repeat history when we don't remember it. They haunt globalization and are the historical windows through which we can see it most clearly.

This first chapter is devoted to ghosts because globalization *does* have a history, and it is essential to understand it. Many people see globalization as entirely new. In fact, it is a reinvention of earlier world economies that I call "ancient globalizations." Only by understanding these earlier developments can we see some of the roots of the poverty suffered by so many like Nisran in the world economy today. When we see how history has been a never-ending process of building new kinds of globalizations, it becomes easier to understand that we can do it again.

We all have our personal ghosts. They often are important figures in our family history—relatives with a drinking problem, a womanizing weakness, a face like our own. We may try to deny their existence, but they haunt us anyway, and we can learn much about ourselves by admitting that they're around and by seeing them clearly. Therapists tell us that only by studying our ghosts carefully can we exorcise them and heal ourselves.

I mention Cecil because colonialism runs deep in globalization's own history. This does not mean that globalization *is* colonialism, although many leaders in the Third World, including the president of South Africa Thabo Mbeki and Arthur Mbanefo, spokesperson for a group of 133 poor nations called the Group of 77, have made the comparison bluntly. And after September 11, many debate intensely whether globalization in the Middle East, as well as in Africa, Latin America, and Asia, is the twenty-first-century brand of colonialism. American power, globalization, and colonialism are now equated or blurred in the thinking of millions of people across the entire Third World.[2]

But to many U.S. workers, globalization is like colonialism in reverse, shifting valuable investments toward the Third World and draining the United States and other First World nations of good jobs. Don't tell a displaced U.S. autoworker whose job just flew to Mexico that he or she is the beneficiary of a new American colonialism. Yet, despite the differences in perspective, colonial history shapes both the reality and perception of globalization. I believe it is useful to look at the Spanish, Dutch, and British colonial empires of centuries past as ancient globalizations that can give us surprising new insights into our very different model today.[3]

I have named colonialism's ghost after Cecil Rhodes, the serotonin-loaded nineteenth-century British entrepreneur and adventurer who along with Rudyard Kipling virtually invented colonialism's logo, "the white man's burden." Rhodes founded the British South Africa Company and De Beers, the huge diamond corporation and the world's richest company of his time. His companies built railroads connecting Cape Town to Cairo, and they literally ruled nations such as Rhodesia, now Zimbabwe. Rhodes himself became the prime minister and effective dictator of Cape Colony, now South Africa. Rhodes saw colonialism as an idealistic mission spreading prosperity and civilization to the newly conquered colonies; he fiercely believed that the English were a superior race and had a moral responsibility to spread British companies and values across the whole continent. Today, he would be leading the chorus of those who see globalization as the West's latest and perhaps best effort to deliver growth, opportunity, and civilization to the world. The persistence of global poverty among people such as Nisran would not discourage him, because it did not make him rethink his business in Africa. The extremist Islamic reaction against the West that exploded on September 11 would also probably not change his views, since tribal resistance to his own African adventures only strengthened his resolve.[4]

My second phantom, J.D., is the ghost of the Gilded Age, the era that virtually invented the large modern corporation. It will not surprise you that I have named this lean and hungry ghost after John D. Rockefeller, the greatest and greediest of all the robber barons and the quintessence of the Gilded Age itself. While many historians have connected dots linking colonialism and globalization, fewer have seen the Gilded Age as a historical window into globalization's soul. This seems hardly surprising since the robber barons in the Gilded Age were busy taking control in the United States itself and were not ready to take on a global mission.[5]

Nonetheless, the Gilded Age is a source of surprising insight. The robber barons ran sweatshops in the United States that were a sad preview of today's factories. One small snippet of Jenrain's story could come right out of J.D.'s factory:[6]

On the production line there are thirty machines with thirty operators and ten helpers. The supervisors give us a production target of 370 caps per hour, but we can barely complete 320 caps per hour, so we have to work as fast as we can. But because of this, we sometimes make mistakes, and then the supervisors shout at us and call us bad names, or they slap us, or hit us with a stick or a cap, or jab us with scissors. Sometimes we cry because of this rough treatment, and then they threaten us not to cry.

I have to ask permission to use the bathroom, and they give you only two minutes. The supervisor checks the time. If I need more than two minutes, the supervisor yells at you and calls you bad names.

We only have tap water to drink, which is filthy and makes us sick. The workers often have diarrhea, jaundice, and kidney problems. Because we have to sit on stools with no backs working so many hours, the workers also suffer from backaches.

The factory is cloudy with dust. It is not well ventilated; it is without enough air and light. The air of the factory is polluted with dust from the cloth. This dust goes into our noses and makes us sick with coughs and respiratory problems.

In listening to Jenrain's story, one begins to believe that globalization is bringing a new version of Gilded Age conditions to millions of global workers.[7]

The Gilded Age was a coming attraction, in a more literal sense, to a kind of economic "globalizing" in the United States itself. The robber barons were immersed in a stunning project of market expansion and integration, moving the country from local commerce to a great interconnected national corporate economy. In a few short decades, the robber barons knit together a huge new market, a feat of extraordinary imagination and boldness. In this sense, the robber barons were "globalizers" within a single nation, and the Gilded Age can be seen as a key historical story about economic integration.

A few caveats here before we proceed with our ghost story. First, Cecil and J.D. may seem like old gloomy ghosts who are not up to the job of giving us the real scoop about globalization. Colonialism and the Gilded Age, you might be thinking, are the past. Globalization is the future, one full of adventure, excitement, and hope—or so it seemed before September 11. Let me try to reassure you. Cecil and J.D. are just globalization's ghosts—they don't tell us everything we need to know about the world today. History never repeats itself in quite the same form. Although the ghosts are telling us about a side of globalization that we might not be hearing about as much as we need to, they can't tell us the whole story.

Let me also acknowledge that these ghosts appear to unfairly stack the deck against globalization. Colonialism and the Gilded Age are not the proudest moments of Western history. Both were built on forms of brute labor exploitation and political corruption that we like to hope no longer exist. But the ghosts as I see them tell us several things. One is that we haven't progressed as far as we thought. Although it is unfashionable to dwell on it in the United States, global exploitation, as people in Africa, Latin America, and the Middle East keep loudly protesting, is still a reality for billions around the world.

Second, Cecil and J.D. have their sunny sides. Few eras in history are all bad, and even colonialism and the Gilded Age had some redeeming qualities. Both were periods of bold growth and change, and both were associated with dramatic technological advances that made the world a better place. Both upset existing systems of power that had exploitative features of their own, and both set into motion new movements for freedom and social justice.

Third, globalization differs in important ways from its historic ghosts. Its legal, technological, and political foundations are all unique. As you will see, my ghost story does not try to reduce globalization to a sad or one-sided historical stereotype. Instead, I will be discussing the parts of globalization that are unpredictable and positive. As noted before, I see globalization as a progressive force in many ways, and I hope to show that those challenging it make a great mistake by demonizing it or creating a nostalgia for the world that came before.

Many of my friends think of globalization as "the Internet thing." They find it nearly impossible to separate the computer e-mail, and the Internet from the process of globalization. They understand that high tech liberates money to fly across national borders, and allows markets and companies to go global faster than the Concorde can rev up its engines. My friends see frightening new dangers after the terrorist attacks but feel that globalization is upbeat because they associate it so closely with exciting new technology. They also believe that high tech makes globalization inevitable, because nobody, not even Osama bin Laden or future terrorists, can undo the information revolution. New, faster, and hotter technology will shrink the world further and rewrite national boundaries in disappearing ink.

I believe that people in the United States and many other Western countries have bought into the technology-centered globalization mystique. Thomas Friedman, who has shaped the public's view of globalization as much as anyone, is a contributor to the technology mystique. He says if his child were to ask, "Daddy, where does globalization come from?" he would respond that it is all about a 1980s and 1990s technological "whirlwind" that blew down the old walls of the preglobalization world. It involved minirevolutions of "computerization, telecomunications, miniaturization, compression technology and digitization." It is about you and me being able to communicate with anyone anywhere at the speed of light, not in the First World or the Third World, which are things of the past, but the one new "Fast World." For Friedman, globalization means you "can call *to* anywhere cheaply, you can call *from* anywhere cheaply, including from your laptop, your mountaintop, your airplane seat or the top of Mount Everest."[8]

I can appreciate his point. Not long ago in the Bangkok airport I was peering into the waiting section reserved for monks. I remember seeing many of the monks, in their saffron robes and bare feet, seemingly deep in ninth-century meditation, suddenly reaching into their robes and taking out *their cellphones.* The image of the monks chatting merrily away on their wireless devices caught me up short and made me think, yes, this is globalization in action, the world of the Buddha married to the postmodern era of electronic gadgets.

Osama bin Laden's high-tech command posts in the caves of Afghanistan brought home the point. From one of the world's poorest nations, terrorists sent e-mails and satellite communications to "sleeper cells" around the globe. And in Egypt and Saudi Arabia, Islamic clergy in nearly every village now use their own Web sites to argue the religious merits of bin Laden's jihad. "Whoever helps America and its fellow infidels against our brothers in Afghanistan is apostate," writes Saudi cleric Sheik Hammoud on his own personal Web site. Hammoud is part of a buzzing Internet dialogue among turbaned and bearded clerics glued to their PCs in their desert huts or mosques in Saudi Arabia, Syria, and Pakistan.[9]

But while images like this help me understand the power of globalization-as-technology, they don't make it true. It is a compelling myth that distracts us from understanding what globalization is about, and our friendly ghosts will help us cut through the fog. Cecil and J.D. offer historical perspectives illuminating the intimate but misunderstood relation between new technology and globalization. Much of the romance of globalization flows from the technology with which we sometimes confuse it, and this was also true centuries ago.

Colonialism and the Gilded Age make it obvious that "globalizers" of any historical epoch have their roots in transportation and communications breakthroughs often connected to the technology of war. Spain, the Netherlands, and Great Britain all turned themselves into empires by harnessing bold new naval technology and using it to trade and conquer. Making better ships and guns depended on advances in mechanics and steel made possible by the industrial revolution. The tie between colonialism and the industrial revolution is probably as close as that between globalization and the information revolution. Few of us, though, would mistake the technological advances greasing colonial empires with what colonialism was really about.

The Gilded Age offers another view of how globalizations of every era feed off great technological innovations with which they can be easily confused. Who were the first robber barons? They were railroad entrepreneurs and Wall Street tycoons such as Jay Gould, who collectively built a national market by financing and hammering in the tracks that knit the country together for the first time. The railroads were to the Gilded Age what the Internet is to globalization. They were the industrial age's information highway, and they help show that globalizing always is anchored in a new physical and technical infrastructure that links people and places that couldn't communicate before. Alexander Graham Bell's invention of the telephone, a second technological miracle of the Gilded Age, may have been as important as the railroads, allowing people to talk and do deals across the country without getting on a train.

What we learn from former globalizations is partly the obvious: we can't create globalizing projects without technological breakthroughs. No ships, no colonialism; no railroads, no Gilded Age; no computer or Internet, no globalization. We just can't blow out the limits of the existing markets without technologies that allow us to economically integrate on a grander scale. New technology makes globalization in any era possible, but that's quite different than saying that technology drives globalization, or that it has the longevity or sexiness of its technology, or—the biggest mistake of all—that it *is* its technology. We could have had ships and guns without colonialism, railroads without the Gilded Age. The Internet makes possible many worlds other than the one globalization is constructing. The essence of globalization lies outside the new truly fantastic technologies that now grip our imagination. This is good for you, the reader, and me the author because, while the technology is fascinating, the real plot is more exciting.

At least in parts of Africa, Cecil is a ghost who is kicking up more than just metaphorical dust. At Makokoba M'kambo market, near Cecil Rhodes's burial site at the Top of the World, some *n'angas* (healers) worry about Rhodes's roaming evil spirit. Local activists appease their worries: "We have ways of directing the energy of spirits."[10]

"If not harnessed, Rhodes's spirit will haunt and harm the British," warns Sangano's resident spirit medium, Mathisa. Sangano Munhumatapa, an activist group in Zimbabwe, the country where Rhodes was buried, has threatened to throw his interred bones into the Zambezi River if someone doesn't remove them first.[11]

The controversy over Cecil Rhodes's burial site suggests the potency of his power as a symbol of colonialism. African leaders still talk with emotion about Rhodes's "evil deeds," including his swindling of early tribal chieftains for the sacred land where he is now buried. But the real issue is the continuing legacy of colonialism, now resurfacing, as many Africans see it, in the new face of globalization.

Rhodes was a crusader on a grand mission who believed that God had divined Britain as his agent to create a new planet built on British civilization. In his youth, Rhodes had heard a famous lecturer at Oxford say, "We are still undegenerate in race; a race mingled with the best northern blood. . . . Will you youths of England make your country again a royal throne of Kings, a sceptered isle? . . . This is what England must either do or perish; she must found colonies as fast and far as she is able."[12]

In contemporary terms, colonialism was a vision of a new *world system*—and I italicize this phrase for a reason. Before colonialism, there had been no vision of the *world* as an integrated entity; there were only hundreds of splintered regional markets, nations, and tribes. True, trade and earlier empires began to integrate the world long before European colonialism, and colonialism itself never went global in today's sense of replacing national with global sovereignty. But in a preview of globalization, colonialism was giving new weight to a novel idea: that we can create something called a world order and really mean it.

Cecil makes it clear that we are also speaking meaningfully of a new *system*. Colonialism was serious about tearing up the economic, political, and cultural pillars of the old world and building a master plan for a new order. The political architects would be the great commercial nations of Europe, and their blueprint was a true system overhaul designed to maximize capital accumulation in the global colonial economy. The dream of Cecil's British Empire was to see the Union Jack flying high all around the world "from sea to shining sea."

The important idea about both ancient and modern globalizations is the breathtaking ambition of the project. My Jewish grandmother would say, "Some chutzpah, this globalization idea!" Globalization is about rewriting all the rules for people everywhere; it's hard to imagine more chutzpah than that. It's also why I write about globalizations as creating Constitutional Moments, periods in which the basic rules are put into play because somebody is serious about inventing new rules and making everyone in the world play by them.

Any new world system, made possible by new technology and often justified in God's name, has human architects. Rhodes saw the divine inspiration of God in the British Empire, and John D. Rockefeller said bluntly, "God gave me my money." But globalizations are always missions by very human actors. This point seems too obvious to mention except that it is so widely ignored or denied in current conversations. With hindsight, it is easy to see that the earlier globalizations of colonialism and the Gilded

Age were designed and enforced by people with immense power and much to gain.[13]

The common sense about today's globalization is that it "runs itself," suggesting that it is conspiratorial to believe that self-interested people run it. Since hardly anyone would deny the greed and self-interest at the heart of colonialism or the Gilded Age, one can only draw two conclusions. The first is that globalization is different from the "ancient globalizations" precisely because nobody is in charge. The second is that the idea of nobody in charge is a myth that helps disguise the prime movers themselves. My own view veers toward the second. We can't speak of globalization without thinking of those who make it happen for their own ends.

One example is media tycoon Rupert Murdoch. He seems to me a modern-day equivalent of the swashbuckling Cecil Rhodes. The Australian-born Murdoch, now an American citizen, built News Corp., owner of the sprawling worldwide Fox media conglomerate and hundreds of other publishers, record companies, newspapers, and magazines. Murdoch now owns *TV Guide,* the *New York Post,* the *Weekly Standard,* the *Sunday Times,* the *Australian,* the *Daily Telegraph,* ChinaByte, HarperCollins, Columbia TriStar Netherlands, Street.com, and many more. The global leader in satellite communications, Murdoch operates nine media on six continents. News Corp. is a huge force in the United States and Europe, and the biggest corporation in Asia. That's saying a lot when you think about Toyota, Honda, or Sony. Murdoch seemed the first to smell a global audience. He was buying satellites to build his planetary ratings, while U.S. media were still delivering newspapers by bicycle. Nobody has had more fire in his belly for globalizing, and nobody has been better at it. Ted Turner, a world-class globalizer himself, accuses Murdoch of being "out to conquer the world." Along with some of his friends running two hundred of the world's largest corporations, Murdoch's made a pretty good start.[14]

tion sounds reasonable, but it ignores the fact that countries create "natural" advantages through subsidies and other political incentives. Nonetheless, conventional international trade analysis does what good academic theory does; it is rigorous within its own assumptions, and it has an intuitive commonsense nature about it.

But it is blind to history. This is not surprising since economic history is out of fashion with today's economists. Colonialism was obviously a system of economic integration and trade, but hardly a win-win proposition entered into, as Ricardo writes, by "a common tie of interest." The colonies went along because they had a chain around their necks with a very short leash. Colonialism led to bloody anticolonial revolutions and wars, and some who see globalization as a new form of colonialism have already begun to pick up their guns.

The most powerful evidence against the win-win view comes from the school of "world system theorists" who have studied a range of ancient globalizations, of which colonialism is only one form. The reigning figure is Immanuel Wallerstein, who believes that Westerners have been looking at the world with the wrong set of glasses for about the last five centuries. We look through the glasses of our respective nations, seeing national economies, national interests, and feeling like a member of our own country. I am an American, we say proudly. Or a Brazilian or French. Wallerstein suggests we are seeing an illusion when we see the world in this way. Or more precisely, we are missing the forest for the trees. For several centuries now, he argues, the nation has been simply an interdependent part of a much larger reality of economically integrated world systems. It's these systems that we must acknowledge. The nation doesn't stand alone or have a true autonomous identity, but we hang onto it for dear life as if it's everything.[3]

World system development has been going on for at least seven hundred years: some believe that the process actually goes back almost to the dawn of civilization itself. Through much of history, what we might call "globalizing projects" have knit together distinct tribes, city-states, or nations. The knitters are most often traders—like the Venetian merchants who traveled the famous Silk Road to join Europe with the exotic markets of the Orient. But whether they are ambitious traders, conquering generals like Alexander the Great, bold explorers like Christopher Columbus, or ruthless entrepreneurs like Cecil Rhodes, they help build a larger integrated market and a new regime. In the more successful of these ancient globalizations, a world system is created that may not actually encompass the whole world (in fact, it can be only a small geographic slice of the earth), but that blooms into a far greater order than the tribes or societies comprising it. Examples range from the Renaissance Mediterranean economy built around the city-state of Venice to the British Empire. Some believe that the first world system and global economy was Mesopotamia in 3000 B.C.[4]

The punch line here should be very sobering to the apple-pie thinkers of today and to all of us concerned about the relation between global inequality, poverty, and violence. The historical research finds one universal idea: that all globalizing projects through history have created world economies polarized into "cores" and "peripheries," winners and losers. If the scholarship is as accurate as it is voluminous, all ancient globalizations have historically been wired more as a win-lose than a win-win proposition—and often degraded into wars and sickening violence between the core and the periphery.[5]

Distinguishing the core and periphery is not rocket science. In the Roman Empire, Rome was the core, and all its far-flung dominions the periphery. In the "world-economies" of the Italian city-states such as Venice, Florence, and Milan, the core was the center city itself, and the periphery its smaller and weaker trading partners. In the British Empire, London was the core, and the colonies (from India to Palestine to South Africa) the periphery. Colonialism can be defined as a world system in which the core and periphery are legally and militarily linked as colonizer and colonized in an exploitative division of labor. But, and this is perhaps the more telling historical conclusion, virtually all ancient globalizations seem to have been built around some variant of the core/periphery divide.

Core and periphery are historically intimate partners that function a bit like spouses in what the Oprah-world calls a co-dependent relationship. There is a deep and unhealthy interdependency. Like dysfunctional marriages, world systems wed economic partners on troubling terms but create binding ties and constraints that make it difficult to exit. Codependency, however, suggests a kind of equality or eager mutual complicity that is misleading when it comes to ancient globalizations. Core and periphery are not created equal; the inequality is raw and naked in colonialism, but it recurs in mild to virulent forms in virtually every world system. "Unequal exchange," which history suggests is a more apt phrase in globalizing projects than "free trade," has polarized core and periphery from the Egyptian Empire of the pharaohs, to the Renaissance Italian city-states, to the last colonial empires of the twentieth century (whose vastly extended peripheries included much of diamond-rich Africa and the oil-rich Middle East).[6]

Today, globalizing projects continue to integrate and divide the core (the developed nations of Europe, Japan, and the United States) and the periphery (the Third World). The core uses skilled labor, while unskilled and cheap labor dominates the periphery. The core enjoys high profits and accumulates capital rapidly relative to its periphery. The core is higher on the "commodity chain," meaning that it tends to rely on its periphery for raw materials and to reserve for itself the production processes requiring the most sophisticated technology and skill. Net wealth tends to flow from the periphery to the core rather than vice versa. Not surprisingly, then, the end result is a wider and more tragic wealth gap between core and periphery than existed when the globalization project took off.[7]

Let us personalize this depressing line of analysis by thinking again of Samima and Nisran. Bangladesh is the periphery, and if history tells us anything, it is that Samima and her fellow Bangladeshis are not going to see their living standards get closer to ours or even take them out of abject poverty. The Western core countries, if history repeats itself, will take more money out of Bangladesh than they will bring in unless Samima and her fellow workers gain a new voice in deciding how the global economy works and who runs their factories.

But why do globalizations seem to always polarize in such tragic "unequal exchange," with such serious potential for violence and war? Trading partners start at different levels of development. They are often integrated through conquest, as colonialism illustrates. Even before colonialism, trade was often historically intertwined with military tribute or forced expropriation of property, raw material, or profits from the periphery. Free trade, the mantra of today, has almost always involved rules and terms of trade imposed by the more powerful trading partners.

And power is the key idea here. It is absolutely central and yet constantly neglected in the apple-pie free-trade conversation. History teaches us that you never ever have trade without power. Trade in oranges, oil, sneakers, or microchips is always shaped by the power of the businesses and the governments selling the sneakers or buying the oranges. In trade between core nations— for example, France and Germany—the power balance can be relatively equal. But when the core (the United States) trades with the periphery (El Salvador), the power imbalance calls to mind the dominatrix in black stockings holding the whip over her prostrate partner.

The core/periphery distinction is now being de-territorialized. That is, we find large parts of the periphery increasingly in the core. Think of all the impoverished immigrants from Mexico, China, Pakistan, or Nigeria who work in the sweatshops of New York or Los Angeles under conditions very similar to those of Samima and Nisran. And we find more members of the "core" in the Third World: superwealthy business leaders in Saudi Arabia, Thailand, Chile, or Mexico who are part of a new globalized plutocracy. This denationalization of core and periphery is one sign of the end of a thousand years of national sovereignty and the rise of a global sovereign that makes today's globalization a radical departure from all former systems.

The power difference between the core and periphery today (still largely a distinction between the First and Third Worlds) is immense, and the deeper the power imbalance, the more the risk of exploitative trade. Yet the win-win idea of trade fills the airwaves. Only two things can explain this out-of-touch discourse. One is that it simply reflects our desire to ignore how our own power stacks the odds in our favor, something that Third World nations have been trying to tell us for two centuries. The second is that our beliefs about trade are rooted in economic theories that never talk about power. Go to any leading international economics text, and search the index for *power*. Look in the table of contents for chapters on the historical power imbalances that shape trade. You will come up empty. This scandalous intellectual dereliction has made much of economics irrelevant to a real-world discussion of globalization.

Despite this gloomy picture, trade can be good and mutually beneficial. Even in the context of great power imbalances, it can bring gains to the weaker party. In the Roman Empire, for example, many regions were eager to gain the privileges that Roman protection and investment brought. The lesson is to recognize that those who make the rules will reap the spoils. The danger is that the periphery will resent, hate, and then rebel, and the core will never feel secure.

J.D. has something important to add about the economic dimension and its mythology. When we think of the Gilded Age economy, a globalization within the United States, we see two key stories. One can be called "go sweat," and the other is "grow the gap." Both reinforce the world-system historical perspective about why Samima and Nisran are likely to be losers rather than winners.

The famous Gilded Age muckraker, journalist Upton Sinclair, ventured into the terrifying meat factories of Chicago. In his classic 1906 book, *The Jungle*, he described a world of sixteen-hour workdays, paying pennies per hour, in slaughterhouses making meat rotting with bood and hair. A century later, Sinclair's graphic look at the sweatshop economy still scorches the brain and shapes our understanding of the nature of the robber-baron economy.

The Upton Sinclair of today's global economy is Charles Kernaghan, the New York–based muckraker most famous for his exposé of sweatshops producing the Kathie Lee Gifford line of clothing for Wal-Mart. Mostly young girls worked at the factory in Honduras. Wendy Diaz was one of them. At a press conference in Washington, Diaz described her seventy-hour work week for approximately 31 cents an hour in an ovenlike plant where the bathrooms were kept locked. She told of nights of forced overtime, threats, physical abuse, and sexual harassment.[8]

Ground zero of the global workshop is China, with its one-billion-plus workers. In 2000, after numerous trips to Chinese factories, Kernaghan writes: "When you see an Ann Taylor suit on sale for $198, do you ever imagine twenty-year-old women in China being forced to work ninety-six hours a week, from 7 A.M. to midnight, seven days a week, and being paid just 14 cents an hour? When you think of Ralph Lauren or Ellen Tracy do you imagine women in China being paid 23 cents an hour to work fifteen-hour shifts six days a week?" Global companies, he writes, "are actually lowering standards in China, slashing wages and benefits, extending forced overtime hours, and weakening respect for human rights while relocating their work to a growing sector of unregulated foreign-owned sweatshops in the south of China."[9]

The harsh reaction against unions is a defining mark of global free-trade zones, evoking memories of the robber-baron hatred of organized labor. After crushing the Homestead union and killing many strikers in the infamous 1894 labor dispute of the Gilded Age, Homestead Steel robber baron Henry Clay Frick wrote to his boss, Andrew Carnegie. "We had to teach our workers a lesson and we have taught them one they will never forget. . . . Do not think we will have any serious labor trouble again." Carnegie, who had been the only robber baron once supporting the idea of unions, joyously wired back, "Congratulations all around, life worth living again."[10]

As in the Gilded Age, any force that gets in the way of cheap labor must go, leading to an all-out assault on unions throughout the world's global export zones. The struggle of workers to associate freely and form independent unions has become the new civil rights movement. While most nations have agreed to this right as codified in the UN's International Labor Organization, global production is increasingly organized to escape or crush unions. Companies flee to safe union-free environments such as China, El Salvador, or Honduras, which typically also offer the freedom to pollute and avoid regulations on health and safety, sexual harassment, or working hours and conditions.

Listen again to Nisran, whose story suggests that the "go sweat" rule, especially the virulent opposition to unions that marked the Gilded Age economy, has reemerged in force:

> In my factory the supervisors treat us like dogs. I would like to be treated as a human being. If we try to make any demand or to argue, the supervisors threaten us and say they are going to fire us, or they fire us immediately without our Pro severance pay. For this reason we cannot make any demands, we have no power, we have no possibility to organize. We would like to form a union, but for all these reasons it is impossible for us to organize.

The robber barons viewed their immigrant workers as just a step above animals or inanimate objects, more like children, and thus developed "scientific management" to shift all mental decisions from the workers to engineers and other managerial experts. They completely rejected the view that such "undeveloped" workers should unionize or have a voice.

Listen now to Samima's story:

I cannot support myself with the wage I am getting. I have rice and lentils for breakfast, rice and mashed potato for lunch, and for supper rice and vegetables. I eat chicken once a month when I get paid, and maybe twice a month I buy a small piece of fish.

If we want to use the bathroom, we have to get permission from the supervisor, and he monitors the time. If someone takes too long for any reason, the supervisor shouts at her and humiliates her, calling her names. If someone makes a mistake, the supervisor docks four or five hours of overtime wage, or lists her as absent, taking the whole day's wage.

In my factory there is no day care, no medical facilities. The women don't receive maternity benefits. The overtime is mandatory, but we are always cheated on our overtime pay. The supervisor makes us sign two separate payroll sheets. One tells the truth—that we worked four of five hours of overtime each day. The other says that we only worked two hours of overtime a day, as our labor law requires. That is the one they show to the buyers.

Our lives have been stolen. We are treated like animals, and any workers who attempt to get together a union are fired immediately and may be blacklisted. We feel we have been born only to serve the needs of the owners.

As in the Gilded Age, the antiunion regime is a prescription for exploitation masked by the eagerness of workers to participate. In 1890s America, desperate Polish, Italian, or Russian immigrants waited in line to work in Carnegie's steel mills in Pittsburgh or in horrific sweatshops in Manhattan. Now, Samima and Nisran still want their jobs, and Mexicans flock to work in Mexico's forty thousand foreign assembly plants, like the Kukdong plant at Atlixco that produces sneakers for Nike. An international human rights team found that the factory refuses to pay legally mandated sick pay and maternity benefits, denies workers five hours' wages each week, and forces workers to eat in a plant cafeteria where food is spoiled. It imposes a company union while beating and firing workers seeking to organize an independent union. At another sweatshop, an Alcoa employee, Isidro Esquivel Sanchez, who clings to his job in Ciudad Acuña, Mexico, said, "They work us like donkeys, and we come back to this," pointing to his one-room, dirt-floor hovel. His coworker, Oscar Chavez Diaz, showed a *New York Times* reporter a weekly pay stub for $60; Diaz lives with his wife in the rusting shell of a school bus and says he lacks money for food and clothing. Economist Ruth Rosenbaum, who has studied purchasing power in eleven border communities where foreign plants proliferate, says the misery is getting worse. "You study these wages for a while," she says, "and it makes you sick to your stomach."[11]

Yet the workers keep coming, prompting influential scholars and journalists to conclude that even the worst sweatshops are better than the feudal conditions in the countryside. Harvard's Jeffrey Sachs suggests that the only problem with sweatshops in poor countries is "that there are not enough of them." Sachs is right that millions in the new global workforce are clamoring to work at and hang on to sweatshop jobs. Says one Mexican female sweatshop worker, "Without these jobs, we would have nothing. We would have no food, and our children would die." But this reveals globalization as a system organized to take advantage of extreme human vulnerability, with the new captains of industry as eager as the old to capitalize on it. We make a terrible mistake if we think that the sweatshop workers desperate to hold on to their job are grateful to us. Nisran and Samima are fighting for their humanity and their survival, and these gentle souls, while not disposed to violence, will not go softly into the night.

"Grow the gap" could have been the slogan of the Gilded Age, and it too has come back to haunt us. In 2000, the three top shareholders of Microsoft owned more wealth than do all six hundred million people living in Africa. The three richest people in the world have accumulated more wealth than the combined GDP of the forty-eight poorest countries. The UN reports that

458 global billionaires have acquired a combined wealth equal to that of half of humanity.[12]

A huge gap between rich and poor defined the Gilded Age. When John D. Rockefeller became the country's first billionaire, more than 90 percent of Americans lived in poverty. In the 1890s, when millions of poor people in Philadelphia, Chicago, and New York were living in some of the most densely populated slums in the world, robber barons were building their fabulous summer palaces in Newport. A leading scholar in 1900s concluded that "the poorest seven-eighths of the families hold but one-eighth of the national wealth while but one percent of the families hold more than the remaining ninety-nine percent."[13]

Splendid economic growth and high employment did not close the gap. Eighty percent of Gilded Age workers, who toiled twelve to sixteen hours a day, stayed poor. The reason was very low wages that robber barons created by exploiting the huge immigrant labor pool and successfully destroying unions. The combination of low wages and high profits grew the gap until the Progressive Era's reforms in wages, working conditions, and progressive taxation finally ended the Gilded Age.

Globalization resurrects the Gilded Age growth model that spectacularly increases wealth while expanding poverty. The wealth gap today is growing between and within nations. The average income in the world's richest twenty countries is thirty-seven times the average in the poorest twenty, and the per capita income gap between rich and poor nations *tripled* between 1960 and 1993. Globalization might someday level the huge differences between the First and Third World, but by the present rules it does just the opposite. As experts say, instead of win-win, the name of the game is "divergence." Could anything be more dangerous in our already deeply polarized world?[14]

At the teargassed 2001 Quebec trade summit, the leaders of the Americas laid down their new battle cry: "Globalization = Democratization." The new U.S. ambassador to Canada, Paul Cellucci, said, "The purpose of the summit is to help democracy.

We want to strengthen democracy, the rule of law . . ." President Bush repeated that free trade is the foundation of freedom. He said he was putting his money where his mouth was by backing an "action plan" of $20 billion dollars to build up democracy in every nation joining up with the massive new free-trade zone forged at Quebec.[15]

Like the idea of trade as apple pie, the mythology of globalization as democracy has become part of the new common sense of the day. But is it true? Is globalization the brave assassin of African dictators or oil-rich sheiks of the old authoritarian world? After the events of September 11, the new spotlight on Middle East politics raises serious doubts. We are painfully aware that unreconstructed oil monarchies that give their increasingly discontented people no vote and hardly any free expression are as much a part of the globalization system as are liberal democracies. And we are newly aware that our support of antidemocratic Mid-East regimes that keep the oil flowing in the global economy has opened us to new and terrible dangers. At the 2001 antiglobalization Quebec protests, protesters saw the hated ten-foot-high chain-link fence keeping them out as a symbol of the "un-freedom" of globalization. If globalization is the spirit of democracy, why do they need to build a "wall of shame" to keep the people out? Said one protester, "This fence is an offense to justice and freedom. Tell your Dubya Bush he can cringe but he cannot hide behind this barrier."[16] Nonetheless, there is reason for hope: globalization has supported new "emerging democracies" in many parts of the world, even if it bolsters other ancient repressive regimes. The relation between globalization and democracy is the most contentious and important of all questions in today's world—and it does not reduce to simple formulas.

The neglected lessons of former globalizations are important here. Remember that all globalizing systems throughout history have three dimensions, and while the economic one holds our attention today, the historical record shows that the political one may be the true father of any "world system" trinity. No one reminds us more of this than J.D. I have said that the robber barons were "globalizers in a single nation"; the new vast U.S. market they created was bigger and richer than many European colonial empires. But while the robber barons are most famous for building Standard Oil, U.S. Steel, and the Morgan banks and making fabulous profits by ruthlessly breaking up unions and exploiting immigrant workers, their greatest accomplishment was rewriting the Constitution and changing the entire balance of sovereign power in American democracy. The Gilded Age is a historical window into a brave new form of corporate rule.

In 1892, tycoon Jay Gould telegraphed the new president, Grover Cleveland, a Democrat, this message: "I feel . . . that the vast business interests of the country will be entirely safe in your hands." Cleveland assured corporate America that "no harm shall come to any business interest as the result of administrative policy as long as I am president." Republican president William McKinley succeeded Cleveland in 1896 with an even deeper commitment to a new corporate democracy. His campaign manager and close adviser, Mark Hanna, one of the most famous robber barons, staged huge fund-raising parades down Wall Street and raised millions to pay for McKinley's election.[17]

With McKinley's 1896 knockout blow to the populist Democrat William Jennings Bryan, the robber barons sealed the political side of their own "globalization within a nation." As they knit local economies into a national U.S. economy, sovereignty shifted in two directions: (1) from the states toward a newly powerful federal government and (2) from the people toward the large corporations and financiers. The new system of American government, essentially federalized democracy with a corporate logo, was described bluntly by 1890s populist, Kansan activist Mary Elizabeth Lease, as "a government of Wall Street, by Wall Street and for Wall Street."[18] As the robber barons integrated the economy from New York to California, they deformed democracy and unhinged the social order. A leading Gilded Age scholar makes clear that the robber barons led not just a business crusade but a wholesale societal and political transformation. "Like earlier invading hosts arriving from the hills, the steppes, or the sea," he wrote, the robber barons "overran all the existing institutions which buttress society . . . they took possession of the political government, of the School, the Press, the Church." Business, that is, began to absorb all of society into itself.[19]

The unexpectedly swift rise in the size and power of large corporations helped create this revolution. Before the Civil War, corporations had been local businesses, and they were balanced in power by craft guilds, state legislatures, and other organs of community or citizen power. But after the Civil War, the robber barons beefed up their businesses to conquer the emerging national markets, while labor and community groups found themselves struggling to survive in the new scale of enterprise. Corporations had become businesses on steroids with huge concentrations of capital never seen before, while contending popular forces of unions and governments remained small in scale.

When you hear "balance of power," you no doubt think about Congress checking the president and the Supreme Court checking both. But the more fundamental balance of power is in society itself, involving the balance between business, on the one hand, and the "countervailing" forces of ordinary citizens and their unions, communities, and governments on the other. Democracies always require a delicate balance here and are undermined when the balance shifts too far in one direction. Democracies also require that popular forces remain supreme, even though they must respect important rights of property.

One lesson of the Gilded Age is that "globalizing" projects tend to tilt the social, and then political, balance of power dangerously toward corporate and financial entities. Money can move a lot faster than people. The information revolution has made investment capital astonishingly mobile, with General Motors or Sony able to shift operations across borders with a few flicks of the computer key. There are no emotional roots or family bonds to tie money down, but one can hardly say the same of the workers left behind or the organizations that are supposed to protect them. Unions are largely local or national affairs, as are governments that are stuck in fixed territories. They are contending with global corporations, the most exquisitely mobile large organizations in history. We can say that corporations are now jet streams, while unions and government are still quicksand organizations.

As anyone in a marriage knows, one of the great sources of power is the freedom to exit. In any relationship, the person who can leave has enormous leverage over the person who has to stay because he or she lacks the emotional or financial resources to leave. Now extend that way of thinking to globalization. Corporations enjoy huge new forms of exit power. By threatening to leave, they can exact enormous concessions from unions or governments. In the 1980s and 1990s, companies such as General Motors, AT&T, and Ford repeatedly forced frightened unions to open up contracts and "give back" wages or benefits. Entire countries confront the same extortion. For example, if El Salvador doesn't lower its taxes or change its environmental regulations or labor standards, the Gap will relocate to Guatemala. This is globalization as the proverbial "race to the bottom," with corporate exit options shifting the balance of power in every society away from the quicksand organizations to the jet streamers.

The Gilded Age offers an ominous warning of the implications for democracy. Exit across state lines by the big robber-baron companies became a corporate craze. In the 1890s, thousands of New York companies threatened to move across the Hudson River to New Jersey, a neighbor who offered not only lower taxes but far less restrictive corporate charters. In 1896, New Jersey created a revolutionary new chapter, which permitted unlimited corporate size and market share, removed all time limits on the corporate charter, and legalized new mergers and acquisitions for Standard Oil and other companies already big as an octopus. Corporations were so pleased that by 1900, a total of 95 percent of big U.S. companies decided to become New Jerseyites.[20]

This triggered a furious bidding war among states not unlike the one going on between countries today. New York, Maine,

Delaware, Maryland, and others competed to see who could shed fastest any hint of corporate public accountability in their charter. "For a state to be conscientious," wrote one law-school commentator, "would be synonymous with cutting its own throat." The eventual winner of this suicidal competition was Delaware, which, as one legal commentator put it, was "determined to get her little, tiny, sweet round baby hand into the grab bag of sweet things before it is too late." Virtually all big corporations began slowly migrating to this tiny state in the twentieth century, after it passed a revolutionary new general incorporation law that turned the corporation into the lord of the kingdom, a sovereign accountable mainly to itself.[21]

"The certification of incorporation," the new law said, may "contain any provision which the incorporators may choose to insert." As Ralph Nader notes, "These little words literally turned corporate law inside out." States had previously retained for themselves all powers not expressly given to the corporation. Delaware blew away this fundamental tenet of state sovereignty by allowing corporations to define their own powers and make their own laws as long as they didn't go against explicit state prohibitions. This Delaware law was the Magna Carta of modern corporate sovereignty.[22]

It succeeded, but far more important, Delaware inaugurated the *political* race to the bottom that profoundly changed democracy in America. For a hundred years, the United States had used its state charters to keep companies in check and harness them to the public interest. Before the Civil War, companies were subjected to harsh limits on acquisitions, capitalization, debts, landholdings, and even profits. Moreover, they had to show that they were contributing to the civic well-being, or they would be dismantled. In fact, Americans since Jefferson had been so afraid of concentrated financial power that many states in the pre–Civil War era limited banks to ten-year life spans.[23]

But this kind of popular sovereignty went the way of the buggy whip when the robber barons economically integrated the nation. Using their exit power, they forced states into a madcap rush to free them of the slavery that Jeffersonian democracy had imposed. This is a ghostly preview of globalization's new politics that would make J.D., the greatest robber-baron power wielder, shiver with delight.

The creation of corporate sovereignty in the Gilded Age required a retooling of the American Constitution and was part of the great shift of sovereign power from the states to the federal government. Earlier globalizers such as John D. Rockefeller and J. P. Morgan triumphed not just by creating a race to the bottom among states but also by subordinating local and state authority to a more business-friendly, federal sovereign government. This globalizing of sovereignty within the nation eerily foreshadowed the secret of today's globalization.

Rockefeller and Morgan unleashed a constitutional revolution that blessed corporations as citizens of the republic, endowed them with protection under the Bill of Rights, and turned them into legal "persons" who would be kings of the castle. The property rights of these new "corporate citizens," enforced by the federal government, would come to reign supreme and trump the human rights of flesh-and-blood citizens. What the Gilded Age ultimately achieved was the reconstruction of democracy to fit a corporate world. Gilded Age constitutionalism is a precautionary tale of the legal revolution led by the World Trade Organization, today quietly drafting a new property-centered constitution for the world.

George W. Bush seems like a plain-spoken man to most Americans, and he says that globalization is just plain common sense. It's good for the United States, good for the Americas, good for the world, good for democracy, good for hungry people, good for economic growth, and good for civilization and peace in an age of terror.

But is his common sense right in this case? Our friendly ghosts Cecil and J.D. remind us again that earlier globalizations also created their own common sense. And while there is much to praise about globalization, a peek into history suggests that globalizers have tended to think a bit too kindly about their own enterprise. Globalizers always create a set of cultural values and beliefs by putting the best possible light on what they are doing. The cultural system props up the globalization trinity and creates a third mythology crucial in sustaining the new world order.

Cecil haunts us with the memory that the colonialists defined their endeavor as a moral responsibility. Rudyard Kipling's 1899 poem, "The White Man's Burden," is generally regarded as colonialism's creed. It begins as follows:

> Take up the White Man's burden—
> Send forth the best ye breed—
> Go, bind your sons to exile
> To serve your captives' need;

Throughout Kipling's poem, the refrain of sacrifice by a more advanced race in the service of a less-developed people recurs. He says the colonial globalizers "seek another's profit and work another's gain." The primitive state of those being served demands a heavy moral responsibility and lays a "heavy harness" and "weariness" on the colonizers:

> To wait, in heavy harness,
> On fluttered folk and wild—
> Your new-caught sullen peoples,
> Half devil and half-child.

> Take up the White Man's burden—
> Ye dare not stoop to less
> Nor call too loud on Freedom
> To cloak your weariness.

Not all the elites of the time bought into this "common sense" of sacrificial colonialism. Ernest H. Crosby, in *The New York Times*, wrote an 1899 rejoinder, "The Real 'White Man's Burden,'" that begins:

Take up the White Man's burden;
Send forth your sturdy sons,
And load them down with whisky
And Testaments and guns.

Throw in a few diseases
To spread in tropic climes,
For there the healthy niggers
Are quite behind the times.

Crosby ends his parody, for good measure:

Take up the White Man's burden;
To you who thus succeed
In civilizing savage hoards
They owe a debt, indeed;

Concessions, pensions, salaries,
And privilege and right,
With outstretched hands you raise to bless
Grab everything in sight.

But if more than a few skeptics remained, virtually all the business, political, and intellectual leaders of the European nations were fervent believers and avid propagandists for their global expansion. Cecil Rhodes spread far and wide their view of colonialism as impassioned idealism. As a young man, in 1877, Rhodes wrote a famous "Confession of Faith," in which he proclaimed, "I contend that we are the finest race in the world and that the more of the world we inhabit the better it is for the human race." Although he got fabulously rich through his global businesses, Rhodes always portrayed colonialism as both sacrifice and "duty." In establishing the criteria for Rhodes scholars, he talks repeatedly of "duty, sympathy for and protection of the weak, kindliness, unselfishness and fellowship." He established the scholarships to create a cadre of leaders who would put into practice his view of colonial globalization as a grand civilizing endeavor. This idea, in new language, has become part of globalization's creed today.

J.D. reminds us that the robber barons had cultural myths essential to their "globalizing" endeavors. When Rockefeller said, "God gave me my money," he was expressing the Gilded Age common sense that the robber barons were carrying out a divinely inspired plan. Like the colonists, the robber barons were religious men who saw their own ancient globalization as serving the highest moral ideals. The religion of the Gilded Age was couched in the rhetoric of social Darwinism, a distinctively American common sense. It made poverty, competition, and exploitation all part of the natural struggle for existence. Said one railroad baron, "Society as created was for the purpose of one man getting what the other fellow has." Rockefeller frequently used Darwinist language: "The growth of a large business is merely a survival of the fittest. . . . it is merely the working-out of a law of nature and a law of God." In other words, the integration of a national market, the robber barons' globalization within a nation, was entirely in harmony with nature and God. Like global business leaders today, the robber barons believed that the market was not a creation of people but part of a natural order of things. As markets expand and larger businesses swallow up smaller ones, business leaders are simply acting out the age-old morality of evolution.[24]

Globalization today has softened its self-justifying rhetoric. Business leaders, backed by the world's most respected economists, continue to see global markets, commerce, and trade as part of the natural order of things. To refrain from globalization today would be to stand against the laws of economics and nature. But today's globalizers do not tend to read God's mysterious purposes into the misery of the poor. Rather, the new common sense is that globalization is the only viable way to bring the world's poor out of poverty.

Consumerism and the mystique of the market have replaced social Darwinism as the common sense of today's globalization.

To challenge it seems to challenge the sovereign right of all the world's peoples to consume burgers at the golden arches or to dream of driving a Mercedes. Those who raise doubts tend to be viewed, at least within the United States, as just as strange as those a century ago who questioned social Darwinism or the white man's burden. When those outside of the United States, like Islamic fundamentalists in the Middle East, attack the new cultural creed, they tend to be viewed as relics of a doomed premodern era.

Some view this cultural revolution as the real explanation for the terrorist attacks on New York and Washington. Samuel Huntington has written of a new "clash of civilizations" now exploding between Islam and the West and pitting globalization against traditional values all across the world. It is a powerful idea, but not the prime source of the conflict between the Islamic world and the West.[25] But without question globalization *is* an explosive cultural and secular force that exports the American dream and melds the idea of consumerism and freedom. Global culture is immensely seductive, even in the Middle East where anti-American elites mimic the lifestyles of the rich and famous, watching reruns of *Dynasty* and sipping Pepsi even as they decry U.S. values and policy. The cultural magic is most explosive among the global poor, awakening desires for earthly comforts that they will never enjoy.

The culture of globalization is based on the vision of billions of people newly liberated to make their own choices in a market offering dignity and endless delights. Even when you recognize that it is a fantasy for most of the world's people, you see the seduction while walking down the main drag in the Sanjuku district of Tokyo at night. The hundred-foot-high, brilliant neon lights of thousands of well-stocked stores and boutiques selling brands from all over the world illuminate the nocturnal landscape. Engrossed shoppers rush around frantically, buying and buying as if making up for centuries of deprivation and serfdom. It makes you a believer and makes clear that globalization will not disappear until a new, even brighter vision takes root.

CHAPTER 3

ONE WORLD UNDER BUSINESS

Democracy is a word all public men use and none understand.
GEORGE BERNARD SHAW

GLOBALIZATION ENTHRONES THREE INTERTWINED INSTITUTIONS. THE first are the global financial markets and transnational companies at the heart of the world economy. The second are national governments that are business-oriented regimes linked to each other in economic and military alliances led by the United States. The third are rising "global governments" such as the World Trade Organization, the International Monetary Fund, and the World Bank, also strongly led from the White House. These three power centers increasingly operate as a system. The new sovereign is not an individual such as George Bush or Rupert Murdoch, or a single organization like the U.S. government or the World Trade Organization. Instead, global power lies in the system itself and the new corporate elites who seek to manage it.

This new world system can be called a *global corpocracy*. By joining the words *corporation* and *democracy*, this appellation perfectly evokes a corporate-driven system that celebrates the idea of democracy more than any earlier global order. It's true that globalization has helped bring free elections to many nations. But it comes with a price tag that ultimately subverts the people's voice, especially that of the global poor, in the economic and social decisions that matter. The crisis of globalization and a sure recipe for violence is the contradiction between the rhetoric of democracy and the realities of corpocracy.[1]

The commanding role of business has become the key element of the new system. This partly reflects the astonishing new size and global reach of transnational corporations, the largest being virtually world empires in their own right, with their own global rules and private armies. The biggest global corporations are each far larger than most countries in the world. General Motors's annual sales are larger than the gross domestic product of Denmark. Wal-Mart is bigger than Poland. Ford is larger than South Africa, and DaimlerChrysler is bigger than Greece. Philip Morris's sales are greater than the GDPs of 148 countries.[2]

Of the hundred biggest economies in the world—counting both corporations and countries—fifty-one are global corporations. The top ten alone in terms of sales—GM, Wal-Mart, Ford, Exxon Mobil, DaimlerChrysler, Toyota, GE, Royal Dutch/Shell, IBM, and BP Amoco—are each larger than about 140 of the 190 nations in the world. The top five corporations are each bigger than 182 of 190 countries.[3]

Corpocracy globally joins these giant transnational companies and governments in an entangled and unequal partnership. In a robust democracy, there is a firewall between government and business. The firewall ensures that people rather than business control the government and make the rules. It is legitimate for business and government to communicate, but they should not be in bed together. The wall acts as a checks-and-balance system that limits the power of both and keeps business from taking over.

In corpocracy, the story line is different. The firewall between big business and government is chipped away, flooding money into government and eroding popular control. The American example of Enron, which for many years paid thousands of dollars to the highest-ranking Washington officials of both parties, symbolizes the corrupting new ties. Business and government forge an intimate relationship, both within the nation-state and the larger world order. In the new system, government still wields formal

ONE WORLD UNDER BUSINESS | 61

sovereign authority, but sovereign power has actually been transferred to a partnership increasingly dominated in times of peace
by the business sector.

The business and government partners maintain separate
identities but also join to create a new system. Business increasingly wields more influence, but there are serious power struggles. In times of war, as occurred after September 11, military
and political leaders reassert their own claims to dominance.

The incestuous melding of business and constitutional government makes governments look and act more like corporations
and corporations look and act more like governments. Governments act to protect profits, and corporations speak the language
of social responsibility and democracy. Business takes on the
planning and rule-making roles of government, and government
becomes increasingly about money. The global fire-wall seems
nearly as obsolete as the Berlin Wall. This must change. In order
for globalization to become a truly democratizing force, it must
acknowledge and reconstruct the relation between business and
government to ensure popular control.

The new union of global business with U.S.-led constitutional
democracies and "world government" is a breathtaking development. Unlike any prior world system, it creates the aura of a
new global constitutionalism. Business now speaks a global language of transparency and accountability, and its leaders call for
a more democratic world. Many see hope in the rise of a more
lawful commercial world and the practice of global corporate
responsibility. But the increasingly incestuous ties between global
companies and the governments charged with regulating them
undermine the prospects for global democracy. Corporate social
responsibility cannot replace government as a basis for law or a
way to ensure that business serves public needs. And the new
marriage of business and government undermines the hope that
people can rely on the political system to serve their needs.

In the past, global business waltzed with dictators in Latin
America and sheikdoms in the Middle East who used brute force
to stabilize their nations and protect lucrative business deals. Af-

ter September 11, Western governments and business continued alliances with repressive regimes that deliver valuable goods, such as oil, and strategic military assets. But the legitimacy of globalization and global business rests on a shift toward a less repressive system of political sponsorship and ever closer ties to governments that are increasingly unified by markets, U.S.-led alliances, and a common commitment to elections. The shift toward formal democracy legitimates globalization while veiling the antidemocratic collusion between business and government that it represents.

Wrapping business in the arms of constitutional democracy began in the United States more than a century ago. Optimists subscribing to the mystique see globalization as the spread of American-style liberal democracy around the world. The American Constitution will, in this view, become the basis of a unifying democracy in nations everywhere and in the WTO and the other emerging global governments. The presumption is that government regulation and corporate responsibility will combine to humanize the rising global capitalist order, a deeply misleading conception of the meaning of both regulation and responsibility in a corporate-driven system.

After the attack on the World Trade Center, much is up for grabs. Globalization seems newly threatened, and the ties of global business with many governments around the world will be reorganized according to new military and security imperatives. The U.S. government and military leaders will take more overt command, and business will depend on new political and military alignments dictated from Washington. But whatever the future holds, global business has established its global authority in a way that no terrorist can undo. Giant corporations are everywhere, and the magic of their logos has captured the world's imagination. It is becoming impossible to find a person on the planet who hasn't heard of Nike or been enchanted by a Disney cartoon. I recently saw a picture of a shoeless boy in rural Africa who had had scratched the Nike swoosh logo onto his bare foot. The Beatles once got into trouble by saying they were more famous than Jesus. Corporations can now truthfully claim that more people have heard of them than most of the worlds' political leaders.

The truth behind globalization is that business, whether national or global, simply can't survive or wield its great power over all of us without government. Part of what government delivers is military stability, a huge issue after September 11. But economic and political intervention by government is essential to ensuring stability, profit, and the very survival of business—in peace as well as war. We all learn that the last thing business wants is an intimate affair with government. Both national and global corporations portray government as a burden and themselves as swimming or sinking on their own. This is a key tenet of the globalization mystique: that business and the markets run themselves and leave governments in the hands of the people rather than seeking to take them over for their own ends.

While this idea is at the heart of the new global mystique, it has always been mostly rhetoric. From the historical origins of the corporation in seventeenth-century Britain to its development in the United States after the Civil War, the corporation has long been intimate with government. The nature of the intimacy has changed over the centuries, but the importance of it to business—and its danger for democracy—has always existed.[4]

Writing about the history of the corporation in the United States, political economist Gabriel Kolko vividly unmasks the myths about business and free markets at the core of the mystique. Kolko has written extensively on the Gilded Age and the Progressive Era, when the robber barons were crying out against big government and promoting the new religion of laissez-faire. He is one of many scholarly chroniclers of the secret marriage between the robber barons and the government they denounced. The robber barons spent fortunes to elect politicians and yoke democratic governments to their own agendas. They needed jurists who would rewrite the corporate laws, the tax laws, and the Constitution itself in the late nineteenth century in order to protect their new corporate property under the Bill of Rights. While railing against regulation, they were the primary drafters of the Interstate Commerce Commission and many other government agencies that worked closely with big business to outlaw upstart competitors and bring order and stability to the market. While they propagated the free-market idea, they built and bought government at the expense of their workers and ordinary citizens.[5]

Government had to create the uniform national regulations, nationally enforceable contract law, and new intangible property rights that made a national market and the corporation itself viable in the first place. The major Supreme Court decisions of the era—including the 1886 Santa Clara Act, which defined the corporation as a person with the rights of flesh-and-blood citizens—allowed the corporation to claim protection for the first time under the Bill of Rights. Several major Supreme Court decisions in the 1880s and 1890s reinterpreted the Fourteenth Amendment, originally written to protect freed slaves, to extend due-process protections to corporations in order to ward off regulation. The Court held for the first time that corporate "liberty of contract" was protected under the amendment and that the regulatory powers of the state were restricted under the due-process clause. Without such major and sustained state intervention, neither the national market nor the corporation itself could have emerged and flourished in its modern form.[6]

As I showed in detail in my book *Corporation Nation,* this government and judicial activism led to profound changes in the American view of the corporation. Before the Civil War, corporations were legally defined as creations of the government to serve public purposes, and their charters could be dismantled by state legislatures if they did not demonstrate their commitment to the common good. The Gilded Age courts redefined the corporation as "private enterprise," a sacred contract between private parties for profit protected from public intervention. Ironically, this "privatization" of the corporation occurred as the new companies were relying increasingly on government to establish their limited liability, secure the rights of intangible corporate shares, and subsidize core business operations.[7]

The enormous role that government has to play in creating the property rights and a constitutional framework that business requires is obvious today in a country like Russia. The Russian government has thus far created neither a sustainable framework of enforceable property rights and national regulation nor transparency in the financial system and a functioning tax system. This has made it difficult for a viable corporate structure and market system to emerge, endangering the rise of a successful Russian national corporation and the prospects of global business taking root there.

In Africa, Asia, and Latin America, there are many weak or crumbling governments barely able to provide order of any kind. This creates major obstacles for companies who need functioning governments to deliver stability, resources, and commercial protections. Anarchism is anathema to business, and corporations will work hard to establish protective governments everywhere, increasingly democratic in form, but often corrupt and tyrannical in practice.

The corporation is inherently a political creature, and the free-market order itself is a government-based system. The idea of free markets, a core tenet of the globalization mystique, obscures the reality that markets are always constructed by governments and can survive only with multiple forms of government intervention and public subsidy. There can be no market without state power establishing, regulating, and militarily defending property and no corporations without state charters and governments managing and stabilizing the economic and social order. And all market systems rest on abundant forms of "corporate welfare" involving not just tax breaks and subsidies, but expenditure on education, infrastructure, and research and development without which the economy would collapse. Most important, the government stands as the ultimate guarantor that contracts will be enforced and laws against fraud upheld so that people's trust in the market remains secure.[8]

The 2002 outbreak of what Senator Joseph Lieberman called "Enron-itis" makes clear just how important that role is today. U.S. and global markets were severely rattled as people worried that their Dow or Nasdaq portfolios might never be safe. How many other Enrons and WorldComs might be betraying them through deception, "creative accounting," and shredding of documents? The U.S. Congress and President Bush immediately responded to ensure the public that government would do everything necessary to restore trust. Bush declared in his 2002 State of the Union message that government must intervene to create "stricter accounting standards and tougher disclosure requirements." In other words, even the most zealous defender of the free market understood that government activism is essential to the survival of the market itself.

This was true of national capitalism before globalization, and it is the essential truth of the new world system that globalization is creating. Global companies are now looking to create and control the political system at the world level that earlier corporations found in both state and national governments. This requires a system of economic stabilization international law and the beginnings of a constitution for the world economy, backed up by military enforcement power. In recent decades, the United States provided the global economic management and political and military sponsorship that business needs. But globalization is leading toward a world government that is likely to gain greater autonomy from the United States over time. It will be harnessed to global business and more concerned with profits than people, a direct contradiction to the globalization mystique's message about a win-win world.

The global business groom dominates the ruling marriage I call corpocracy, but he is very dependent on his government brides. He needs government to manage and stabilize the system, keep order, and sustain the democratic image on which the globalization mystique rests. He has confidence that he can remake his government partners in his corporate image and harness them to his mission. But the power struggle is never entirely predictable and this makes global business nervous. He gets even more nervous in periods of war, which potentially threaten his reach abroad and his safety at home.

The events of September 11 point to this vulnerability. Hundreds of powerful financial companies were devastated by the attacks on the Twin Towers, and corporations everywhere are facing new crises that could bankrupt them. Violence has threatened their very identity as global players. Within weeks of the New York attacks, thousands of Western apparel and electronic companies had withdrawn from Pakistan, Bangladesh, and other nations in Asia, war zones deemed too unsafe even as new security challenges loomed at home. The new military climate will intensify business dependency on government and may dangerously expose the illusion of the free-market religion that sustains both global business and globalization itself. Global business, though, will survive September 11 and remains, even in an era of war, the dominant and unifying force of our time. It is itself a partnership of two huge institutions: global financial markets and global corporations. Together, they control more wealth than any institution in history and create a network that increasingly unites all of us, whatever our culture or religion.[9]

Global financial markets are best seen as the brain—and global corporations as the muscle—of global business. The financial markets are something like an electronic cortex sending out billions of buy and sell orders from millions of investors. Meanwhile, the global companies race to make sure they understand and comply with the message the markets are sending. When the corporate muscle acts against the will of the financial brain, the markets will starve it of its oxygen—that is, global capital.

Globalization is often associated with direct corporate foreign investment creating jobs. But the mushrooming of the global financial markets is the more eye-opening development. By 1997, more than *$1.5 trillion* in such foreign-exchange transactions took place every day. Analysts have noted that "only one to two percent of these transactions are related to trade or foreign direct investment. The remainder is for speculation or short-term investments that are subject to rapid flight when investors' perceptions change." Between 1980 and 1995, the value of world merchandise trade increased 400 percent, while the value of the world stock exchanges increased 970 percent and foreign-exchange transactions 2,100 percent. The amount of money exchanged globally *each day* "is more than the total value of world trade in goods and services each quarter."[10]

The rising power of the global financial markets is a leading theme of nearly all commentators on globalization. Thomas Friedman calls the global markets "the Electronic Horde" and celebrates them as the centerpiece of globalization. He recognizes, though, that they put nations into a "Golden Straitjacket," eroding national sovereignty. "As your country puts on the Golden Straitjacket, two things tend to happen: your economy grows and your politics shrink." Your "political choices," Friedman summarizes, "get reduced to Pepsi or Coke." But he believes that this loss of control is acceptable because the markets are forcing nations to make rational choices promoting growth that they can't or won't do on their own. These include "making the private sector the primary engine . . . shrinking the size of its state bureaucracy . . . eliminating and lowering tariffs . . . privatizing state-owned industries . . . eliminating government corruption, subsidies, and kickbacks . . . opening its banking and telecommunications system to private ownership and competition."[11]

Some of these virtues are real, but the notion that such critical national policies should be imposed by investors is hardly a democratic idea. Decisions about size of government, financial regulation, and the role of the market are at the heart of democracy. Take them away, and you really *are* electing leaders just to decide whether they prefer Pepsi or Coke. Friedman accepts such a drastic assault on democracy because he takes on faith the economic theories that markets allocate money most efficiently and maximize efficiency and growth. But what if countries do not view economic growth as their highest priority? What if preserving their antipoverty programs or democracy itself is more important to them? And what if, as the Argentine debacle, the traumatic setbacks in Thailand and other Southeast Asian nations, and America's own post-Enron crisis suggest, leaving it all to the markets does not promote sustainable growth?[12]

Beyond the fundamental concern about democracy, there are other serious issues. The mushrooming of global exchanges in currency, derivatives, and other short-term investments represents an effort by investors to exploit new global rules permitting vast sums of money to be invested and withdrawn at lightning speed without national controls. This was not part of the original globalization system or the concept of trade developed by American and British planners after World War II. They worried that speculators or other short-term investors, whether finance firms or rich individuals, could exploit such freedom for enormous profits while destabilizing whole nations and regions of the world. They created initially a strongly regulated trade regime, with special protections for national banks and financial systems to prevent such possibilities.

The new freedom of money to race anywhere creates enormous dynamism as well as frightening instability. The Clinton administration led an aggressive financial deregulation campaign in the 1990s through the International Monetary Fund and the World Trade Organization. Globalization leaders overturned long-standing restrictions by governments that limited foreign ownership of their banks, deregulated currency exchanges, and eliminated restrictions on how quickly money could be withdrawn by foreign investors. Most analysts now believe that such deregulation helped give rise to the catastrophic Asian financial meltdown in 1998 that devastated Thailand, Malaysia, Indonesia, and South Korea. In late 1997, when short-term investors precipitously withdrew huge sums, they helped bankrupt these Southeast Asian economies that had reconstructed themselves around the large foreign sums originally loaned and invested. The same chaotic pattern hit Mexico in 1994 and Russia and Brazil in 1998.[13]

The liberalization of financial markets has helped globalize the unstable, "irrational exuberance" of stock markets described by Federal Bank chief Alan Greenspan, and also helped produce a cesspool of unsupervised global "hot money." As one analyst argues, "International financial transactions are carried out in a realm that is close to anarchy. Numerous committees and organizations attempt to coordinate domestic regulatory policies and negotiate international standards but they have no enforcement powers. The Cayman Islands and Bermuda offer not only beautiful beaches but also harbors that are safe from most financial regulation and international agreements."

U.S. leaders have led the charge for deregulation of the world's financial system for many reasons, including the dazzling financial opportunities it offers for U.S. and other global financial companies. Once opened financially, the ability of these countries to develop their own economic models or regional economies independent of American influence erodes substantially. This is viewed by U.S. leaders as another core benefit. But after the Enron scandal, in which the giant Texan company created thousands of such offshore havens to conceal its financial dealings and debts, Americans can newly appreciate the dangers of redefining free trade and globalization itself as the creation of a deregulated and often anarchistic global financial order.[14]

There are now more than 45,000 corporations worldwide, with 300,000 affiliates. But the top 200 global companies, including such giants as General Motors, Shell, Citigroup, Sony, AOL Time Warner, Exxon Mobil, Siemens, Mitsubishi, and Microsoft, dominate the world economy and are the heart of global business. The majority are headquartered in the United States (82), Japan (41), and Germany (20), with many of the rest in other European countries, but they all have branches and contractors in nations everywhere. Their profits exploded 224 percent between 1983 and 1997, a far faster rate than the 144 percent growth in the world economy as a whole during the same period. Their sales are bigger than the combined economies of 180 of the 190 countries of the world, and eighteen times the combined income of the world's 1.2 billion poorest people.[15]

The sales of the top 200 account for more than 25 percent of the entire output of the world economy (global GDP), and thus the entire world economy is increasingly a proprietary production of a few giant firms. The top 200 hold 90 percent of the world's patents; grow, refine, and sell much of the world's food; supply the oil that runs our cars and heats our homes; operate the global media and entertainment companies that reach billions of people; and create most of the world's software and manufacture the computers it runs on. They build the airplanes and cars we travel in, make most of our clothes, provide most of the world's banking and financial services, and increasingly dominate services from health care to financial services to retailing. Finally the top 200 produce nearly all the weapons that cram the arsenals of nations everywhere.[16]

It sounds almost old hat to say that the globalizing of business produces these huge wealth monopolies. But it is integrating and controlling the world more profoundly than ever before. This is happening through a corporate version of the process that my sociological colleague, Diane Vaughan, calls "uncoupling" in her study of divorce. Globalization is the process of corporations (and financial markets) uncoupling from the nation-state in a strategy to accumulate astonishing wealth as well as unify the world. It is something different than simply choosing to operate in many different countries, which corporations have always done. And it is also not quite the same thing as divorce, because the corporation remains legally tied to its old partner while in effect marrying a new set of partners.[17]

This new corporate uncoupling is *not* from national government. As is obvious after September 11, when the airlines and insurance companies in the United States rushed to Washington for bailouts, global companies are snuggling ever closer to national governments. Corporate uncoupling is from the nation itself, and it involves abandonment of loyalty to any particular nation's interests or those of its citizens, even as ties to the nation's government may intensify. This endangers the well-being of insecure middle classes and the poor in every country.

Uncoupling is a strategy to further corporatize all aspects of life in *every* nation by freeing companies from responsibility to any particular country. By claiming loyalty to all countries equally, and moving from national monogamy to a kind of global polygamy, corporate uncoupling actually binds nations to corporations in a far deeper way and turns both national government and social life everywhere into an expression of global corporate values. Corporate uncoupling, in this sense, is a "denationalization" of business but a far more intimate coupling of corporations and global social life. It integrates the world politically as well as economically, begins to build a worldwide business civilization, and is the foundation of the "denationalizing" of sovereignty and the weakening of democratic states.

The authoritative chronicler of corporate denationalization is Leslie Sklair, a British sociologist. Just as Vaughan interviewed couples who were divorcing, Sklair went directly to the companies (about 80 of the global top 500) to talk to executives. Almost all of the executives he interviewed in the 1990s described themselves as going through a profound shift. Their companies had long operated with subsidiaries in foreign countries. But in Sklair's words, they saw themselves now as global citizens and no longer as "national companies with units abroad." This is a sign of a total, revolutionary shift in their identities and loyalties.[18]

As early as the 1970s, the chairman of Dow Chemical painted a graphic picture of where the new corporation was going. "I have long dreamed of buying an island owned by no nation and of establishing the World Headquarters of the Dow Chemical Company on truly neutral ground of such an island beholden to no nation." GE's famed former leader Jack Welch has been quoted as saying he thought the corporation should be headquartered on a barge floating free in the ocean, free of national identity and moral obligations to any nation and empowered to speak for the world as a whole.[19]

Such uncoupling is far from consummated, and it should not be viewed as conspiratorial or nefarious. It also should not be overestimated. Global companies remain dependent on their home countries for economic subsidies, and they also rely on favorable trade and other political and military policies essential to their global business prospects. Moreover, while uncoupling can be part and parcel of the "race to the bottom," a strategy for pitting vulnerable workers and states against each other, some of the most highly uncoupled companies, such as Unilever, which is based in the Netherlands, have also created highly developed global codes of conduct and model forms of global "corporate citizenship." There is no simple relation between the social responsiveness of the corporation and its degree of uncoupling. Foreign companies can bring higher standards of performance to nations where the norm has been abysmally poor. As with globalization generally, the problem is not uncoupling per se, nor the integration of global operations, but the lack of global accountability systems and of worldwide countervailing power to limit abuse and provide checks and balances to global business.

Not long ago at Kennedy Airport, I noticed big, bright signs at many airlines proudly announcing new partnerships with one or more major airlines from other countries. Your frequent-flier miles with United can now be used on Lufthansa. Miles accumulated with British Airways are now valid for travel on American Airlines. Global business is no longer one corporation but a planetary network of hundreds of the biggest companies. National business was also an alliance system, involving not only two-party partnerships between Disney and McDonald's but companies such as Microsoft partnered with virtually every other major corporation in the United States. But part of the meaning of the evolution of the national corporation into global business is the globalization of the alliance system.[20]

Globalization is creating a vast new system of global part-nerships that looks like a global octopus. As individual companies globalize, they need to merge with or partner with hundreds of allies in other countries to lock in unfamiliar markets, secure adequate capital for playing on a planetary field, and monopolize market share. States and companies must unite into coalitions in order to succeed on the new global playing field. You can't win the game, whether economic or military, without a global team operating under loose common command. This is novel for countries in a world of sacred national sovereignty, and it is even stranger in an economy based on the god of competition. Global coalitions of companies do not eliminate competition, but they undermine any traditional notions of free markets by turning the two or three dominant players in every global industry into kissing cousins with huge new power to influence the markets and all of us with lives bound up in them.

Telecommunications has now been carved up into three rapidly changing global partnerships. One, called Source, is an equity arrangement in which BT (British Telecom) bought a 20 percent share in MCI, linked to the Spanish carrier Telefonica. Telefonica engaged in an equity swap with Portugal Telecom (bringing a strong Latin American market to the alliance), which is also marketed by a Canadian company, Stentor. A second global alliance in the industry is made up of Sprint, Deutsche Telekom, and France Telecom. The third alliance is World-Partners, formed by AT&T and Unisource, a European alliance including Telecom Italia, Telia of Sweden, Swiss Telecom, and KPM (of the Netherlands), as well as KDD (the international carrier for Japan), Telstra of Australia, and Unitel of Canada.[21]

The alliance system also bridges different industries. In the Gilded Age, John D. Rockefeller, J. P. Morgan, and Andrew Carnegie sat on each other's corporate boards and ultimately merged steel, banking, railroads, and oil to create an American octopus integrating the whole national economy. Today, most of the global top 200 are partnering feverishly, not only with thousands of subsidiaries and contractors, but also with many other top 200 firms within and across industries. In the auto industry, GM and Toyota are hopping into bed with each other on numerous new projects following their initial joint venture of the Nummi plant in California. Chrysler is negotiating with Mitsubishi to engineer all its small cars. In big oil, Texaco and Royal Dutch/Shell have long been partners in refining and marketing, while Texaco is marrying Chevron to catch up with Exxon Mobil. The truth is that all the biggest auto, energy, media, computer, financial, and other global oligopolies are already partnered with nearly all their competitors in nearly every global industry.

It goes further, as the biggest global firms link up with other gigantic firms outside their own main industries. GM is hooking up with News Corp. to run global satellite-based media operations, but that is just one of hundreds of partnerships of both corporations. For more than a decade, the German giant company Siemens has been so intimately partnered with the likes of Microsoft, Fuji, GE, Corning, Phillips, Toshiba, and scores of other giant firms that it led scholars to wonder whether the single firm is becoming an extinct species. Microsoft is partnered with nearly every other top 200 global corporation, making me wonder whether the global octopus is better described as giant corporate Windows.[22]

The globalization of the alliance system leads inexorably toward the creation of a transnational financial and corporate elite. The corporate leaders all over the world are now a small, closely knit club. They are not a conspiracy of tycoons running the world from smoke-filled secret dens. They do not share the same cultural values, religion, or view of foreign policy. But they are increasingly intertwined in transnational political and lobbying associations as well as joint business ventures. The creation of a genuinely global, corporate-dominated governing elite uncoupled from nationality not only in its membership but its institutions, cultural sensibilities, and business strategy would be truly unprecedented. No earlier world system has created anything like it. It would be the most impressive achievement of globalization and the most alarming, because it would concentrate global power in the hands of the few and thus doom democracy.

In the United States, workers and citizens spent a century building unions and civic groups that balanced the power of business elites with countervailing forces and kept Washington from being a pure handmaiden of business. But in much of the world there have never been unions or civic associations that are counterweights to business. Globalization has allowed business to unravel much of the power of unions and community groups in the First World by exiting to union-free Third World environments without any history of civil society or democracy.[23]

As global business uses exit threats to gain influence over First World unions and governments, it has an even easier job yoking Third World governments to its cause. Many such governments, even those with the formalities of elections, have never been accountable to their own people. Easily seduced by the money and jobs that global companies can dangle in front of them, they have become increasingly hostage to the global financial markets and institutions, such as the International Monetary Fund, that control credit and their ability to survive in the world economy.

The question then is this: Who can protect the people in either First or Third World nations when their governments are in a race to seduce and please the global giants that bring money and jobs? Many corporations champion self-regulation and "corporate responsibility" initiatives that have brought higher standards to some nations than ever existed in domestic businesses. These are important developments and should not be dismissed as pure public relations, although they are often are.

But such self-policing is not enough. Even when well-intentioned, it leaves it up to the businesses themselves to define responsibility, and it offers outsiders no public means of verifying information and claims of good business conduct. The monitoring and disclosure arrangements presented by Nike and Reebok have helped create improvements in global factories, but public-interest groups have uncovered a long string of broken promises that are the inevitable product of a system lacking public transparency and accountability, as Enron proved in the United States itself.

It took countervailing power by new American unions and progressive community groups to finally tame the robber barons, end sweatshop conditions, and begin to recapture government for the people in the Progressive Era and New Deal years. But countervailing power in the world seems vanishingly small compared to that in the United States following the Gilded Age. Building global democracy is going to require organizing unions for Samima and billions of workers like her. And it will take a wider coalition of global civic groups that can create worldwide, citizen-based power and build a New Deal for the world.[24]

Global business is itself a work in progress, far from fully consolidating global unity or power. As the liability suits against Enron and the antitrust suit against Microsoft demonstrate, giant corporations are far from omnipotent in their own home countries, let alone in the world at large. The erosion of countervailing power is something quite different than the capture of absolute power, and corporations are far from accomplishing that end in the United States or the rest of the world. To consummate that power, global corporations need to further build the global octopus and its political capabilities and overcome huge political and cultural differences across the world. We are seeing a rapid proliferation of new corporate partnerships and transnational, politically oriented business associations spanning the Atlantic and the Pacific. But the International Chamber of Commerce and all such rising global business associations have not demonstrated yet the ability to create a new basis for enduring control and remain vulnerable to new movements for democracy and human rights.

Global business needs to legitimate its already immense worldwide power and authority as the will of the people. This leads to the presentation of the corporation as a new global citizen and the corporate system itself as a new kind of socially responsible democracy.

The "democracy of the market" has become the phrase of the day. The concept goes something like this. The will of the market is nothing but millions of consumers and investors democratically voting their preferences. When you participate in the market, you are exercising a kind of global citizenship. And your market vote may be even more important than the one you make in your local polling booth. This idea of market democracy is seductive. It is based on the reality that the consumer's choice of a brand or the investor's purchase of a specific company's stock does represent a kind of vote in the world economy. Consumers and investors are emotionally invested in this kind of choice or vote. And it has some impact, when combined with the choice of millions of other consumer and investors, on the economy and larger society. When I talk to my own students, they tell me they feel powerless to affect government, but they perk up because at least they can still choose what brand of coffee to buy or boycott.[25]

Corpocracy depends on people accepting the view that market choice is a meaningful democratic exercise. As people become more disenchanted with government, believing that their vote in the polling booth makes no difference because of the dominance of special interests (mostly large corporations), they will become rebels against the system—unless, of course, they feel they have another way of exercising their voice. Market democracy, our choice as consumers or investors, provides this sense of empowerment. But while it can make us feel good, it is something different than democracy. Market democracy is based on the principle of one dollar, one vote. Real democracy is one person, one vote. One dollar, one vote, is the logic of the market, but it is the opposite of the equal representation of all citizens that democracy is about. As a sovereign principle, one dollar, one vote, is inherently undemocratic, and it ensures a growing gap between the rich and poor because it gives the rich far more political representation.

Choosing what brand of sneaker to buy, the kind of vote market democracy offers, is not like electing a president, and it cannot create the accountability of the government to the will of the people. For that to occur, both national government and global government will have to abandon their servile marriage to business and start serving ordinary people.

CHAPTER 4

THE AMERICAN UMPIRE

If a nation values anything more than freedom, it will lose its freedom; and the irony of it is that if it is comfort or money that it values more, it will lose that, too.

SOMERSET MAUGHAM

O N APRIL 16, 2000, THOUSANDS OF HIGH-SPIRITED PROTESTERS DE-scended on Washington to call for the radical reform or out-right abolition of the International Monetary Fund and the World Bank. These global agencies offer aid or credit to poor nations on controversial terms. I was a participant in the protest. It was a beautiful sunny weekend, and I decided to stroll over to the White House. I walked up from Constitution Avenue and turned right on Seventeenth Street. From there, I thought I would turn left at the old Executive Office Building and walk down Penn-sylvania Avenue a few blocks toward number 1600. But as I got closer to the Pennsylvania Avenue intersection, I saw there was no way I was going to get anywhere close to the White House. A fleet of police vans and several lines of gun-toting, gas-masked D.C. police made sure that nobody was getting within blocks of number 1600. Seeing this Darth Vader–outfitted army fanning out in all directions, I stopped dead in my tracks and turned back, sensing a potential for violence that I had not seen since protests in the Vietnam era.

The protesters believed that the IMF and World Bank dictated ruthless policies that hurt the poorest people in the world. By virtue of money and political influence, the White House called the shots at the IMF and the Bank. Many demonstrators, in open defiance of the globalization mystique's view that globalization runs itself, said that these global financial agencies were window dressing for an American government out to run the world.

The protesters found support for their view from an important source. During the protests in Washington, the Group of 77 was holding meetings in Central America. The Group of 77—actually a coalition of 134 countries, including virtually all the former colonized countries in Africa, Latin America, and Asia—is a leading Third World voice on issues of trade, development, and globalization.

In a ringing declaration, over forty presidents of poor nations as well as other official delegates to the Group of 77 signed a statement making clear that many Third World nations see globalization as a collective "dictatorship" by rich nations led by the United States Belize's prime minister, Said Musa, insisted that instead of helping poor nations grow and stabilize their economies, globalization was only "stabilizing poverty." South African President Thabo Mbecki said that the protests show that "consciousness is rising, including in the North [the rich nations], about the inequality and insecurity globalization has brought . . . [and] the plight of poor countries." Nigerian Arthur Mbanefo, spokesperson for the Group of 77, said that Southern leaders were being silenced and marginalized by the United States and other G8 nations. He announced that the Group of 77 was "very supportive of demonstrations" and would join the protesters in opposing the "one size fits all" globalization rules drafted in Washington.[1]

The fact that 20,000 protesters and many Third World leaders see globalization as the new face of colonialism does not make it so. But in virtually every poor nation of the world, a public debate rages about whether globalization is *neocolonialism,* colonialism without legal colonies. Poor countries once again feel vulnerable to foreign corporations and governments who come with noble rhetoric and business deals backed by armies. In nearly every country but the United States itself, we hear a growing tide of outrage from those who see globalization as an American agenda to remake the world in its own image. Those outside the United States have lots of prejudices about America, but they have put their finger on an obvious truth. The Stars and Stripes has replaced the Union Jack as the symbol of power from sea to shining sea. Despite deep differences from earlier colonial empires, globalization can be seen as a polite phrase for a world system dominated by a nation far more powerful than England at the height of the British Empire.

We can now speak conservatively of an American Umpire system. It is fundamentally new, but it retains important similarities to an empire. Its economics produces a new but still exploitative relationship between the First and Third Worlds. Its politics takes the form of a U.S.-led order that—despite the legal equality of nations—involves huge power imbalances between rich and poor nations. And a globalizing military system dominated by the United States polices the globalization game with extreme force.

Violence and anarchy still run rampant in the age of globalization. But in contrast to Empire, globalization roots itself in rules of property protection. And as in baseball, there are now global umpires with the authority to enforce the new rules. Because of its enormous economic, political, and military power, the United States has emerged as the head umpire behind the plate.

In baseball, the umpire calls the balls and strikes and lets it be known who is safe and who is out. While he claims to be bound by universal rules, nobody can challenge his interpretations. As the supreme arbiter, this potentate, protected by his iron mask, can tip the outcome of the game. On a trip to Old Sturbridge Village, a Massachusetts tourist site that reenacts life in 1830s rural New England, I listened to a guide explain how early Americans played baseball. There was, he said, no firm rule book. Groups of "gentlemen clubs" fielded teams and negotiated with each other about the rules. On different occasions and among different clubs, the rules could vary a great deal, and each club tried to lay down rules that favored its strengths. Typically, the most influential club, the one with great resources or standing in the community, got the rules it wanted.

Today's umpire regime of globalization looks more like baseball then than baseball today. This is hardly surprising, because those were the earliest years of baseball and today is the formative era of globalization. There is the appearance of rules and the beginnings of what might eventually evolve into a genuine rule-based game. But the emerging rules play to the strength of the biggest and strongest teams, and they can be rewritten and broken when the bigger clubs or umpires proclaim it in the interest of the game. In such a game, the umpire is far more powerful than in today's baseball and far more partisan.[2]

Globalization has transformed the empire system of colonialism into an umpire system based on legal equality among all nations. It is a new regime of international commercial law replacing a colonial system of raw plunder, and has the air of constitutionalism rather than brute force. But the special role of the United States as head umpire places a single nation with overwhelming national power at the center of the globalization regime. This is a systemic fault line creating enormous instability.

Globalization today would weaken drastically without the power of the American state behind it. In truth, the U.S. government is betwixt and between, since it continues to field and favor the red, white, and blue team and to use its immense power for its own national interests, as all great powers historically do. But as it partially melds with global business, it increasingly represents global business and the globalization system itself.

The colonial empires relied on a system of "rip and ship," whereby the natural resources of the colonies were nothing more than ripe fruit to be plucked. The colonial economic system made sure that virtually anything could be ripped from the ground in the resource-rich colonies and shipped with little cost or interference to the mother country. Empire economics turned the Third World into a captive source of raw materials and the First World into an eager manufacturer who would send the finished goods back for a pretty profit. This enriched the First World while depleting the Third World of their most valuable natural resources. Now, even though oil, diamonds, and other lucrative raw materials are still ripped and shipped in huge volume from the Third to First World, much of the action is elsewhere. While empire economics promoted manufacturing as the monopoly of the rich countries, globalization and the new umpire economics involve the shift of manufacturing to the Third World.

Something genuinely new is taking place. Globalization and its umpire economics have unleashed a stream of investment and capital flow from rich to poor nations that could—*under a truly fair and democratically administered set of rules and regulations*—help stimulate sustained development for the Third World. And we have examples of countries, from Taiwan to Chile, proving that a limited form of success is possible even under the current flawed umpire model. Even large, extremely poor countries, such as India and China, have seen progress, although only by bending the current rules.

Thinking about the new umpire economics, the image of Popeye popped into my mind. I hadn't thought about Popeye since I was a child. When I looked Popeye up on the Internet, I was surprised to find he is still one of the most popular cartoon characters on the planet. There is even a Popeye canned spinach that is the second biggest global brand behind Del Monte. A Popeye cartoon, according to his fan club's Web site, airs somewhere in the world nearly every minute of every day. Popeye is the sailor who is magically transformed when he pulls down a can of his beloved spinach, rips it open, and swallows it in one huge gulp. Spinach turns Popeye into a superman with bulging biceps and a sense of vitality that makes the Energizer Bunny look lazy. Only spinach allows Popeye to develop and realize his full powers.

According to the globalization mystique, globalization creates a kind of "Popeye economics" for the global poor. For centuries, poor nations have remained undeveloped and unable to realize their full potential. But the real meaning of globalization and the new umpire economics, so the story goes, is that big companies and global financial markets began to pour huge amounts of spinach down the throats of the poor countries. These global investments are theoretically regulated by the new commercial rules of an umpire-based property-law system rather than by the lawless plunder of old colonial empires. As we can see by looking at success stories like Singapore, Hong Kong, or Taiwan and semisuccess sagas like Brazil or South Korea, globalization's new spinach can turn Third World nations into fast-growing adolescents with rippling economic muscles.

Globalization's spinach is, to be perfectly clear, the new flow of financial capital and foreign direct investment in a property-based international order that creates new jobs and development in former colonies. When Third World countries get loaded up on the spinach, they can presumably grow faster than they can while eating any nutrients they can find in their own country. According to Popeye economics, globalization seems almost like colonialism in reverse, because it transfers capital, jobs, and wealth from the former powers of the old colonial empire to the former colonies, making it likely that the fastest growth in the world economy will take place in the Third World.

Popeye economics is the most important story line in globalization's mythology, morally as well as intellectually soothing. Popeye economics appears to make umpire economics a lawful global investment system far more beneficial to the Third World than the transparent looting and thievery of colonial economics. It fleshes out the new economic common sense that globalization is a happy win-win proposition for both rich and poor nations. Unfortunately, Popeye economics is more fiction than fact.[3]

The idea that globalization promotes rapid growth in poor countries is more than an argument in the globalizers' arsenal; it is a creed of faith so central that if you prove it wrong, virtually the whole case for globalization collapses. Yet faith in the Popeye effect is so strong that even the most influential writers on the subject often don't bother to examine the evidence. Thomas Friedman, whose book *The Lexus and the Olive Tree* has helped build public enthusiasm for globalization, offers virtually *no data at all* showing that globalization has increased growth rates in poor nations. This is remarkable because he clearly wouldn't have written the book if he didn't believe it.

But new powerful data have emerged in the last few years that makes us wish that Friedman had actually looked at some figures. In fact, the new findings offer evidence for the unthinkable. To wit, globalization and the new umpire regime, rather than catalyzing a splendid burst of economic growth in Africa, Latin America, and other parts of the Third World, have slowed it to a snail's pace. Much of the startling new data comes from official bastions of globalization such as the International Monetary Fund and the World Bank. The Bank reported that worldwide growth actually shrank from 3 percent in the 1980s to a paltry 2 percent in the 1990s, the decade of accelerating globalization. The slowdown was especially notable in the Third World. In an understated but remarkable admission, the World Bank summarized its findings covering both the 1980s and 1990s as follows: "Indeed, growth in the developing world has been disappointing, *with the typical country registering negligible growth* [emphasis added]."[4]

I feel sorry for the World Bank economist who had to present these figures to his boss. The Bank's data show that the only part of the Third World showing high growth rates was Southeast Asia. Even there, growth was higher in the two decades before globalization took off, and the 1998 Asian financial meltdown reversed much of the gains, turning success stories like Thailand and Indonesia into economic nightmares. Meanwhile, sub-Saharan African economies actually shrank, while in much of the rest of Africa and Latin America growth hovered close to zero.

In a stunning report called "The Emperor Has No Growth," the Center for Economic and Policy Research shows that the era of globalization and umpire economics between 1980 and 1998 created a massive slowdown. Growth rates in individual living standards fell all over the planet, especially in the Third World. Between 1960 and 1980, average per capita growth in all countries of the world grew 83 percent, while in the globalization era (1980–2000), it fell to 33 percent. In Latin America, between 1960 and 1980 per capita growth grew by 75 percent, but under globalization (1980–1998) it fell to 6 percent. In sub-Saharan Africa, per capita growth was 36 percent between 1960 to 1980, and then it collapsed completely under globalization, actually *falling* 15 percent between 1980 and 1998.[5]

While looking at statistical data may not exactly be your idea of fun, I recommend taking a peek at Harvard Business School professor Bruce Scott's charts on global trends in wealth and income. Using a much longer time frame, and relying on data from official sources such as the World Bank and United Nations, Scott confirms that only a tiny percentage of nations, mostly the East Asian tigers of Hong Kong, Taiwan, and Singapore, have shown dramatic growth and poverty relief under globalization. World Bank studies in 2000 and 2001 suggest that Scott needs to add to his list China, India, and even Vietnam, all also showing strong growth and some reduction in poverty rates as they "globalize." But the huge majority of poor nations have remained desperately poor over the entire course of the twentieth century. The growth rates of most Third World countries on Scott's charts look like the EKG flat-lines of a brain-dead patient.[6]

In a chart with the dry title, "The Incomes of Rich and Poor Nations Continue to Diverge," Scott shows an amazing picture. The line representing the per capita income of poor nations remains almost absolutely flat, hovering close to zero (meaning almost no disposable personal income) for the period from 1970 to 1995. The line representing per capita income in rich nations starts in 1970 high on the chart at over $10,000 and skyrockets upward to about $20,000 in 1995. So the gap between the two lines on the chart—one showing the fate of the First World and the other the Third World—gets bigger and bigger. The gap in personal income between the First and Third Worlds *tripled* between 1960 and 1993. In 1960 the per capita GDP in the richest twenty countries was eighteen times that in the twenty poorest nations, but by 1995 this gap had ballooned to thirty-seven times. Subsequently, there are millions more poor people in the world today than there were twenty-five years ago. The World Bank minces few words about the horror of the problem. "The world has deep poverty amid plenty. Of the world's 6 billion people, 2.8 billion—almost half—live on less than $2 a day and 1.2 billion—a fifth—live on less than $1 a day. . . . While in rich countries fewer than 5 percent of all children under five are malnourished, in poor countries as many as 50 percent are." Globalization is doing what colonialism was designed to do: massively increase the wealth gap between rich and poor nations without reducing the number of horrifically poor.[7]

Why doesn't the global spinach of foreign investment work its magic on poor countries? Globalization leaders point their fingers at *political* problems: internal corruption, lawlessness, and bloated state bureacracies. Third World leaders are doing deals with foreign companies and stealing the profits for themselves, leaving the people no better off. No amount of foreign investment will save poor nations if they do not rewire their internal programming to make sure the money doesn't just go into the pockets of ruling plutocrats and kleptocrats who rip off their own nations.[8]

True, corruption by Third World leaders and the plutocracy in many Third World countries is a huge problem and a major element in the equation. But while internal reform of Third World countries is essential, the fact that the rich nations keep winning the globalization game over and over at the expense of the poor ones suggests the problem may lie also in the political design of the game itself, specifically in the umpire and the rules. Blaming the Third World nations can become a version of blaming the victims, because they did not design globalization and are not the ones taking home the spoils.

There is not enough space here for a detailed explanation of why the investment spinach fails, and the truth is that nobody has a complete explanation. Many forces other than globalization affect the growth of both rich and poor nations, and it is exceedingly difficult to sort out causes. But the failure of globalization to create sustained and rapid economic growth in poor countries is so startling and so important that we need to consider at least a few of the key reasons. The overall problem lies in the internal wiring of the poor nations *and* in the political design of the globalization system itself, a blueprint largely shaped by the rich nations in their own interests. The following seven points help explain why Popeye succeeds but Popeye economics fails.

- First, Popeye decides when he wants spinach and how much he'll consume. The poor nations don't control their own access to foreign investment. They are dependent on foreign companies and nations that make that decision for them.
- Second, and closely related, Popeye consumes his spinach only when his sense of injustice is awakened. Poor countries get foreign investment only when outsiders feel it is in their own interests. It has little to do with what the Third World nations want or need, and nothing to do with justice.
- Third, Popeye "keeps" all of the nutritional yield of the spinach he consumes and metabolizes. But outsiders cream off the vast majority of the metabolic return of the spinach (that is, the economic yield or profit from the foreign investors). Foreign companies repatriate much of the profit on their Third World operations to their First World shareholders. Foreign investors of all kinds demand a huge return on their capital, whether or not poor nations can afford to pay it.
- Fourth, Popeye doesn't have others giving him spinach one moment and taking it away the next. But foreign investors will withdraw their spinach the instant it pays to do so, regardless of the effect on the poor nations who have come to depend on it. Foreign companies will invest only as long as conditions are ripe for huge returns; when another country becomes an even more lucrative cash cow, they will disinvest and take the spinach with them. Poor nations become

dependent on the spinach, paying huge prices to get it and losing the capacity to survive and thrive when it is withdrawn.

- Fifth, Popeye doesn't have to rearrange his life to get his spinach. But Third World nations have to sell land, reallocate government spending, and accede to many other economic and political changes to get any spinach at all. These transformations, required by the WTO and IMF, the rich nations, and the foreign companies and investors, sometimes are beneficial but often are devastating. For example, to play the globalization game by the new rules, many poor nations that were self-sufficient in food production before globalization had to sell their most fertile and arable land to foreign agribusinesses that export cash crops. They also had to open their agricultural (and other markets) before they had a chance to grow and become competitive, driving millions of people off their land. This has created a crisis involving the need to import food just to prevent starvation, while also giving birth to a displaced surplus pool of hungry workers who are super-exploitable by the foreigners with the spinach.

- Sixth, and closely related, Popeye is not in a life-and-death competition with others for spinach. But poor nations are trapped in a vicious "race to the bottom" with rivals equally desperate. The only way to win that competition is to cheapen their labor and loosen their environmental and social regulations, making themselves more "spinach eligible" only by degrading their own social compact. Put differently, to get the spinach, poor countries have to continuously weaken their own social health.

- Seventh, Popeye's spinach does not come at the price of entering a system that is inherently unstable and crisis-prone. But for their own spinach, Third World countries have to enter a crisis-ridden globalization system and bear the biggest burdens of each inevitable and successive lurch. The 1998 Asian financial meltdown and the emerging economic crisis shaking Latin America, Africa, and much of Asia are just two examples of the deadly twists and turns of a speculative and financially unstable global regime that is recognized to be crisis-prone even by its champions. Rich nations are also vulnerable to these crises, but have far more resources to ride them out. Their control of the game also ensures that they can shift the burden of system crises onto the weaker players.

What are we to conclude? Despite the facts and figures, many are reluctant to dismiss Popeye economics. Can poor countries really go without the spinach of foreign investment? No matter how many times it doesn't work, won't poor nations have to keep going after the spinach? Do poor countries have any choice but to take the spinach under any conditions they can get it? Isn't a sweatshop job offered by a foreign company better than no job at all?

My own conclusion is that we should take a far more cautious and skeptical view of today's model of global economics. We cannot completely dismiss the current model. First, the data are not entirely one-sided or conclusive, and there are enough partial success stories to suggest that *under the right political conditions* globalizing can realize some of its growth promises. The varied Asian success stories have globalized, but not by toeing the neoliberal rules about privatization and deregulation. All rely on major government intervention in their economies, and countries like China and Vietnam have as much as 50 or 60 percent of their economies under direct government ownership. Other much touted successes, such as Chile, have exercised "capital controls," political controls over the inflow and outflow of global capital that are seen under neoclassical rules as heresy. In other words, the success stories prove what's wrong with the current system as much as what's right.[9]

I am not arguing that we should end foreign investment or trade. Maybe, as many globalization champions propose, we just haven't given globalization enough time. Maybe many Third

World nations would be even worse off without the spinach they have gotten. Maybe they just need more spinach over a much longer period. I am a believer in Popeye economics to this extent: I think foreign investment and trade can help poor nations develop, and I think we need to find the right way to get the spinach delivered.

President George W. Bush, when confronted by 100,000 people in Genoa protesting globalization, was blunt. According to *New York Times* reporter David Sanger, Bush simply "declared the people on the streets plain wrong, saying they should just accept as a matter of fact that free trade is the only path out of poverty. He appeared not the least bit interested in entertaining the intellectual arguments about whether borderless competition worsens the gap between between rich and poor."[10]

"I know what I believe," he said, "and I believe what I believe is right." Well, this arrogance and blind faith are a huge part of the problem of globalization's leaders, but I agree with Bush that spinach is generally a good thing and we should not be shutting down trade or foreign investment. But let us also agree that it matters how fast you eat the spinach. It matters how much it costs. It matters whether someone can decide to take your spinach away. And spinach can be dangerous if it comes with conditions or fine print that throw your whole system out of balance. If we want to hold on to some version of Popeye economics, we have to agree to suspend blind faith, look more carefully at the evidence, and renegotiate all the rules of the game with all the players at the table.

Under colonialism, poor countries stayed poor because that is precisely what the colonial system was designed to do. My seven Popeye points suggest that globalization might be politically stacked the same way. To consider this requires moving from economics to politics.

Globalization is *not* a political clone of colonialism. In addition to the economic distinctions, three basic *political* differences separate the umpire and empire systems. First, legal colonies have been abolished in the umpire era. Rising from the still-smoking ashes of the crumbling European colonial empires, globalization created a new global order in which all nations are formally sovereign and legally autonomous. Trying to reintroduce legal colonies into the globalization system would be like trying to reintroduce legal slavery into capitalism; it would destroy the ideological and constitutional foundations of the new system.

Second, under the empire system, the master nation ran things by brute force and made no legal pretenses of equality or universalism. In the umpire system, though, the whim of the master nation is formally replaced with global rules administered by financial markets and the global "governments" of the WTO, the IMF, and the World Bank. Colonialism did not bother to create "surpranational" institutions or global rules, but the umpire system depends on the existence of presumably fair rules that define the game for *all* nations. So globalization comes with the aura of global constitutionalism and world government. In the process, the entire nation-state system is subject to an Alice-in-Wonderland potion that shrinks and redesigns sovereign nations, including the United States and other very powerful countries, into new entities subordinated legally to a new and growing system of international law.

While the most powerful teams often make and break their own rules, a rule-setting process has been launched that is not just a fig leaf. It is creating powerful global legal and judicial bodies. The making of a constitutional game has started, and it is not likely to disappear. As the new game matures, the constitutional and rule-based processes will make global corpocracy look more radically new. Certain tragic outcomes, such as growing disparities between rich and poor and the continued dominant military power of the United States, are similar to empire. The power of the United States or other leading nations may persist. But the umpire system is likely to evolve further toward global, rule-based forms of power, whether managed through the United States, WTO, or the UN, than we have never seen before.

Nation-states remain extremely powerful in globalization, but a third political difference from colonialism is in the rise of a new type of national and global discussed government: the corpocracy. As discussed in the last chapter, nation-states have become formally democratic with all the trappings of free elections, rule of law, and an independent judiciary. But the new democratic state in the age of globalization is so incestuously intertwined with big corporations that the business of the state is increasingly, well, just business. In countries such as Italy and Thailand, the presidents *are* the richest business leaders (i.e., President Silvio Berlusconi, Italy's fabulously wealthy media tycoon, and President Thaksin Shinawatra, Thailand's billionaire cellphone magnate).[11]

Colonialism was also a deal between national governments and the corporation, but it was a different arrangement. The government literally created the corporation, like the British East India Company or the Massachusetts Bay Company, to sail forth and become its business agent in the colony, rewarding it with subsidies and backing it with guns. Very often, as in Massachusetts, the corporation not only was given economic monopoly rights but it also became the formal governing arm of the British crown; the directors of the Massachusetts Bay Company were the first legal government of Massachusetts. In return for its services to the crown, and the risks of doing business in dangerous and unknown lands, the corporation could make fabulous profits, but it could lose its charter if it failed to hew to its main mission of building the empire.[12]

In colonialism, the corporation served the crown. The corporation was the junior partner whose mission was to expand the empire and serve the nation more than the shareholder. The colonial state—think sixteenth-century Spain or nineteenth-century France or Britain—was not a corpocracy, because it was not driven by the corporation. The goal was to extract loot from the colonies and thereby enrich both crown and corporation, but most of all to build the power of the state and the glory of the empire itself.

Today state and corporation have an even tighter marriage, but the state increasingly serves the corporation rather than vice versa, although this may be disguised and partially reversed in periods of war. George Bush's job is to make Bill Gates's job easier and more lucrative, but Bill Gates's job is no longer to build George Bush's power. Microsoft sees the whole world as its oyster, and its loyalty to the United States is secondary to its allegiance to its global shareholders.

Colonialism put loyalty to the nation, for corporations and everyone else, above profit. In corpocracy, however, profit rules the state as well as business. Nations are loyal to the corporate agenda, but the corporation knows loyalty only to itself. Can you imagine the nineteenth-century British East India Company saying, as Coca-Cola or General Motors does today, that it had no loyalty to its nation but serves only its global investors? In colonialism, the marriage of government and corporation was ordained and managed by the crown for its own glorious ends. In globalization, the marriage is consummated again, but this time it is run increasingly by the corporation for mammon.

The complex political reality is that while globalization is not colonialism, there are nonetheless startling political parallels between the new umpire and the old empire systems. Visualize the baseball field again to understand the political side of the new globalization umpire system. The head umpire behind home plate is the United States. The umpire at first base is a group of G8 countries in Europe, such as Germany, France, and Britain. The umpire at third base is Japan. The umpires tend to agree on the general rules, and they have some rule books to go by. On tough calls, the various umpires sometimes disagree and start yelling at each other, but the tall guy in red, white, and blue behind the plate usually wins these arguments, and the others then fall into line.

Every now and then, the various umpires come together to talk about the rules. They have formed various organizations to discuss how and when to modify the rules. They even invite representatives of all the teams in the league to join them in these meetings. At places like Seattle, Washington, and Quebec, the fans (consumers), who never get formal invitations, come and noisily try to get their voices heard too.

There are almost 190 teams in the league, but the peculiarity of the globalization game is that in addition to all the other teams, the umpires each field their own team. The head umpire—in red, white, and blue—has by far the biggest and wealthiest team of all. This begins to hint at the problems of a level playing field. The umpires claim only to be bound by the rules of the game and deny favoritism. But all the other teams are constantly crying foul about the obvious problem of the umpires having their own teams. Even the first-and third-base umpires get increasingly upset with the head umpire, claiming that he is using his "hyperpower" to favor his own team.

The head umpire is naturally sensitive to these charges and insists that the game is run, not by him, but by a set of rules that govern all teams equally. In fact, he and the other umpires point out that they are not technically umpires at all because the formal rules do not assign them any special referee roles or decision-making power. The real umpires, they claim, are the millions of anonymous investors in the global financial markets and the global organizations (the WTO, IMF, and World Bank) that craft and adjudicate the rules of the game. The head umpire points out that all teams are represented in these organizations, which write and amend the rules as well as make the calls on tough plays. For example, when two teams disagree about how to interpret the rules about trading bananas or hormone-treated beef, they take them to the judicial panels of the WTO, where an interpretation is handed down by arbiters who represent the league, not individual teams.

Unlike the global games that came before, especially the colonial game, globalization is, as noted earlier, a technically rule-bound system. The rulebook consists of a growing body of international law governing trade, investment, and production— a legal corpus that is the beginning of a constitution for the world economy. And unlike earlier historical games, we have for the first time serious international organizations entrusted with the responsibility of making and applying the rules. Prior global games never created such a proto "world government" that stands above all nations and can issue legally binding judgments. Colonialism knew nothing about global constitutions, world law, or global governments. The force of the Spanish Armada or the British navy sufficed.

And in today's globalization game, the rules and rule-making bodies make judgments against even the most powerful team. In 2001, the WTO ruled that the U.S. export tax-credit system, a major subsidy by the United States to American exporters, violated WTO free-trade rules. In 2000, the WTO had ruled that the Foreign Sales Corporation tax-credit law was itself a violation of the WTO, forcing congressional amendments. This is not the first time the United States has been forced to rethink or rewrite one of its own laws, showing that no team is exempt from the global rules.

While it is true that the head umpire has no technical authority as referee and must legally abide by the new global rules, this is quite misleading in understanding the real power dynamics. The United States is the lead author of the global rules and the autocrat at the table of the new global government. While formally just another team on the field, its overwhelming power sets it apart from all other nations and from the umpires behind first and third bases.

One of the most incisive writers on globalization is Walden Bello, a small, gentle Filipino scholar with a large, powerful pen. Nobody better documents globalization as not an Internet thing, not the coming of the dawn, but an obsessive U.S. project. American leaders virtually dreamed up globalization, lovingly crafted the organizations that make it tick, authored virtually solo the major global rules, and now make the key judgment calls about how to move the system forward, when to amend or modify the rules, and how to interpret them at critical moments. Bello sees globalization as the export of American ideology to the world stage—an effort to persuade the whole world to play the American game of corporate sovereignty dating back to the robber barons.[13]

The history of globalization reads pretty much like a chronology of American-driven decisions. Uncle Sam was the architect of Bretton Woods, the 1944 conference that more or less invented globalization (although it was a radically different system in its earliest days) and created the IMF and World Bank. Britain was in on the original decisions but was turning over its empire to the new U.S. umpire.

The United States launched and blessed each new stage of globalization. In the 1950s, Uncle Sam sponsored new global trade rules called GATT (General Agreement on Tariffs and Trade) that became the first draft of a neoliberal, global economic constitution. In the 1960s and 1970s, the United States redesigned the IMF and World Bank into new institutions to run indebted Third World nations according to American market ideology— ideology that the United States often does not apply to itself. In the 1980s and 1990s, the United States decided that the entire game needed to be restructured and centralized under what would eventually become the World Trade Organization. Today, against growing popular resistance in Europe and the Third World and among many American citizens, it is the United States who promotes neoliberalism and American-style economics as the only game in the global village.[14]

When we connect the dots, we see a consistent pattern: the United States acting with persuasion when possible and with force when necessary to rebuild the world on an American foundation. Bello sees the globalization project as "missionary idealism that is out to remake the world in America's image." It is not entirely mistaken to imagine globalization as a new manifest destiny, reshaping the world along the lines of our own business model and American dream, even though globalization has already technically curbed American sovereignty and could do so in a more more powerful way in the long term.[15]

While the umpire system is not a traditional empire, the head-umpire role is a commanding one. Unilateral power dressed in the trappings of global institutions and multilateral rules is harder to see and easier to exercise. The very fact that globalization subjects the United States to a higher legal authority has veiled and legitimated America's unique role.

This brings us back to the basic contradiction in globalization. While it promotes global authority and rules not rooted in nationality, it depends ultimately for its enforcement on one nation. Globalization is torn between transnational global governance and U.S. global hyperpower. The contradiction is beginning to create a major political crisis, not only regarding the legitimacy of the WTO and IMF as instruments of U.S. power, but the entire functioning of globalization as window dressing for an American view of the world.

If the United States is the head umpire, what is it is trying to achieve? And since it has no special legal or formal authority to play this commanding role, what allows the United States to get away with it?

The United States has two contradictory goals as head umpire. The first is to build globalization as a system. In this respect, it represents not just the U.S. team but the league and the game itself. Its goal here is to firmly establish an ideology and set of rules (those typically called neoliberal) and to codify them into a rule book all players at least rhetorically endorse (this rule book is the growing body of international trade agreements and law evolving in the WTO). The United States also aims to build and legitimate the global organizations (the WTO, IMF, and World Bank) that enforce the rules and stabilize the game.

The task of building and managing the world economy is a complex and delicate one, requiring that the United States look beyond its own immediate interests. It must use its own economic strength, its currency, and its political influence to enhance the stability of the entire system, and this requires sacrifice of short-term national concerns to promote broader goals. After World War II, when the United States was the only nation powerful enough to play this global role—one that master nations in colonial systems pursued in different ways—it used the dollar as a global financial reserve and source of liquidity. It also helped rebuild both Europe and Japan, not simply to promote its own trading interests, but to ensure that these regions would not weaken the world system, either by failing to recover or by forming their own autonomous trading blocs.

Why does Uncle Sam seek such an intact global system? First, the United States as a corpocracy speaks for both U.S. corporations and foreign-based global corporations. Both groups, and they are becoming harder and harder to distinguish from each other and from the American government itself, have a stake in seeing a stable, ideologically coherent and tightly managed, profitable global system. Contrary to conventional wisdom, government and a highly developed legal and regulatory system have always been the oxygen allowing business to breathe and prosper. In the Progressive Era, U.S. business supported the development of a federal regulatory system in order to achieve predictability, enforce contracts, and control unruly competition. J. P. Morgan promoted federal financial regulatory powers for the entire U.S. banking system, and his lieutenant, Henry Davison, bluntly told Congress in 1912, "I would rather have regulation and control than free competition." The need to create order and rationalize competition is equally strong today in the global economy. Richard McCormick, former CEO of US West and chairman of the United States Council for International Business, wrote in 1997 that global corporations "rely on having consistent rules of the game" and support a full panoply of international standards for business and all its stakeholders.[16]

This ironically leads corporations to be advocates of global constitutionalism and to push the United States hard to build something close to a true world government. The United States is pulled in two different directions. On the one hand, it embraces the constitutional route as a major goal, both because it wants to serve its corporate base and because as head umpire it has an allegiance to building the global game itself. And from a more self-interested point of view, the stronger the whiff of constitutionalism, the more it legitimates the U.S. power in the system. At the same time, the United States is afraid of allowing the global constitutional process to go too far. The construction of a true world government could ultimately undermine American power, and a true rule-based system would destroy the current U.S. ability to call the balls and strikes or to bend the rules as it sees fit.

What makes globalization new is precisely that the United States is creating a game that could ultimately weaken the nation-state itself, a system in which stateless capital rules through financial markets, supranational institutions, and subnational public entities as well as national governments redesigned as business handmaidens. This is the first goal of U.S. corporate globalizers and their political allies: to create a new world in which states survive but have become so thoroughly corporatized that they essentially function as subsidiaries of global corporations. But the United States also has a second and somewhat contradictory set of aims that are much more old-fashioned: building the power of the United States itself as the greatest and most commanding nation in world history. The traditional pursuit of U.S. foreign policy and military power can collide with its new role as head umpire, making the United States look transparently like an advocate for its own team rather than head umpire for the league.

In fact, this second aim, building U.S. global power, is seen by many critics as the more important force driving the United States. Chalmers Johnson, in his powerful work *Blowback*, treats globalization as simply the economic side of the United States' continuing mission to build a classical empire. Globalization is best seen, Johnson argues, as America's economic weapon to control other nations by forcing them to play on its terms.[17]

This could be dismissed as simpleminded anti-American rhetoric, except that Johnson is a widely respected academic researcher and Asian expert. He has made a powerful case that globalization in East Asia grew out of U.S. foreign-policy interests in keeping the region from falling under Soviet control during the Cold War and keeping it firmly under our own dominion in the post–Cold War era. He argues that the United States helped build up Japan and the East Asian "tigers" after World War II to create American client states in the Pacific and contain Soviet influence. After the Soviet collapse, U.S. and IMF policies requiring the tigers to build export industries, privatize, cut government spending, and open their capital markets increased dependency on the U.S. economy and contributed to the financial meltdown devastating Thailand, Malaysia, Indonesia, South Korea, and other Asian states.

Johnson writes that this horrific debacle "had its origins in an American project to open up and make over the economies of its satellites and dependencies in East Asia." Its purpose was both to diminish them as competitors, prevent them from developing a regional economic bloc independent of Washington, and to assert "the primacy of the United States as the globe's hegemonic power. . . . The globalization campaign significantly reduced the economic power and capitalist economic independence of at least some of the United States' 'tiger' competitors . . . and was from a rather narrow point of view a major imperial economic success."[18]

By this view, the line between head umpire and empire narrows substantially. It suggests that the U.S. interest in building a world safe for global capital is part and parcel of the drive to assert American global political and military dominance. And it suggests that the underlying forces driving globalization are not just global businesses seeking fabulous profits in a planetary market but also the world's sole superpower seeking to secure its global hegemony against any military or economic rivals.

The truth is that the United States, like the globalization system itself, is entangled in the incomplete transition between national and global sovereignty. All national governments today are schizophrenic in their dual commitment to traditional concepts of national interest and the new commitment to global sovereignty and a world serving transnational business rather than the nation-state. U.S. policy remains suspended between the logic of the old and new system. In the rising globalization order, the United States acts as head umpire representing the global business league, while in the old nation-state system it wraps itself firmly in the red, white, and blue uniform and acts to keep itself globally on top.

The secret of globalization has rested on the United States' success in reconciling these two aims. Building a world safe for global business has been almost entirely consistent in recent decades with increasing and consolidating American power in the world. By imposing the neoliberal ideology around the world, the United States has simultaneously created a dreamworld for global companies, while creating a Pax Americana that appears to be a constitutional democracy of, by, and for the world.

All this reflects the shrinking fire wall between global business, with its thousands of lobbyists spread across Washington, and the U.S. government itself. The distinction between the U.S. government and global business is blurring. American politicians are elected only with the huge campaign contributions of global companies, and while national leaders must speak in the name of the people who elect them, they tend to pay back the companies by representing them first. In wartime, traditional patriotism and "America First" sentiment come into the foreground, and the U.S. government is all red, white, and blue. But the war on terrorism, like the Gulf War and other U.S. military campaigns in the age of globalization, serves two intimately related ends. It builds American political and military power against terror networks and any regimes around the world viewed as hostile to U.S. interests. But it simultaneously protects the oil supply that keeps the global economy running and protects regimes in the Middle East and around the world that serve as handmaidens to global corporations.

The happy melding of global business interests with U.S. hegemonic aims will not survive forever. The new globalization order will evolve toward forms of transnational authority eroding national sovereignty and national power, including that of the United States itself. The smooth integration of American imperial power with globalization will at some point collide with the shift in governance toward the WTO and other global bodies that will not remain forever under U.S. domination. We have already seen WTO rulings that challenge American policy and laws, as well as new struggles within the WTO by nations rising up against historical U.S. dominance. For now, however, we live in a U.S.-led globalization order that largely succeeds in papering over these looming contradictions. The United States seamlessly blends its hegemonic agenda with that of global business, postponing for the future the conflicts between Pax Americana and the rising global business order that ultimately has no greater loyalty to the United States than to any other nation.

The umpire system, and globalization generally, has both more danger and more promise than did earlier world systems. The danger is that the consolidation of the world under rules dictated by the corpocracy is not a pleasing prospect. We could have a world run by money with the aura of global democracy and the respectability of international law and world government.

The more hopeful possibility is that the umpire system could evolve into a genuine system of global constitutional democracy. Currently, the umpires serve commercial and First World masters, but new social movements could change the rules and turn the game around. A global constitution and transformed umpire regime could serve human rights and people rather than money and perhaps create a new kind of Popeye economics that builds the economic muscle of even the poorest nations on earth.

CHAPTER 5

THE WTO AND THE CONSTITUTION

All the world's a stage and everyone wants to be the property man.
UNKNOWN

I N 1787, LEADERS FROM THE THIRTEEN FORMER COLONIES RODE THEIR horses to Philadelphia to write a new constitution. Cloistered in ornate rooms in Liberty Hall, the framers with their elegant poufed wigs and cloaks represented the best and brightest of the propertied elite. Two hundred years later, the Constitution they drafted is a hugely important foundation of both globalization and the movements rising up against it.

The boisterous 1999 gathering of world financial and political leaders that turned into the battle of Seattle might seem to have little in common with the legendary Constitutional Convention in Philadelphia. For one thing, the Seattle WTO leaders did not proclaim the majestic purpose of writing a new constitution. They wanted to create new, binding global rules protecting property, but they were not yet bold enough to call for a new world government or a planetary constitution. Nor did they succeed in drafting the WTO document they had hoped to achieve. While the WTO elites in Seattle faced rioters in the streets, the Constitution makers at Liberty Hall had no tear gas or angry crowds at their door.

Yet, for all the differences, Seattle and Philadelphia are both signposts of a Constitutional Moment, a period when the basic rules of the social and political system are rewritten, or written for the first time. In the barricaded streets of Seattle, I saw pictures carried high by WTO protesters of a colorful globe under construction, a potent representation of the real meaning of a Constitutional Moment.

While the WTO elites in Seattle did not say so, they were involved in an embryonic constitutional process. In some ways more bold than the Philadelphia framers, they were helping lay the ground for a new world government and a global constitution. A Constitutional Moment unfolds over decades, not days. While they failed in Seattle, their efforts continue today in new WTO negotiations and in other global agreements.

In Constitutional Moments, making history is a realistic prospect for ordinary people, as they find themselves caught up in seismic struggles over the basic rules of the world they inhabit. Just witness the drama of the hundreds of thousands of protesters spilling into the streets of Seattle, Quebec, and Genoa. In Constitutional Moments, there is the hope of fundamentally changing the way things are, rather than living as we always have.

Over the last several years, I have spoken to many public audiences about globalization as a new Constitutional Moment. The idea quiets the room quickly. People seem to understand this is of vital importance to them, their children, and the world at large. Explaining this moment completes the story of the global power system run by business, the United States, and new "world governments" like the WTO. It sheds more light on the tight relation between globalization and U.S. power, and it clarifies why equating globalization with democratization is mythology. But it is also a hopeful chronicle, the beginning of the story about how ordinary people around the world have been working to reinvent globalization in a more democratic spirit.

Seattle marked the most recent phase of our global Constitutional Moment, and the first in which ordinary people in the United States mobilized to take a place at the table. Our present moment began in 1944, as American and other world leaders began to reconstruct the world. Britain and Europe lay in ruins and were no longer capable of securing the global order organized around the British Empire. Two world wars had destroyed the global system based on centuries of colonialism, thus plunging the world into a new Constitutional Moment. As with others, this one would be shaped by titanic shifts in the organization of power, enshrining the new dominant power of the United States.[1]

There is no way of understanding Seattle and our Constitutional Moment without recognizing the emergence of the United States as military superpower and head umpire in the new world system. Remember that the umpire system depends on the rise of global constitutionalism and the appearance of a rule-based system. The "global governments" with constitutional teeth, including the International Monetary Fund and the World Bank, were crafted by U.S. and British policy makers at the famous 1944 conference in Bretton Woods, New Hampshire, to help create a new world based on American leadership and global markets.[2]

The founding period between 1944 and 1948 was like the few seconds before the cosmic big bang. This period gave birth to both the United Nations and the Bretton Woods institutions. They came to represent two competing visions of global order, each drawing from different and conflicting sides of the American Constitution.[3]

The UN vision, which draws inspiration from Jeffersonian democracy and the Bill of Rights as well as from social-democratic European traditions, was founded on human rights, including socioeconomic and social welfare entitlements, and democratic representation of all citizens and nations. Its constitutional vision is spelled out in the UN Charter and the 1948 Universal Declaration of Human Rights. I call it "Citizens' Globalism," and it could have created a very different world order than the globalization of today evolving out of Bretton Woods. The Bretton Woods framers hoped to integrate democratic ideals with global trade and property rights, and they too were inspired by the U.S. Constitution. But over time, Bretton Woods came to express the more conservative, business-oriented constitutional vision of commerce and contract molded by Thomas Jefferson's adversaries: Alexander Hamilton and the most influential U.S. chief justice, John Marshall. Bretton Woods would come to enshrine the economic individualism and property-centered vision of the great British political theorist, John Locke, as globalization's common sense.

The Bretton Woods system created the IMF, the World Bank, GATT, and a short-lived, now forgotten predecessor of the World Trade Organization called the International Trade Organization (ITO). These were the founding political institutions of globalization. The structure and aims of these bodies have changed over the years, but they were established as international authorities charged with managing trade and stabilizing the global financial order. These embryonic "world governments" are financed by contributions of each member state, with voting power or influence linked to the amount of money invested and the United States enjoying dominant influence. They have become the global enforcers of the property-centered, or neoliberal, constitutionalism that helps define globalization today.[4]

While drawing on American roots, Bretton Woods evolved into the kind of constitutionalism feared by Jefferson. Its triumph, as just noted, parallels the victory of Chief Justice John Marshall in American constitutionalism: a victory of property, especially commercial and corporate property, over other human rights. Jefferson fought Marshall unsuccessfully to his grave, a struggle much discussed by Charles Beard, Edward Levy, Max Lerner, and other American historians and constitutional scholars. Max Lerner writes that Marshall viewed Jefferson's followers as "Jacobins" and "Jefferson as Robespierre." He describes Marshall as the judicial agent "of his class" and that his thirty-five-year tenure on the Court spearheaded a struggle "by propertied groups" against the "agrarian-labor masses" about the meaning of the American Revolution and democracy itself. Lerner argues that Marshall developed judicial review, the new controversial system in the early nineteenth century allowing the court to overrule legislation, as a check on populist state legislatures and a critical constitutional protection "of the new monied groups." Lerner makes clear that this was not just an American struggle between elites and ordinary citizens "but part of a world wide movement of social struggle fought out in France and England as well as America."[5]

Jefferson's own flawed conception of democracy and human rights, including his compromised practice of slavery, helped contribute to the success of his rivals. Jefferson also did not espouse the social democratic vision of economic and social rights that were part of European constitutional traditions and that became strongly integrated into UN constitutionalism and Citizens' Globalism. Yet just as the Jeffersonian alternative never died in U.S. constitutional history, so democratic constitutionalism, including the forms espoused by Jefferson in the United States and by social democrats in Europe and large parts of the Third World, never passed from the global scene.[6]

Our Constitutional Moment is a story of the ideological battle, not only between the two faces of American constitutionalism, and conflicts between American and European constitutional traditions, but also of a second closely related ideological and constitutional conflict between the developed and poor nations. While I strongly endorse the constitutional challenge led by the poor nations and citizens' movements and while I embrace much of the Jeffersonian tradition and the European social democratic visions, this is a complex historical struggle with contradictions and hypocritical tendencies on all sides. Third World leaders speaking for human rights have often grossly violated or distorted them in practice. The same is true of some UN commissions and bodies, that have made lofty pronouncements while implicitly tolerating unacceptable violations of rights by member states drafting the resolutions. Meanwhile, the U.S.-led Bretton Woods forces have historically wrestled with the tensions between their own visions of market philosophy and human rights traditions. They have historically championed in rhetoric and often in practice key individual and political rights in the United States' own domestic constitutional order.

These contradictions play an exceptionally important role. U.S. constitutional ideals, particularly those regarding individual and political rights enshrined in the Bill of Rights and in the first twenty articles of the UN 1948 Declaration of Universal Human Rights, helped catalyze the UN's founding vision and Citizen's Globalism itself. At the same time, American individualism and its constitutional neglect of socioeconomic or "positive" rights clashed with key elements of the UN's constitutionalism. In Article 23, the UN Declaration spells out the universal right to a job with "just and favourable remuneration ensuring . . . an existence worthy of human dignity." In Article 25, the Declaration proclaims, "Everyone has a right to a standard of living adequate for the health and well-being of himself and of his family, including food, clothing, housing and medical care and necessary social services, and the right to security in the event of unemployment, sickness, disability, widowhood, old age or other lack of livelihood in circumstances beyond his control." Article 28 states, "Everyone is entitled to a social and international order in which the rights and freedoms set forth in this Declaration can be realized." The United States affirmed these rights when it became a signatory to the Declaration. However, in multiple subsequent UN resolutions reaffirming rights to food, work, shelter, and employment (detailed in Chapter 8), the United States voted against these rights, thus implicitly violating the commitments it made in 1948. Moreover, in its guidance of the WTO, IMF, and the entire Bretton Woods regime, the United States has supported the more restrictive tradition of constitutionalism developed by John Locke and John Marshall, one that rejects the positive rights spelled out in Articles 23 and 25 of the UN Declaration.[7]

Citizens' Globalism and UN human rights constitutionalism emerged in the immediate postwar years with surprising force. They sought a global order based on the United Nations as an embryonic new world government, representing all nations and enshrining human rights and democracy as its guiding light. The

1948 Universal Declaration of Human Rights was a global document of resounding constitutional significance. Soon, the UN adopted hundreds of other global rights agreements and resolutions affirming and expanding these rights, including Conventions on the Rights of Women and Children as well as the Conventions on the Rights of Workers enshrined in the International Labor Organization, a UN agency.[8]

The unexpected early influence of Citizens' Globalism and global, social democratic constitutionalism reflected the agony of the world after the Holocaust and two horrifying world wars, and the widespread desire for a different, more humane world. The greed and power of colonial empires had to be tempered. The UN symbolized these new hopes, and its dream of global peace based on collective security helped propel a vision of global constitutionalism based on human rights and social welfare. For a brief moment, the most noble human aspirations seemed like they might reshape the world.[9]

Few nations were prepared to cede to the UN the sovereign powers necessary to become a robust federal world government, and the Great Powers helped mold the Security Council as the real decision-making body. The UN was thus flawed in many ways from the beginning, vesting disproportionate influence and veto power in the most powerful nations and enjoying little respect among the leaders or people of the member states on which it depended for resources and legitimacy. Moreover, few nations lived up to the rights they espoused in the 1948 Declaration. But the UN's human rights covenants were an important step toward a global constitutional order, and the principle of one vote accorded every nation in the General Assembly was a first step toward a more democratic world.

In their earliest years, the Bretton Woods agencies embraced many of the human rights principles and the social development vision associated with the UN Charter. The Bretton Woods institutions—the IMF, World Bank, and WTO—are technically UN agencies, and they started with a healthy dose of Citizens' Globalism, including a commitment to both political and socioeconomic rights. This reflected the New Deal politics of President Franklin D. Roosevelt and the philosophy of the two architects of Bretton Woods: the famed British economist John Maynard Keynes and Roosevelt's trusted aide, Harry Dexter White.

Keynes and White were progressives who tried to reconcile U.S.-led globalization with a world based on both liberty and social justice. Keynes, one of the most important economists of the twentieth century, insisted that trade must permit governments to promote full employment and social welfare policies. White, among the most left-leaning of the New Dealers, shared this view. While supportive of globalization and expanded trade, neither man wanted to see human dignity nor social policy weakened by global financial markets, and both supported social regulation of the world economy. They insisted that national governments should not be forced to open their financial institutions and markets in a way that would undermine full employment and social democratic policies practiced in many European nations. They also preserved exchange controls that prevented unregulated capital flow and currency trading.[10]

Keynes and White sought a balance between the dueling constitutional traditions of property and social democracy. But the rise of the Cold War was the beginning of a dramatic change of course. The division between the United States and the Soviet Union undermined the UN's ability to act as a force of collective security. American isolationists and conservatives, fiercely opposed to the UN and to European social democratic ideology, organized to limit the UN, helping discredit its constitutional agenda among many constituents at home and influential allies abroad. American financial support of the UN collective security and social development agendas largely evaporated. New American internationalists were committed to sustaining globalization and American global leadership, but on very different constitutional terms than Keynes and White had hoped.

After Roosevelt died and the Cold War intensified, the United States reoriented politically and militarily to focus on Soviet containment, build U.S. global power, and challenge social democratic ideology. President Harry Truman appointed the conservative Missouri senator Carl Vinson to replace the liberal Henry Morgenthau as Treasury secretary, and Vinson fired Harry Dexter White. The country's policy toward Bretton Woods dramatically changed, repudiating much of the Keynesian approach to global social and financial regulation.

The Bretton Woods institutions, although effectively controlled by the U.S. Treasury, were kept weak by Harry Truman, Dwight Eisenhower, and U.S. congressional leaders, who feared any loss of U.S. sovereignty to global institutions. U.S. central bankers, in conjunction with military planners at the White House and Pentagon, took the lead in shaping the new world. The Keynsianism they retained took the form of massive military spending and the economic reconstruction of Europe, funded through Marshall Plan aid, and of Japan, to stem the Communist tide and stimulate the world economy. Keynes's development policies, encouraging government intervention and regulation of capital markets to ensure full employment and social welfare, were gradually weakened.[11]

Under the supervision of the United States, the General Agreement on Tariffs and Trade (GATT), a successor to the International Trade Organization staunchly committed to market constitutionalism and economic liberalization, became the arena for writing the rules of the new economy. Nonetheless, the world economy through much of the 1950s and the early 1960s remained highly regulated. Both in developed and developing countries, much of Keynes's vision and constitutional compromise survived. The Bretton Woods regime continued to support unions and social spending, global capital flows were limited, and strong regulations over banks and the financial sector survived and supported national social development and provisions for the poor.

In the late 1960s and 1970s, global economic integration accelerated rapidly. The United States and other developed nations began investing large amounts of petrodollars and other surplus capital in Third World nations. As part of this transition to a more globally integrated order, the Bretton Woods system shifted toward a more aggressive, property-centered constitutionalism. The IMF and the World Bank became more vigorous sponsors of global privatization and deregulation, the core of neoliberal constitutionalism. At the same time, many Third World intellectuals and policy makers tried to preserve elements of Citizens' Globalism and the Keynesian vision of Bretton Woods. A more polarized struggle between the two global constitutional visions began to crystallize.

The Bretton Woods constitutional shift was associated with the rapid acceleration of global capital flows and global political and economic changes in the late 1970s that posed great challenges for poor nations. Many were becoming newly independent, and experienced significant growth as they received significant loans and investments from the United States, Europe, and Japan. But while rapid growth in many poor nations occurred, the new postcolonial forms of global trade and investment were creating severe problems. Third World economies increasingly based on cash commodity exports suffered adverse terms of trade. Global inflation and higher interest rates contributed to the rise of substantial debt burdens throughout large parts of Latin America and other regions that had received loans of Eurodollars and petrodollars. The harsher market-driven constitutionalism of the new order coincided with greater dependency and the feeling among poor nations of the rise of a new velvet colonialism.

Third World countries thus not surprisingly led the first great challenge to property-centered globalization. Before Seattle, these protests were below the radar screen of the American public, but from the 1960s to the 1980s Third World leaders and intellectuals championed a more socially regulated vision of globalization drawing on Citizens' Globalism and the earlier Bretton Woods constitutional compromise. They forced the United States to accept compromises that slowed the globalization train and the transition to a new neoliberal constitutionalism. U.S. leaders accepted important compromises with the UN Conference on

Trade and Development (UNCTAD), a UN trade body that prioritized the special needs of poor nations and rejected the free-market ideology espoused by American leaders.[12]

UNCTAD was the most important of several Third World bodies to challenge globalization as early as the 1960s. Others included the Group of 77, the Non-Aligned Movement, and the New International Economic Order (NIEO), all inspired by the Argentinean political economist Raul Prebisch. Prebisch's theory of the "structural dependency" of Third World nations attacked the new mystique of free trade as "win-win." Prebisch argued that the South would stay dismally poor under Bretton Woods because of both deteriorating terms of trade for agricultural export staples and global rules that forced poor nations to reduce tariffs while developed nations protected key sectors of their own economies. Prebisch's ideas gained wide acceptance among Third World intellectuals and policy makers, who used their positions at UNCTAD and other trade and development posts to puncture the globalization mystique and suggest new directions.

UNCTAD's greatest success was the General System of Preferences (GSP) which gave poor nations differential treatment in global tariff-reduction agreements. The GSP ratified the Third World idea that trade and development had to be linked, and that trade policy which undermined the economic sovereignty or development capacity of poor nations was unacceptable. In the 1970s and 1980s, UNCTAD pioneered other agreements to stabilize the price of export commodities and helped craft IMF financial packages to protect the South against foreign exchange crises created by declining prices for coffee, sugar, and other export commodities. But the most important contribution of UNCTAD and the NIEO was to insist that global rules should be democratic, responsive to the needs of the global poor, and based on UN human rights principles. They challenged the view that more liberalization and free trade was the key to a better world, arguing that only a shift of global power from Bretton Woods and rich nations to the UN and poor countries could stimulate development and lead to a humane global order.[13]

The Third World challenge inevitably targeted the IMF, which from the 1970s onward became the leading enforcer of globalization. As noted earlier, in the late 1970s, poor African, Latin, and Asian nations incurred huge debt that created chronic financial insolvency and desperate long-term dependence on external credit. This new "debt trap" transformed the goals of the IMF and World Bank. Now that Western Europe and Japan had revived, the United States turned to the IMF to solve the global financial threat posed by the debt trap and help manage and integrate Third World regimes through new economic levers.[14]

As the world's designated loaner of last resort, the IMF became a "government within the government" in more than seventy-five desperately indebted poor countries, dictating the neoliberal policies that ensured political compliance with U.S. power and a property-centered world. Harvard economist Jeffrey Sachs called the IMF a permanent "neocolonial" force in scores of countries, drastically eroding their sovereignty. The IMF's structural adjustment policies opened a new stage of aggressive neoliberal constitutionalism. It forced poor nations to open their markets, privatize and deregulate key industries, and cut wages and social programs such as health and education, all to increase exports and reduce imports. Sachs, a leading mainstream American economist, summarized the IMF role in harsh terms: "Not unlike the days when the British Empire placed senior officials directly into the Egyptian and Ottoman finance ministries, the IMF is insinuated into the inner sanctums of nearly seventy-five developing country governments. . . . These governments rarely move without consulting the IMF staff, and when do, they risk their lifelines to capital markets, foreign aid and international respectability." Sachs concludes, "It is time to end the IMF's artificial monopoly on policymaking in the developing world."[15]

The Group of 77, the NEIO, UNCTAD, and a growing number of nongovernmental organizations mounted numerous campaigns for debt forgiveness and radical change in IMF policies, including democratization of the IMF itself, which is dominated overwhelmingly by the United States. Their demands, thirty years before Seattle, raised all the concerns about American power and neoliberal constitutionalism that antiglobalization protesters have turned into a worldwide social movement. Despite their limited success, these early Third World campaigns helped raise questions about the IMF and the WTO that have now become a subject of intense controversy.

The Third World challenge, however, remained incomplete and inconclusive, lacking money, power, and a politically viable alternative vision. Southern challengers need allies in the United States and Europe, but had not clearly articulated the dangers to labor, the environment, and national sovereignty that globalization and property-centered constitutionalism poses in the North as well as the South. Nonetheless, the challenge from the poor nations led to a strong American reaction. U.S. policy makers sought to strip UNCTAD and other UN development agencies of much of their authority, while dismissing their economic prescriptions as backward-looking and protectionist.[16]

As the American commitment to neoliberal thought racheted up in the 1980s and early 1990s, U.S. leaders sought to drastically accelerate liberalization, especially of financial markets. In the early 1990s, the *New York Times* reported that President Bill Clinton and his Treasury secretary Robert Rubin "took the American passion for free trade and carried it further to press for freer movement of capital. Along the way, they pushed harder to win opportunities for American banks, brokerages, and insurance companies." While UNCTAD had been severely weakened, and its official functions stripped back to analysis and technical assistance, it issued alarms about the dangers of deregulating capital markets and "the ascendancy of finance over industry."[17]

The squeeze on UNCTAD and the UN, and the intensified ideological and policy campaign supporting financial liberalization and global deregulation, was part of a larger constitutional strategy to reshape globalization based on property rights and the ideology of free trade and markets. The creation of the World Trade Organization in 1995 was the most important institutional innovation to consolidate the new order. The WTO quickly became a flash point of contention about U.S. global power and the nerve center of the evolving and increasingly divisive and polarized constitutional battle.[18]

The WTO emerged out of the Uruguay Round of GATT negotiations lasting from 1986 to 1994. Before the Uruguay Round, GATT embodied a constitutional compromise favoring First World corporate interests but accepting a small number of global labor standards and the need of poor nations for special protections to promote industrial development and sustain poor farmers. But U.S. corporations were impatient to gain greater market access for agricultural and manufacturing exports and were chafing at the bit to liberalize the "new economy"—services, biotechnology, and finance—under their own global umbrella. Presidents Ronald Reagan, George H. W. Bush, and Bill Clinton all aggressively promoted the Uruguay Round, a kind of booster shot to globalization with an ambitious agenda of worldwide deregulation, tariff reduction, and expanded liberalization. In the 1990s, GATT moved to slash tariffs and nontariff barriers in all sectors, including the protected areas of agriculture, finance, and services. It also pioneered new agreements in intellectual property rights and investments and promoted a new form of global enforcement. But greater liberalization and profitability would require rooting out the remnants of Citizens' Globalism in GATT and creating a new and more powerful entity.

The WTO was created to constitutionalize sovereignty of property and further entrench principles of deregulation and privatization in all sectors of the global economy. But while designed and dominated by the United States and operating in a deeply antidemocratic spirit, unlikely to change, it is not helpful to treat the WTO as a conspiracy against national sovereignty. In any form of globalism, supranational bodies are essential to create global rights, rules, and responsibilities. The problem is not the existence of supranational entities or "world governments" but designing them to ensure they express a democratic constitutionalism, protect political and economic human rights, and apply fairly to rich and poor nations alike.

Before Seattle, the American public saw the WTO as a narrow trade body with little relevance to ordinary people's lives. After Seattle, it became clearer that the WTO is emerging as one of the world's sovereign powers, writing the rules that can supersede the laws of nations. As such, its creation in 1995 opened the second great stage of our global Constitutional Moment that exploded into public consciousness in Seattle.

The WTO is nöt a formal world government nor does it proclaim itself as a framer of global constitutionalism. Legally, it is simply an international organization with powers to enforce trade agreements. It lacks the status of either a federal or even weaker confederated world government such as the UN, because nations have not delegated it powers to define global citizenship, create a world parliament, or assume a role in fighting wars or keeping the peace.

The WTO is also far weaker than the "private world government" that it has been created to support and regulate. Global financial markets and corporations write the operational rules and policies that increasingly control the lives of the planet's workers and the future of whole nations. The director of the WTO (in 2002, the little-known Australian, Michael Moore) is a figure of pitiful authority compared to Bill Gates. The dictates of Microsoft or the daily investment decisions of the world's richest private traders and speculators shape the world as powerfully as does any WTO decision. The WTO creates the public and constitutional framework that allows global business to operate, but it is the junior partner.

Historically, both the WTO and IMF have been so tightly controlled from Washington that they can be seen as surrogates carrying out either economic policy emanating from the U.S. Treasury or the foreign policy of the State Department. But the current limits of WTO autonomy should not diminish its potentially revolutionary sovereign powers. Along with the IMF and

World Bank, it is the only global governance system with real economic enforcement powers, and while WTO decisions are sometimes brazenly flaunted or manipulated by the most powerful companies and nations, they have a bite that even the United States has seen necessary to respect. The United States under the Clinton administration interpreted international law to mean that all nations, including itself, must amend their policies to conform to WTO rules and standards. The United States has already weakened its clean-air standards (in response to a suit by Venezuela complaining that our standards discriminate against their own oil producers) and other environmental laws in this spirit. And in 2002, in a strong blow to U.S. policy, the WTO ruled that offshore tax havens for U.S. companies constituted an unfair trade subsidy, a decision that could cost American companies billions.[19]

No other international organization or treaty has the "self-executing" capacity of the WTO to enforce its decisions and punish violators who refuse to make their laws WTO-compliant. Other supranational governance institutions, including the UN, must rely on the good faith of member nations themselves to carry out international covenants and treaties. While the UN must gain the universal consensus of Security Council members to enforce its most important decisions, WTO enforcement kicks in automatically without the need for any agreement by the member states.[20]

Such enforcement power takes on special meaning in the context of the surprising constitutional significance of trade. The word *trade* makes most people's eyes glaze over. Trade seems abstract, technical, and unimportant, something best left to corporate lawyers and government bureaucrats. But just as one sage said that war is too important to be left to the generals, trade is far too consequential to be left to business and political elites. The world has slowly awakened to the reality that trade law and philosophy impact every aspect of every nation's social and political life, and is revolutionizing sovereignty and democracy itself.

Because of the dominant role of the United States in the WTO, and its overriding interest in expanding and protecting global business, it is hardly surprising that the WTO's constitutional vision is Lockean, based above all on property rights. John Locke, the British political theorist who inspired the American Founding Fathers, has undoubtedly been, along with James Madison and Chief Justice John Marshall, the most important influence on American constitutionalism. He has now become the patron saint of *global* constitutionalism and is destined for a revival as a superstar of globalization. Locke defined the sovereign's primary role as protection of property from governmental and citizen intrusion. The WTO has translated Locke's constitutionalism into a global vision that privileges corporate property and seeks to extend it maximum protection everywhere.[21]

In the United States itself, Locke's constitutionalism has created a society protective not only of property but also of personal freedom. A more enlightened version of Locke, closer to the Jeffersonian ideal, would be a different story, but the WTO embodies a narrow form of Lockean constitutionalism, squeezing out values conflicting with the cash register of the market. The WTO has no mandate to make or enforce human rights laws protecting labor, the environment, or women and children. Its sole purview has been to make global rules and judge national laws based on their safeguarding of property. The WTO has dressed up globalization in the Lockean vision of liberty—that is, property protection and freedom of contract—while rights for the world's workers are left to other global authorities without comparable enforcement powers.

The language of free trade is central to WTO constitutionalism but should be understood as largely rhetorical, because the United States, Japan, and Europe all remain selectively protectionist. The United States has historically been aggressively protectionist, and these policies contributed to its economic development. Charles Beard and other renowned historians argue that the United States fought both the Revolutionary and Civil Wars partly to protect New England manufacturing against British competition. American leaders continue to protect textile, steel, and many other industries, while Europe refuses to abandon high levels of agricultural protection. As the poorer countries have long charged, free trade has been applied in practice mainly to weaker developing nations that lack the power to resist. This hypocrisy helps explain the infuriated response in much of the Third World to the WTO and IMF policies forcing them to open their markets in the name of global free-trade principles.[22]

Despite their selective application, Lockean principles have vested the WTO with a global constitutional basis for overriding the sovereignty of both weak and powerful nations. The WTO's famous overturning of European laws banning hormone-treated beef symbolizes the priority of narrowly conceived Lockean property rights over social and environmental rights. The WTO's constitutionalism married Locke's British constitutionalism with the American tradition of Marshall and Gilded Age justices such as Thomas Beck, who defined the only role of government and the courts as protecting corporate contracts and other property rights against public intrusions. Locke's shadow hangs over the expanded core mission of the WTO, which now involves extension of a radical American vision of property rights into the frontiers of the new economy.[23]

The creation of global intellectual property rights protection through the new convention known as TRIPS (Trade-Related Intellectual Property Agreement) is central to the WTO's constitutionalism. Intellectual property rights, democratically arrived at and enforced, are essential to promote innovation and ensure fair return to inventors and developers of creative and commercial products. But the WTO's aim is to provide the most stringent form of property protection to every global good or service, without consideration of the human costs. TRIPS extends global patents for twenty years, giving companies longer monopoly-pricing powers in many countries, including the United States. American patients will spend billions more as pharmaceutical companies under the TRIPS regime can profit from the prohibition of rival generic drugs for an additional three years. Promoted by U.S. pharmaceutical, biotech, and agribusiness companies, and media and software corporate giants, TRIPS has more severe effects on poor nations, radically constraining the ability of Third World farmers and industries to develop their own inventions or apply the technologies of the developed world.[24]

In Africa, where AIDS threatens 25 percent or more of the population in many countries, TRIPS prevents "parallel importing," which has been used by poor nations to import generic affordable drugs. As noted earlier, only after September 11, when the United States and Canada challenged Bayer's patent rights on the anthrax antidote Cipro, were poor nations able to get some WTO support for generic drugs to treat their own medical epidemics. In India, Monsanto has patented seeds used by subsistence farmers for centuries, forcing them to pay unaffordable royalties on each seed purchase. The cost in lives is staggering, but the situation has no legal standing within the WTO framework.

The assault on "nontariff trade barriers" by the WTO is another sign of the radical Lockean compulsion. These can include anything from subsidies for poor farmers to domestic content laws mandating that companies hire a percentage of their workers from the host nation or community. The United States subsidizes its own farmers, a sign of double standards at work here. Likewise, Taiwan, South Korea, and other Asian tigers developed successfully in the pre-WTO era because they had strong governments that were able to effectively leverage domestic content laws to transfer technology and skills to their own workers and businesses. Under the WTO, however, domestic content laws discriminate against foreign corporations and must be struck down. The "nontariff barrier" proviso is a blunt and radical constitutional assault on national sovereignty, because almost any social policy or national development strategy, from food subsidies to business aid, can fall under its shadow.[25]

Nations can still pass laws to protect labor rights or the environment. But the WTO shifts the right to create the standard of protection to itself and its own advisory councils, made up mainly of global trade associations representing the companies. National regulatory codes, both technical and social, are being weakened to conform with international standards developed by world trade groups coordinated under the WTO bureaucratic umbrella. Those regulations still left to nations are now conditioned by new Lockean criteria; they must be the least restrictive of trade and cannot ban products based on the technical process by which they are produced. The Agreement on Technical Barriers to Trade led to the famous invalidating of the U.S. law preventing the purchase of shrimps by producers who failed to use sea-turtle exclusion devices, making sea turtles one of the sainted symbols of Seattle.[26]

Moreover, the burden of proof regarding safety is shifted to consumers. In its Sanitary and Phytosanitary Standards Agreement (SPS), which regulates food safety, the WTO undercuts the precautionary principle that mandates legal caution if there is any evidence of danger to health. The WTO made its beef hormone decision on the grounds that hormones must be definitively proved dangerous. Consumers are now required to demonstrate scientific certainty of harm rather than producers being mandated to offer reasonable guarantees of safety.[27]

The WTO now urgently seeks liberalization in agriculture, media and software, financial services, health, education, and other services. This agenda is embodied in WTO plans for radical expansion of the Agreement on Agriculture and the General Agreement on Trade in Services (GATS). The new focus on services all reflect the U.S. interest in boosting its own leading sectors, something aggressively promoted by the Clinton administration in the late 1990s. As these new sectors promise unprecedented profits, American corporations, from AOL–Time Warner to Citigroup to Microsoft have set the highest store on breaking down barriers on these new frontiers.[28]

For a preview of where this all leads, consider only the "investor rights" provision of NAFTA, known as Chapter 11, that sets up a court allowing corporations to sue governments for passing environmental or labor laws that "infringe" on property rights and profits. The U.S. based Ethyl company sued the Canadian government in the late 1990s for passing a law banning use of MMT, a toxic gasoline additive produced by Ethyl. Ethyl claimed that Canada was unfairly discriminating against foreign firms by passing such environmental protection, since it excluded its own products from the Canadian market. The Canadian government rescinded its ban in the wake of the suit, fearful of trade sanctions and penalties imposed under Chapter 11. In the wake of the Ethyl case, many important U.S. organizations, the National League of Cities, the U.S. Conference of Mayors and the National Conference of State Legislatures, have argued that U.S. local and state environmental and health regulations are at risk. The new global agreements allow international trade courts to override local efforts to protect their own populations in the name of global property rights.

The NAFTA "investor rights" protections and secret courts are a scary forerunner of the WTO judicial tribunals. The WTO tribunals provide corporations globally with a venue to sue governments for passing labor or environmental regulation that infringe on property rights and profits, based on a radically expansive legal vision of unjust corporate "takings." The takings provision is based on a Gilded Age property theory—updated by "contractarian" American legal theorists re-emerging in the Reagan era. It prohibits governments from nearly any regulatory intervention that reduces corporate profit, arguing that it represents an unjustified violation of the "due process" rights of corporations to dispose of or contract property as they see fit. Critics have described the WTO as "NAFTA on steroids," referring to the creation of an unaccountable "world court" based on contractarian principles—essentially Lockianism taken to an absurd extreme. It creates the specter of labor and environmental laws everywhere in the world cut down by WTO judicial panels in the name of free trade, equal protection for domestic and foreign firms, and respect for private property.

In 1816, Thomas Jefferson wrote, "I hope that we shall crush in its birth the aristocracy of our monied corporations which dare already to challenge our government to a trial of strength, and bid defiance to the laws of our country." Jefferson did not oppose a new federal constitutional order, but led the struggle to ensure that it remained democratic. So, too, the protesters in the streets of Seattle, Quebec, Washington, and Genoa see themselves in a new democratic fight. They seek to limit the overwhelming power and wealth of the richest nations and corporations, and to organize the world on more democratic constitutional principles than the WTO and the current globalization system now embrace. As the rising struggle for global democracy erupts across the world, it's clear that this global constitutional fight has only just begun.

CHAPTER 6

THE UN, THE BARBERSHOP, AND GLOBAL DEMOCRACY

I am not an Athenian or a Greek. I am a citizen of the world.
SOCRATES

TINA. *THERE IS NO ALTERNATIVE.* THESE FOUR LITTLE WORDS SEEM the most common in the world today. They are depressing, and they paralyze many people who are deeply uneasy about globalization and would dearly love to help make a better world. I bet you think TINA when you think about "reinventing globalization." But the popularity of TINA reflects a terrible ignorance of history. Think back to the history discussed in Chapter 1. It suggests that reinventing globalization has been a large part of what world history has been about for at least a thousand years.

The world's first great civilizations, such as Mesopotamia and Egypt, invented "ancient globalizations." The Romans reinvented globalization when they created their great sprawling empire. The Italian city-states, such as Venice and Florence, created a merchant-driven "Renaissance globalization" that circled the world with Marco Polo. The colonial powers of Spain, the Netherlands, France, and Britain built a new globalization as they built the foundations of a worldwide industrial order. And, as discussed in the last chapter, the United States with its global business partners reinvented a new model of globalization over the last fifty years.

While much of this history is drenched in blood, the basic story line should lift our spirits. It shows that systemic change is not only possible but is a constant in history. Each time we think reinventing globalization seems farfetched, remember that it is already the reality of our times. With the collapse of colonial globalization after World War II, the reconstruction of globalization was inevitable, leading to our current Constitutional Moment.

It is precisely because we are in a new Constitutional Moment that the idea of reinventing globalization has begun to capture serious attention. We the people can sit back and allow global business and our government to design globalization as they are doing now, or we can choose to enter the fray and reform it in the spirit of our own values. Thousands in the new global justice movements have already chosen to act. Moreover, millions, perhaps billions, of other people not identified with these movements in either the First and Third Worlds are uneasy about globalization. After the events of September 11, they also want to change the world to make it safe and economically secure for everyone.

The struggle to reinvent globalization will be the dominant issue of the coming century. To succeed, it will have to offer a credible alternative and build a global mainstream social movement that can translate it into action. The alternative vision is what I call *global democracy*. In this and the next few chapters, I discuss what I mean by this idea, how ordinary people are beginning to develop the vision and put it into practice, and how and why I think it will change our world for the better.

Global democracy may sound utopian, but it is pragmatic and realistic. However, this does not mean it is inevitable. In the aftermath of September 11 and the darkening global recession, it is clearly possible that the world could take the opposite path: toward a permanently militarized model of globalization rather than the democratic variety I am proposing. The world stands at a crucial crossroads. Without choosing the democratic path, globalization will survive but move rapidly toward the fortress model outlined in the introduction. This possibility looms as the great and most frightening danger of the coming era. The fortress model is a militarized globalization that puts security over freedom in order to contain growing global violence. It will sabotage the prospects for democracy at home and abroad.

The path toward fortress globalization in the United States was laid down only weeks after September 11. The threats to democracy within the United States are obvious. In a rush, Congress passed—and the president signed—a "Patriots" bill that permitted far-reaching new powers of government surveillance, wiretapping, and detention. Authorities would be able to detain illegal immigrants and prisoners suspected of terrorism without formal charges. They could be tried by military tribunals and their conversations with their attorneys could be monitored by government officials. There are sober discussions about the U.S. government using torture against suspected terrorists. Constitutional scholars see major threats to civil liberties and warn of a looming police state.[1]

The war on terrorism, killing many civilians and dislocating wretchedly poor people in Afghanistan even as it helps liberate the country from a horrifically repressive regime, may last for some time. This could easily incite more terrorism and lead to even more American-led military retaliation. The "peace" of globalization could be a chronic state of terrorism and military responses against it.

This would accelerate a turn toward fortress globalization. Under conditions of fear and instability, business will not close down overseas and come home. There are no safe harbors in this new war. But global firms and many frightened citizens will insist on new elaborate security measures. And this will involve a partnership between business and government that could curb political liberties that have been the pride of our society.

Since we are already seeing movement toward the fortress, why is there reason to believe that the democratic path is a realistic alternative? I see several hopes. First, fortress globalization contains the symptoms but doesn't attack the sources of global violence and instability. The fortress model is expensive and in-efficient, committing the world to massive new surveillance and operational costs subverting the efficiency of the markets. The fortress will mitigate terror if billions are invested but will never eradicate it.

Second, global democracy attacks the causes rather than the symptoms of global injustice, and it works in concert with the positive sides of globalization. That is why I have called global democracy a move through and beyond globalization rather than backlash. It empowers the world's poor and pushes in more deeply democratic directions.

Third, historical movements deeply grounded in the Third World and newly explosive in the First World have already begun a struggle for global democracy. They do not share a crystal-clear vision, and they remain in the early stages. But because they attack globalization's core problems and reflect the interests of the world's poor and fragile middle classes, they will be able to build a global majority for their democratic agenda.

Fourth, business itself has a stake in the democratic path. As noted in the introduction, globally extended businesses are the front lines of globalization, and the fortress will impose huge new operating and transaction costs on global companies. They will have to invest billions in new hidden cameras, cyber security, and other security and employee-safety measures, and they will face major new and costly hurdles to cross-border trade and invest-ment. Communication at home and abroad will be slowed and compromised (think only of spreading anthrax in the mail). Whatever the costs of global democracy, they could be less for business than those of the fortress, a possible explanation for the new business rhetoric of social responsibility and "global citizen-ship."[2]

Fifth, the plunge of the United States and the world into re-cession, in association with the economic dislocations caused by the New York attacks and the 2002 U.S. market crisis, has changed the political debate. Free-market credos are being re-considered as government is being asked to bail out industries, protect the public, and create new jobs for millions of unemployed or laid-off workers. Democratic governments are the only ones that will create the necessary jobs and new safety nets in dark economic times. During the U.S. Great Depression in the 1930s, a New Deal was needed to make people feel safe. Today, only global democracy will create the new New Deal that will bring true security to American workers and the world's poor.

After September 11, the growing violence and darkening global recession set global democracy back in the short term, but they may broaden its base of support significantly in the longer term. Religious leaders have begun speaking more urgently about the importance of global justice. Toward the end of 2001, Catholic bishops meeting in Rome passed a document denouncing the growing gap between global haves and have-nots and emphasizing that "the persistence of gross inequalities between nations is a threat to peace." Third World bishops were especially vocal in critiquing global economic policy and called for "drastic moral change."[3]

World political leaders are sounding many of the same themes. Tony Blair strongly supported the war on terror but made eloquent pleas for a new global order based on democracy and justice for the poor. In a now famous speech, Blair focused on the remaking of globalization on a just and democratic basis as the only way to free the world from terror: "If globalization works only for the benefit of the few, then it will fail and will deserve to fail. But if we follow the principles that have served us so well at home—that power, wealth and opportunity must be in the hands of the many, not the few—if we make that our guiding light for the global economy, then it will be a force for good and an international movement that we should take pride in leading." Bill Clinton and Mikhail Gorbachev made speeches with almost identical emphases on the need to reform globalization so that the poor have a new voice and a new deal. These words suggest that the world after September 11 will be one in which global democracy will get new rhetorical support from the most powerful as well as the poorest of the world.[4]

Powerful movements for global democracy started at the end of World War II, the same time that modern globalization itself was born. Over the last fifty years, movements began to conceive the global democratic vision that is still evolving in global justice movements today. They are the foundation of the new democratic path that will help heal the crises of global poverty while promising a reduction in global violence and terror.

Global democrats have in recent years divided into what appear to be two quite different camps. One talks about a "globalization from below" that brings a democratic voice and justice to the world's poor. I call them "UN people," because they see the original vision of the UN and its 1948 Universal Declaration of Human Rights as the inspiration of global democracy.[5] The UN camp is reincarnating the "citizens' globalism" movement discussed in the last chapter. Recall that during the big bang of our Constitutional Moment, between 1944 and 1948, President Franklin Roosevelt and many Third World leaders envisaged one world based on justice and democratic human rights. They imagined a planet free of colonialism and militarism, and capable of making the idea of global democracy meaningful. They founded the UN to be the forum and symbol of their alternative democratic world. While many global democrats have become disillusioned with the UN itself, which they see as increasingly harnessed to U.S.-led globalization, today's global justice movements draw inspiration from the ideas of the UN founders. They see the 1948 UN Declaration and later conventions of the rights of women, children, workers, and the environment as an enforceable bill of rights for the world.[6]

From the beginning, the UN camp embraced the revolution against national sovereignty at the heart of globalization. But it had a very different idea of world government than the WTO version. UN founders sought a new global order for peace rather than profit. After two world wars, they recognized that unfettered national sovereignty meant global anarchy and perpetual war. The UN founders also wanted what Franklin Roosevelt called global "freedom from want." This required a global constitutional vision subordinating property rights to broader human rights and especially jobs for the global poor.

The 1948 Declaration called for "positive" economic and social global constitutional rights for jobs, education, health, and welfare. These simple but revolutionary rights have become the passion of the current global justice movements. Today's UN people see a movement to secure positive human rights, especially rights to employment and free association of workers, as the starting point for a new global vision. Building democratic movements for global positive rights is close to the core of the very idea of global democracy, and it is the only way to create global and national government committed to the needs of the world's people.

This vision has begun to crystallize. It starts with an enforceable system of global labor rights, ensuring that Guatemalan peasants can organize farming cooperatives and Indonesian workers can organize independent unions without being arrested or shot. The positive rights vision also includes a call for global environmental laws. It calls for regulation of worldwide capital flow and global corporations to ensure a more equal distribution of wealth. It demands abolition of racial and sexual discrimination, with special attention to the safety and dignity of a mainly female and nonwhite global labor force.[7]

For the UN camp, the problem with globalization is not too much global government but the influence of money over everything it does. The UN camp recognizes that desperately important human and environmental rights are possible only in a world racing rapidly beyond the old world of national sovereignty. In this sense, the UN camp runs with the tide of globalization but seeks a democratic world government and constitution that delivers positive rights to the 3 billion people living on less than $3 a day.

The second camp of global democrats that has emerged in recent decades speaks for what at first appears a blatantly contradictory idea of global democracy. Rather than stressing world government and global constitutionalism, they see democracy embedded in the revival of community and local autonomy, a way of life rooted in face-to-face connections and active citizenship rather than constitutions and laws. I call them the "barbershop camp."

Barbershops have yet to become a global corporation, and I suspect that they will always remain a community business. This inherent localism symbolizes the barbershoppers' core vision: the democratic economy and democracy itself need a strong local anchor. Once we start rigidly integrating local economies into a global system, we lose not only diversity but start a chain reaction of ecological and human devastation. Businesses get divorced from the local community, the local community gets dependent on absentee companies and loses its economic independence, and then it loses its political control to big business and big government. This undermines its ability to protect its environment and to sustain the community itself. And once community is gone, democracy is out the window, and the possibility of the good life rapidly erodes, as people try to compensate for the loss of human connection with the thrills of headlong consumerism.[8]

The barbershoppers want to "relocalize" the world to democratize it. They see a problem with the UN camp because they do not think global human rights conventions or even the best world government can build life-affirming democratic economies and communities. Only people on the local level can do that. Only local folk can know their neighbors, come out to town meetings or tribal assemblies, and create a vision of how their community can produce a sustainable way of life. If the UN people have politicized globalization, the barbershoppers have personalized it. They see globalization as a spiritual crisis, not just a political or even social one. They consider it a threat to their own capacity to be human. The future of nature and the human soul are on the line.[9]

Like the UN people, the barbershop people have a diverse history to draw on. They have learned from native Americans and their respect for the tribe and the earth, Mexican Zapatistas and their defense of indigenous communities, and Gandhi and his vision of nonviolence and local political autonomy. From the anarchist Emma Goldman, they have learned that how you make the revolution matters as much as where you want to go, and you have to dance while you are doing it.[10]

The barbershoppers want to reinvent globalization by retribalizing the world. This is not just a spiritual dream but a global reinvention vision rooted in carefully designed democratic local institutions networked in new global connections. At this vision's core are not democratized global businesses but sustainable community-based businesses newly networked with other localities. It is not democratized global government but revitalized and reconnected local communities armed with a measure of sovereign autonomy. They want not so much a UN-enforced culture of peace than a peace arising from the cultures of thousands of nonviolent communities.

If there is to be a new movement to reinvent globalization, it needs a coherent vision. But that is not what the UN camp and the barbershoppers seem to offer. Instead they seem to be serving up radically different alternatives that clash with each other as much as they do with today's globalization. Yet, despite real differences, they are looking at two sides of the same global democratic coin.

Many barbershoppers fear the UN, even a perfect UN, as a deadly threat to local sovereignty. And many UN-ers see the barbershoppers' passion for local sovereignty as a huge, outdated hurdle to the global rights and rules we desperately need. But both see the threat today as the creation of a new market-driven world answering only to money. The relentless expansionism of the markets threatens the global rights and rules of the UN-ers as much as it does the localism of the barbershoppers. And they are united by their underlying horror of the global commodification of everything. What both UN-ers and barbershoppers share is a desire to preserve both the local and global community from becoming just two expressions of the same giant cash register. And they instinctively recognize that they need to work together to keep market expansion and the globalization mystique from imperializing our souls as well as privatizing every niche of local community and every nation.

Today's global democrats openly resist a single blueprint for change, and one would not want to paper over the differences in their perspective. They are not party-line people. When asked about their creed, they say "one no, many yesses." The one no is their common opposition to today's globalization. The many yesses is their view that the world cannot be reinvented using a formula. They are not going to go about the arrogant project of speaking for billions of people and laying out a formula tailor-made for all of them. They want people around the world speaking up for them. They want people around the world speaking up for themselves in a new democratized dialogue.

One starts the process of global reinvention, then, by simply moving the conversation out of the closed meetings and into the town square. What both UN people and barbershoppers clearly share is outrage at the secretive process through which elites are inventing today's globalization and imposing a corporate way of thinking on the world. That is why the activists all went to Seattle, Quebec, Washington, and Genoa. They were determined to crash the party and show that it can't be a closed country-club affair anymore. If there is going to be conversation about the future of the world, it has to be open to people and views not heard in the boardroom. And there can't be an admission charge.[11]

In 2001, as the world's financial and political elites were planning to meet in Davos, Switzerland, the traditional site of the World Economic Forum, thousands of people from around the world came to Pôrto Alegre, Brazil, to launch a "people's" Davos. Farmers, workers, clergy, students, and teachers jammed together in huge assembly halls to talk about reinventing globalization. They talked about sustainable development, sweatshop organizing and global labor rights, rights of indigenous communities, regulation of global capital flows, debt relief to poor nations, changes in global patent law, and hundreds of other pieces of a new global agenda. The conversations were broadcast over loudspeakers to people out in the streets and sent over the net to people around the world. These reinventors did not come with a new global blueprint, but they did model a new and more democratic discussion about the future of the world. In February 2002, a second massive people's assembly gathered at Pôrto Alegre to protest the World Economic Forum held in New York City and show that the democratic alternative was more vital than ever.

Democratizing the conversation is the most important first step in creating a democratic world, the passion clearly bringing together the UN and barbershop camps. It is slowly giving rise to a view of global democracy that both camps can embrace. It imagines a world governing itself at many different levels in a robustly democratic spirit. Democracy from the barbershop level to the UN level is indivisible, and inevitably comes together in the emerging idea that neither local democratic association nor global democratic formal governance can do the job on its own. If we think of global democracy as a living organism, the UN camp is building the skeletal system, and the barbershoppers the soft tissue and blood.

Democracy is both a constitutional arrangement, a political system making government accountable to ordinary people, and a way of living that brings people together in multiple, freely formed associations to form a common identity and a way of expressing themselves as citizens. The UN camp is beginning to spell out the political arrangements necessary for this to happen worldwide. The barbershop camp is starting to create the new forms of community and participation necessary to revive the idea of local democracy while also building global citizenship.

Global democracy requires respecting differences while refashioning and integrating the vision of the two camps, something already under way. Few in the UN camp believe the UN can be activated as a democratic government for the world without building a new sense of global community and civil society outside the market itself. Nor do UNers believe that one institution, including the best UN possible, should be vested with anything like the full powers of a global sovereign or planetary Big Brother. They seek a pluralism of global governing institutions that are limited in their authority and strictly democratically accountable both to national and local governments and to global citizens newly organized into thousands of civic associations.[12]

Likewise, few barbershoppers seek a world of totally insular local associations and communities. In the distant past, localities could seek total self-sufficiency and isolation, but few today want to wall off their local communities. The aim is not pure localism, but forms of democratic association that connect communities everywhere through more democratic links than the market. The aim is to revive local democracy as well as create a democratic community of communities, another name for the global government imagined by the UN camp.[13]

Both the UN and barbershop camps are working toward a new intertwined model of local and global citizenship. They are creating new associations of labor, women, environmentalists, and other civil society groups that are locally based and revitalize local communities. But these localists also are "thinking globally" and increasingly forming global networks to create new democratic global rules necessary to save their own jobs and communities. A local labor union in Detroit understands today that it can't protect its own workers without changing the rules governing wage conditions and cross-border investment in Mexico. Increasingly, that union is beginning to form cross-national links with Mexican unions as the only way to defend jobs and dignity in both Mexico and the United States.[14] It takes global democracy to preserve local democracy, while global democracy cannot be achieved without the revitalization of localism and civil society.

The globalizing of markets and states is being haunted by the globalizing of civil society. Over 150 years ago, Alexis de Tocqueville marveled at the proliferation of civic associations in the

United States, which he saw as the basis of American democracy. If he were back today, I suspect he would turn his attention to the globalizing of these same associations, whether they are unions, environmental groups, feminist groups, educational and health groups, public interest advocates, or other new global citizens. These are the new activists of both local and global democracy, and they come equally from the UN and barbershop camps.[15]

The barbershop symbolizes the local level of community and business. The UN is a symbol of the broadest global level of governance and citizenship. And there are many levels in between. The goal of the global democrat is neither to integrate economies nor resist their integration. It is to democratize every level of social and economic organization to maximize participation and equity. The global democrat seeks to encourage a flowering of social connection and popular control outside as well as inside the market, and to build many different democratic levels that enhance global democracy itself.

In globalization today, the integrating principle is the market. Each level, from local to global, is more and more tightly organized around corporate power and finance. Globalization increasingly makes local communities look like miniaturized carbon copies of global markets.

The democratic alternative starts with a rejection of the global market as the integrating principle of the world. It is too radically homogenizing, and it betrays democracy in the service of money and corporate sovereignty. It is the seduction from hell—our consumer self desperately wants to buy it, but we pay the price of losing our job, our community, and our own power as citizens.

The reinvention of globalization requires the discovery of a new set of connecting and integrating principles. Today's global democrats have a few starting points.

One is the idea of "subsidiarity." It says that decisions should be made at the lowest level that can handle the problem, as well as at multiple levels to encourage a democracy that overflows the voting booth. Subsidiarity has a bias toward the local, but welcomes the global, as long as power flows from the bottom up rather than from the top down. It encourages local communities and businesses to manage their own affairs, but recognizes that they face key issues like global warming and global capital flight that they cannot manage without help at higher political levels.[16]

The European Union has become a pioneer in working out the subsidiarity idea, and global democrats are taking note. Rather than shutting down economic integration, the Europeans are trying to get the right mix of local and European-wide communities, which is consistent with the preservation of local cultures and economies, human rights, and democracy itself. They are inching toward a European government and constitution; the idea of a European constitutional convention was floated for 2001, which would create Europe-wide rights and social protections for workers, but in a way that increases participation and pride of place within localities, regions, and nations.[17]

A second, closely related principle is federalism, an idea dear to most Americans. It makes explicit that we need many interdependent levels, and we need to build from the bottom up rather than from the top down. The key words in a federal constitution are that "all powers not explicitly reserved for the federal government are retained by the states or localities." In other words, the upper levels cannot grab powers not delegated explicitly by the people and levels below. The federalist principle gives comfort to localists who fear a centralized Big Brother. It ensures that communities will give away only as much power as they choose, but permits the rise of global bodies that can deal with global problems.

This takes us to the most basic principle: democracy itself. Reinventing globalization is really about reinventing democracy. *Democracy* is the most used and abused word in the world today. It evokes both rituals of reverence and near total cynicism in the public. Even in the United States, which sees itself as the democratic model for the world, more than half the people don't vote. The new vision starts with the recognition that globalization has debased democracy even as it has exported the idea to every corner of the earth.

The alternative to globalization is, at heart, exceedingly simple: it is to take the idea of democracy seriously. This means vesting ordinary citizens across the entire planet with real control in an era when governments have become handmaidens of global corporations and global markets are held up as the model of democracy. Global democrats bring a few fundamental new ideas about democracy. One is that democracy is not the same as free elections. Whether in El Salvador or Iraq, elections are rarely free, and they do not by themselves create the kind of democracy that guarantees real popular control.[18]

We should not disregard the importance of constitutional democratic procedures, or the vital need for elections in societies that have never given citizens the vote, free speech, and freedom of association. But free elections in scores of countries are not delivering democracy serving the poor, the great majority of the population. We need a broader, deeper democracy if we are to wean governments at every level from the grip and greed of global markets. We need to move from the procedural democracy of globalization—which restricts itself to voting while societies are polarized between a tiny wealthy oligarchy and a huge poor majority—toward the social democracy that can attack global corporate power at its roots. This means vesting ordinary citizens with real control over the political and economic decisions that matter. It will involve engaging citizens not only in free and fair elections, but in active participation in local, national, and global politics through civic, grassroots, labor, feminist, and public-interest associations of every stripe. We need citizens who are as passionate about political participation as they are about sports or sitcoms and who have effective rights and vehicles for holding leaders accountable.

Global economic democracy is a second new idea. Because financial markets now drastically limit the choices that any government, even the most democratized, can make, there is no choice but to take democracy directly into the world of business. In any age, but especially the age of globalization, there can be no political democracy without economic democracy. Global economic democracy means making corporations answer to citizens as well as stockholders, and making financial markets accountable to the global public as well as investors. The urgency is so great in the new era of terror and recession that it has become the great passion of citizen activists throughout the world who speak of economic democracy. But it has also become a matter of conversation among global business leaders, who, after Enron, increasingly talk about stakeholder democracy and global citizenship.[19]

A third and most basic new idea is that democracy today has to be globalized. The biggest challenge will be empowering the majority of the world's population who live in the Third World. This will require democratic movements led by the Third World itself, both to take back their own governments and to invent new regional and global bodies that can speak for them. While poor nations claiming their rightful power is threatening to almost everybody in rich countries, democratically aroused Third World peoples are the most important allies workers and ordinary citizens in rich nations can have. They bring the desperation of the hungry and their moral authority, as well as the power of two-thirds of the world's people, to challenge the global monied powers corrupting democracy and riding roughshod over human rights.

If we can't create a democratic world forum in a body like the UN, where the world's majority holds sway, we can't expect to preserve democracy in the town hall or in national governments, and we certainly will not get a democracy taken seriously in the Third World. This leads to a fourth new idea: democracy at any level depends on democracy at all levels. The town meeting in Springfield or Jakarta and the global town meeting at the UN or the World Bank have to support each other's democratic possibilities, or they will both surrender to the "democracy of the market"—the degraded forum we suffer now.

CHAPTER 7

A GLOBAL NEW DEAL

If you have built castles in the air, that is where they should be; now put foundations under them.

HENRY DAVID THOREAU

A VISION OF GLOBAL DEMOCRACY IS ONE THING, BUT HOW DOES IT translate into the real world? What would the world look like based on these new ideas? And is there any real chance that they will become more than a dream?

The truth is, the democratic alternative to globalization will emerge not from a blueprint in some brilliant futurist's mind but from a long process of experimental efforts. Any credible new global vision is going to arise from the messy global politics currently pouring out into the streets, labor halls, and church basements. If we want to see what the new world will look like, we should look at what the activists are trying to do.

Moreover, the new principles discussed here do not imply a complete repudiation of the current order. As noted in earlier chapters, globalization in its present form has brought gains as well as pain. The changes proposed here involve working with forces that globalization have already catalyzed as well as creating new visions and institutions. There are five concrete aims that should serve as a compass for global democrats. These are (1) creating accountable "world governments," (2) reconstructing national democracies, (3) democratizing global business, (4) resurrecting local community with global citizenship, and (5) creating collective security. The ideas here may seem to have a distinctive Western cast, with their focus on equality, democracy and human rights. Speaking of a "New Deal" immediately betrays a relation to specifically American political culture. This is cause for concern, since any enduring alternative visions for the world must arise from the cultural and political traditions of the great majority of the world's people who do not live in Europe or the United States.

Just as Americans should not dictate the principles of globalization, American critics should not presume to dictate the alternatives. I have tried to draw on ideas and practices that have long been promoted by peoples in the Third World and the international community as a whole. Much of the agenda here is already codified in UN covenants and international agreements that have been signed by most nations around the world. While themes of democracy and human rights are closely related to Western constitutional and ideological traditions, many Third World nations and social movements have been the most enthusiastic and dedicated advocates of these values and of many of the agenda items I summarize and endorse here.

I am offering the ideas here less as a wish list than as a marking of new ideas and trends already surfacing. Global justice activists and ordinary people around the world are now advancing much of this vision. In some cases, governments and grassroots groups are already institutionalizing programs based on these ideas. The task, here, is not just to invent new ideas, but feed and water the democratic seeds that have already begun to be planted.

The first aim, the creation of a global government, will be particularly hard for many Americans to accept. But global democracy is impossible without building on existing UN agencies and creating a variety of new and democratically robust international bodies that will collectively comprise a new "world government." By this, I mean not a single centralized Big Brother monopolizing the world's political power but many different publicly accountable global bodies making decisions that can only be made at the global level.

Globalization is creating its own more centralized "world governments" in the WTO, IMF, and World Bank. We have the seeds of democratic alternatives swirling in and about the UN's orbit. The pure localists among global democrats, passionate about dismantling not only the WTO but any global authority, may shudder at my raising the UN specter. But all three principles of the last chapter—subsidiarity, federalism, and democracy—tell us that a democratic and sustainable world is going to need global as well as local governance. This will require a major strengthening of the UN itself, and a broadening of its economic, legal, and moral authority.

Even die-hard localists with no interest in the UN want local communities to reach out and touch their neighbors and committed localists everywhere are hard at work creating networks of communities that can dialogue, cooperate, and barter with one another. The biggest global network of all communities is inevitably going to bear some resemblance to the UN, even though it will need to overcome many of the flaws of the current organization and might evolve into more of a people's assembly or world parliament. Localists can take comfort that global democracy does not seek a single, centralized world government, although it requires a stronger UN. Global democracy will support a pluralistic variety of bodies—either under UN authority or in partnership with it—including UNCTAD, the International Labor Organization, UNICEF, the International Court of Justice, and literally hundreds of other international agencies that each wield only a small slice of global authority. In addition, much of the democratic authority exercised above the national level will be wielded regionally, at the level of the EU or Organization of African States. Such "regional governments" already play a huge role in the world and will be key players in reconciling local cultures and economies with a new federal supra-national system. In other words, big world decisions are not going to be made by a few global bureaucrats in UN back rooms, but by hundreds of hemispheric and global associations that will collectively constitute a more democratic and locally accountable "world government."[1]

The alternative to globalization is going to depend on writing something like a Constitution for the world economy that will guide and coordinate the many "world governments" to come. The WTO is already hard at work drafting its own property-centered version and it will congeal into irreversible hard international law if global democrats do not move quickly to replace it. Writing democratic global rules does not require utopian thinking, since we already have in place the 1948 Universal Declaration of Rights and many later UN treaties that are the beginnings of an exemplary global Bill of Rights for the world. We now need to make these principles enforceable, ensuring that the human rights of workers, women, children, and the environment cannot be sacrificed to property protection.

Is there a place for the WTO, the IMF, and World Bank in the democratic vision? These institutions—having failed to promote development or eliminate world poverty because of their dominance by rich nations and corporate elites—are already suffering a global crisis of legitimacy. Global democracy requires what some call a "decommissioning process"—an analogy to the term used for scrapping toxic nuclear power plants. We need now to decommission the WTO, IMF, and World Bank, historically proven toxic for the great majority of the world's peoples, and supplant them over time with more democratic "global governments." Existing UN agencies such as UNCTAD—a strong voice for the world's poor nations and long concerned with creating a trade order linked to development—must be reconstructed as a leading voice in the new system along with new UN-affiliated trade and development agencies. The new order, which will emerge as the Bretton Woods institutions lose credibility in the face of their corporate biases and economic failures, will be based on a few core democratic principles. It must be transparent, accessible, and accountable to the global public, with all deliberations and documents open to public scrutiny and subject to review and approval by democratically elected representatives of member states. The new governing agencies will shift the constitutionalism of global economic government from the narrow standard of property protection to the broader foundation of global human rights and equality. And they will ensure that trade agreements would promote labor and environmental values and social development as the heart of their mission. Such systemic values sound utopian but are already emerging as common sense in global publics as the existing neo-liberal system begins to collapse under the chaos and burden of its own failed promises.[2]

Many in the global democracy movement as well as in the mainstream call for reform of the Bretton Woods triumverate. I propose replacement for three reasons. First, while a reform effort appears more pragmatic, the changes required are so basic that any serious reform agenda will eventually lead toward fundamentally new institutions. We need a thoroughgoing democratization, and a new labor, human rights, and development agenda inconsistent with the basic design of the triumverate. Second, the fight to replace the triumverate will educate people to the depth of the current crisis and the need for systemic changes, while reform efforts are likely to lull the public, hinting that the current system is basically sound. Third, the Bretton Woods institutions are already facing a crisis of global legitimacy, from both the left and the right, as well as among some in the mainstream. The time is ripe for a radical reconsideration of these profoundly antidemocratic institutions. I am not at odds with radical reformers, as long as they acknowledge that the reforms we need will transform the triumverate into constitutionally new bodies.

In calling for abolition, I am not proposing doing away with global institutions concerned with trade, financial stabilization, and development. Instead, I am suggesting that we already have more democratic alternative institutions in the UN, such as UNCTAD and the ILO, that have long experience with these matters and could be vested with new resources to take responsibilities now vested in the WTO, IMF, and World Bank. It will take time to develop, as well, new institutions proposed here, so that a phase out period is necessary, following a series of UN-sponsored global conferences to plan the new system. The phase out should involve a series of stages in which new WTO and IMF agendas for expanding liberalization into services, agriculture, and other sectors are put on hold, and the Uruguay Round agreements are reviewed and re-evaluated according to democratic, human rights criteria. As the review is conducted, many of the current missions of the WTO, IMF, and World Bank can be shifted to UNCTAD and other new institutions, which will review and redraft trade agreements on the basis of democratic, labor, environmental, and social development values.

Americans can appreciate the need for such democratic, socially oriented global government by drawing on their own history, looking at the reconstruction of the U.S. federal government as it sought to try to civilize the robber baron capitalism of the late nineteenth century. Americans recognized in the Progressive and New Deal eras that it would take major federal government intervention based on social democratic principles to limit Gilded Age greed and exploitation and create a national capitalism respectful of workers and communities. Since we now have a form of a new and largely unregulated world capitalism, we need a global federalism that civilizes the global economy.

To create global democracy, the post–Bretton Woods global government must pursue "a New Deal for the world" based on four policy agendas: *global regulation, redistribution, decommodification,* and *participation.* This set of policies at the global level complements my recommendations for national governments, businesses, and communities outlined in the next chapter. It is a practical program of global reconstruction essential to turn globalization into an attack on global poverty rather than a feeding frenzy for the rich. It might have sounded hopelessly idealistic before September 11, the Enron crisis, and the new global recession, but the Trade Tower attacks changed the political equation as business executives and political elites as well as the protestors on the streets recognized that more inequality and disenfranchisement is an open invitation to more violence. The WTO, IMF, and World Bank have come under withering attack from conservatives in the Bush administration as well as critics from the left and mainstream economists such as Nobelist Joseph Stiglitz and Columbia's Jeffrey Sachs. While they are only now losing credibility in the First World, the WTO and IMF have already lost their legitimacy in many Third World nations because of their failure to deliver the sustainable growth and democracy they have promised. Moreover, in the context of U.S. and global recession, the likely alternative to global New Deal policies crafted by new UN-led global government is a slide into depression, another potential catalyst for violence.

The first New Deal policy is regulation of global money and corporations to end the current global "race to the bottom." It would subordinate all the current WTO and GATT trade laws to an international legal order and trade system based on human rights and sustainable development. It would repeal much of the existing WTO and IMF regime that deregulates financial services, labor, and environmental protections in the name of property rights and "free trade." But it will begin with small practical steps, reining in the global speculative flows of financial capital and embracing new "capital controls," rules to help nations prevent speculators and investors from destabilizing their economies by suddenly pulling out vast sums of money at will.[3] Such financial regulation is now being discussed in the highest circles of global elites as well as among the democratic critics and protestors. Malaysia and Chile have already experimented with their own version of capital controls, although their experience suggests that countries cannot do it on their own or without transforming the Bretton Woods system.

After the 1998 Asian financial catastrophe linked to unregulated capital flows, and the new crises in Central and Latin America as well as Africa, many even within the mainstream, such as financier George Soros and former chief economist of the World Bank, Joseph Stiglitz, are calling for systemic change. Beyond his blistering attack on the IMF, Stiglitz has proposed a broad package of regulatory reforms in the financial system, starting with tax deductions for global investments longer than a year, and imposing a tax penalty on very short-term transactions. Stiglitz proposes reserve requirements on all short-term capital flows as part of a comprehensive strategy to encourage longer-term investment. New taxes on capital originating in off-shore, hot money havens such as the Cayman Islands would help to stabilize the financial order and encourage growth and development. They should be paired with efforts to bring all financial markets up to a minimal global regulatory standard approved by appropriate international financial agencies, a step discussed by Stiglitz, Jeffrey Sachs, and George Soros. Even Stanley Fisher, as deputy director of the IMF, declared after the 1998 Asian crisis, that "the IMF recognizes the problem of surges of capital across borders and the need to find ways to deal with that." Beyond such ritualistic declarations, what is really needed is a return to the original Bretton Woods understanding that nations need the power to regulate capital flows to create jobs and stabilize their own economies. This, in turn, will require rolling back much of the GATT and WTO agenda of the last two decades.[4]

As a step in the rollback process, journalist William Greider has proposed a comprehensive and practical package of financial regulation that would "take the fun and profit out of speculative currency trading and other speculative activity . . . but would not inhibit the flows of long-term capital for foreign investment and trade." His system would tighten credit terms that encourage global speculation, expand transaction taxes to limit corporate or speculative whipsawing of national economies, outlawing unregulated partnerships and offshore bank havens (Enron had more than six hundred of such accounts) and monitoring the impacts of capital flows and corporate flight. But even these changes are only the beginning of a systemic shift that would redefine capital mobility as a privilege granted by nations only when it is consistent with their own democratic needs and development.[5]

The deregulation of financial markets and services is a dagger aimed at the heart of democratic self-rule, undermining the ability of nations to choose their own path to development. But it is just the sharpest and most dangerous weapon in the larger neoliberal arsenal that forces weaker nations to deregulate all industries and sectors, open themselves indiscriminately to foreign ownership, and transform themselves into agro-export economies while their people lack food. These policies, at the heart of the WTO, IMF, and World Bank, can be reversed only by creating new democratic bodies affirming the right of each nation to choose its own development model. This includes the right to reject forms of trade, investment, or foreign ownership that countries view as compromising self-governance or their capacity to feed and protect their own populations. A post–Bretton Woods regime would treat regulation—including the right of nations to regulate flows of money, limit foreign ownership of national assets such as banks and land, and control the conditions under which corporations enter and leave—as the foundation of a trade system based on democracy.

This may seem a return to the "bad old days" of Smoot-Hawley, when global protectionism contributed to global depression in the 1930s. But what I propose here is, ironically, closer to the original Bretton Woods vision of John Maynard Keynes, who clearly saw the need for a regulated financial order to preserve global stability and growth, development in poor nations, and social welfare and full employment policy in both rich and poor countries. Keynes understood that the only way to avoid the global depression of the 1930s was not to eliminate all protectionism but to seek trade agreements and a financial order that subordinated "free trade" and global money to democratic regulation.

The new regulation that we need, beyond subjecting corporate exit power and capital flight to stringent democratic controls and reversing the Bretton Woods shift toward centrally imposed deregulation and export-led economies, must enforce global labor and environmental standards shredded by the current system. The WTO and IMF have sacrificed such social protections on the alter of property rights—and it will take new governing institutions unfettered by existing neoliberal philosophies to create the needed regulatory framework. The UN's International Labor Organization could be a major player in helping craft enforceable global labor standards, and a variety of new international bodies seeking to implement the Kyoto accords on climate change could move us beyond the disastrous environmental deregulation of the Bretton Woods triumverate. Ironically, they are likely to find initial support in this seemingly idealistic mission from leaders of the corporate world. Global companies, under pressure from consumers outraged by sweatshops and environmental destruction, themselves seek minimal public regulation of labor and the environment beyond what the Bretton Woods system has delivered. Richard McCormick, CEO of US WEST and chairman of the United States Council for International Business, wrote to President Clinton in 1997 to ask that he be "more vigorous in using the ILO to bring international pressure to bear on goverments that commit egregious violations of basic workers' rights" and to "work through the WTO, UN, and World Bank to combat extortion and bribery in international business transactions." While the regulation advocated by business is nowhere close to the democratic form of regulation we need, it hints that business can be forced to comply with necessary regulation that in the long run will spare it from the costs of its own current depredations.[6]

A new global regulatory system must end the "extortion economy" by which companies threaten to leave if nations don't lower their standards and compromise the rights of their people. To prevent predatory exit, Greider has proposed that U.S. companies be held to the same standards globally as they are at home, with wages adjusted appropriately to the living costs of other nations. He notes that we do not permit U.S. airlines to lower their safety standards when they are flying in other countries or operating subsidiaries there. Greider makes a compelling case that by holding companies accountable through existing national regulatory authority, we can make significant advances until better global mechanisms are in place. Georgian Democratic Congresswoman Cynthia McKinnon has proposed legislation in this spirit, requiring that U.S. companies operating abroad adhere to U.S. federal environmental laws and regulations, and to laws respecting rights to unionize and health and safety protection well established not only in U.S. law but in International Labor Organization codes and other covenants of human rights enshrined in many UN declarations. The successors to the Bretton Woods institutions will need to globalize new labor, social, and environmental standards, while offering incentives for nations to pursue their own labor codes and social protections well beyond the global floor.

To counter concerns in the South that any such regulation would be veiled protectionism by the North, all global labor, environmental, and other standards must be agreed upon by a majority of poor as well as rich nations. UNCTAD, the ILO and other UN agencies must be structured to ensure that poor nations—representing the great majority of the world's peoples— have a dominant voice in global standard setting. Until this is achieved, a transitional approach would be to hold corporations to the standards in either their host nation or the nation invested in, whichever is higher. Another transitional alternative includes proposals to classify corporations into most favored, favored, and least favored, based on their respect for labor rights (including rights to organize and a living wage) and environmental protection. Most favored corporations, with the best labor and environmental practices as evaluated by independent monitors, would be granted reductions on export/import duties, shipping transactions, and other routine international transactions, thus offering financial incentives for companies to compete by racing to the top.[7]

The era of deregulation, even in America, may be on the wane. The Enron scandal, in which the company evaded regulation through hundreds of off-shore tax havens and unsupervised accounting schemes, led many Americans to associate deregulation with corporate crime and greed—and with fleecing of workers who lost their retirement monies tied up in collapsing Enron stock. If Americans demand more regulation at home, it will have a powerful effect on the global conversation, since the United States has been the messiah preaching deregulation and the most powerful influence behind the deregulation policies enforced by the WTO, the IMF, and the entire corrupt Bretton Woods order.

Redistribution of income and wealth is the second obvious remedy for a global economy that is currently awarding more wealth to a few hundred billionaires than to half the world's population. Globalization has left behind the two billion global poor who lack enough to eat or minimal health care. Put simply, a global New Deal has to be a program of massive investment in and aid to the world's poor—and it has to move fast. Global democrats are proposing a new abolitionism, abolition of debt and poverty of poor nations, that may prove as important as the abolition of slavery and colonialism. There can be no saving of the global poor or freeing of their nations from the IMF yoke under the current crushing debt systems. Debt relief for the world's poorest countries has already been endorsed by rich nations, but far more needs to be done and will not be accomplished without phasing out not only the IMF but the neoliberal philosophy and system that is dedicated to redistribution from poor to rich.

Global democrats have mobilized powerfully to take up the debt issue, even prior to achieving the broader systemic changes that will be required for a fair distribution of the world's wealth. Jubilee South has promoted the idea of a "debtors cartel" and its South-South Summit Declaration underscored "the need for collective action among the South" (i.e., poor nations) for debt repudiation. Thirteen African countries met in Lusaka, Zambia, to call for "collective repudiation of illegitimate foreign debt payment" and to "link our arms across borders" to build strength. A leading Brazilian Presidential candidate has sounded the same theme and Argentina has already suspended its debt payments. Global activists called for the 2002 Pôrto Alegre meetings to put the idea of a debtors cartel on the global agenda that would have the power to collectively bargain with the creditor countries. The debtors plan to act in concert to demand debt abolition for the poorest nations and "a cap on the percentage of export earnings that can be required for debt service." Payment of debt would also be conditioned on assurances that basic human needs and social services be funded first. The key to this new debt strategy is that it "globalizes" the struggle, bringing together indebted countries with supporters in creditor nations and increasing their countervailing power to threaten a collective default that the creditor countries could not disregard. Such a collective organization could become the basis for a more systemic challenge, moving from debt relief to broader and deeper redistribution of the world's wealth.[8]

As a step in this direction, global democrats seek a more comprehensive global fund for development that would be targeted at the poorest nations. It envisions increased foreign aid and development financing at the global level, funded by hot money taxes, new taxes on the profits of global corporations, or higher levels of aid from rich nations. While such reforms fall well short of necessary systemic changes, they help prepare the ground for deeper transformation. Responding defensively to the debt campaigns, world leaders, particularly in Europe and at the World Bank, are beginning to use the rhetoric of a global aid agenda that could eventually help global democrats argue for a system creating real global equity. Greater aid commitments from the rich nations was taken up in world meetings held in New York and Monterry, Mexico, in 2002, although it faced resistance from the United States, which had not increased its foreign aid for a decade. The UN has been calling for an urgent increase in aid for the global poor, involving a commitment of at least 0.7 percent of total economic output of developed nations, far more than the United States will commit even after in its much touted increase in foreign aid at the Monterry meetings. European nations such as the Netherlands, Norway, Denmark, and Sweden have already implemented the UN proposals and most other European nations have promised to do so.

The conversation in the mainstream, prompted by deteriorating global economic conditions and mass antiglobalizaion protests, has begun to inch toward more systemic concerns. Economists Jeffrey Sachs and Joseph Stiglitz have become severe critics of IMF policy, arguing for democratization of the IMF and basic change in its structural adjustment programs. Sachs and Stiglitz are major proponents of increased aid, but now also see the Bretton Woods core policies as locking the poor into chronic emergencies of health, poverty, and environmental disaster.[9]

World leaders, while resisting systemic change, are now talking about a worldwide commitment to end global poverty as the most cost-effective approach to violence and terrorism. Gordon Brown, Britain's chancellor of the exchequer, argued repeatedly and explicitly after September 11 that developed nations had to sponsor a "new Marshall Plan" for the world's poor that would "create a new relation between developed and developing countries." In one address on terror, Blair talks extensively about "a partnership for Africa," in which the developed world would "provide more aid, untied to trade; write off debt. . . . The state of Africa is a scar on the conscience of the world . . . we could heal it. And if we don't, it will become deeper and angrier." This is mostly rhetoric but it signals the possibility in the post–9-11 environment of a new conversation about the underlying systemic conditions creating such deep hatred by the global poor against the world's rich.[10]

Global recession has also made talk about a global New Deal of redistribution from rich to poor more credible, both among those seeking to preserve the current order and those seeking to create a new more radically equitable system. It took a Great Depression to create a New Deal in the United States. Billions of people around the world now live in conditions far worse than did Americans in the 1930s. In an interdependent world, we can no longer afford to turn a blind eye to their desperate plight. But even in the United States, the decline of the high-tech markets in the first years of the new millennium and massive layoffs of millions of workers in the very fragile American economy created a new climate for government activism and intervention. The terrorists attacks and the recession have weakened the free market religion of the Reagan era and created more fertile conditions here and abroad for a new New Deal.

The collapse of Argentina and the massive street revolts against leaders prescribing neoliberal medicine could become a global turning point. Economist and *New York Times* columnist Paul Krugman wrote that much of the world believes that "the policies in Argentina have 'made in Washington' stamped all over them." He compared IMF leaders to doctors who used to bleed their patients, "and if the bleeding made them worse, repeated the process."[11] In early 2002, the new President, Eduardo Duhalde, said he would "no longer play by the rules of the IMF." He brought Argentinian parliamentarians to their feet when he promised to walk away from "an exhausted economic model," referring to the neoliberal policies of the IMF. He would not resume interest payments on the foreign debt and instead would increase spending on social programs for workers and the poor. In a country and continent wedded to free market orthodoxy over the last decade, this was revolutionary and hinted at a possible change in global thinking not unlike the shift from Hoover to Roosevelt at the start of the U.S. New Deal.[12]

The International Forum on Globalization (IFG), a group of prestigious globalization critics, has proposed abolishing the IMF (as well as the WTO and World Bank) and rolling back all IMF structural adjustment agreements, while simultaneously creating a new set of democratic finance and trade agencies under the UN, precisely what is needed. A first order of new business by successor institutions to the IMF would be management of national debts on new terms consistent with development and dignity. A new UN International Insolvency Court would provide for a negotiated process of debt relief or outright abolition for every nation whose debt has undermined its capacity to feed and shelter its citizens or to initiate its own development agenda. It would also permit identification and cancelation of "odious" debt incurred through illegal, coercive, or deceptive processes that offered no public or social benefit. Debt that remained would be restructured according to time schedules consistent with the capacity of the country to deliver affordable food, housing, health care, and other essential social services.[13]

The changing conversation about debt relief shifts the conversation to a focus on how the Bretton Woods system creates endless debt and ever-greater gaps between rich and poor nations. In this systemic approach, a new agency, such as a UN International Finance Organization proposed by the IFG, would assume the broader responsibilities associated with debt management and global finance now entrusted to the IMF and the WTO. Its constitutional mandate would be to promote development rather than simply protect the rights of creditors. It would help monitor and deal with trade imbalances by prioritizing the urgent development needs of poor nations and seeking to help transform the disastrous IMF policy of promoting export economies tragically vulnerable to erratic swings in commodity prices. It would promote national development and domestic food security as well as protect local business until a country felt prepared to compete on a newly leveled playing field in the world economy. It would help limit the flows of speculative capital, close down illicit offshore banking havens, and reallocate any IMF and World Bank surplus assets after "decommission" to a new global fund for short-term emergency loans to countries in financial crisis. It might also create a Currency Defense Fund to help nations defend themselves from undue speculation without radically tightening monetary policy or devaluing currency, consistent with Keynes's proposal many years ago of an "international clearing union" designed precisely to permit social development and full employment policy in poor countries vulnerable to speculative attacks. This would be part and parcel of a successor system to Bretton Woods that rewrites the global constitutional rules to empower the poor, reversing the entire panoply of policies deliberately structured now to enrich the wealthy.[14]

Decommodification, a third New Deal policy embraced by many global democrats, involves radically reversing the global tidal wave toward privatization. This involves resurrecting what economist Hazel Henderson calls the "global commons," recognizing and protecting the earth's water, air, oceans, space and all the resources of the world that belong to the people of the world as a whole. They need to be protected from becoming market commodities if the earth itself is to survive.[15]

Global governments replacing the Bretton Woods triumverate will have to take the lead in reclaiming from business property, goods, or services that should never be put on the market. This includes not only the environmental global commons, but the education, health care, and social welfare needs of the world's people, not to mention the air waves and media, large sectors of world knowledge and culture, and the Internet itself. The global democratic alternative means that large parts of the world will carry a permanent sign saying "not for sale." Some of the most critical fights are now taking place over water, as companies such as Bechtel have negotiated with Bolivia and other national governments to privatize and manage local water supplies. In Bolivia, we have seen the emergence of "water movements" made up of desperate villagers who cannot afford to buy the water at the prices that the private companies charge. Their protests successfully convinced the Bolivian government to cancel its Bechtel contracts.

Decommodification should start by enshrining the sanctity of the "global commons" into the UN charter. There is a close connection between the positive rights to food, shelter, education, health care, and development established in Article 25 of the 1948 Declaration of Human Rights and in many successive General Assembly Resolutions affirming such rights, and the preservation of the global commons. Privatization of everything from water to health care to education inevitably prices millions of the global poor out of access to the commons and leaves them without adequate food, water, and other basic needs. We thus need strong affirmation in the UN charter of the unconstitutionality of privatizing the commons, since this deprives people of the positive rights that the UN has ratified over and over again. The broad global disenchantment with the privatization policies of the IMF and the WTO have made decommodication a key priority of the global justice movements and of national governments and local communities suffering the pain.[16]

The fourth and most important New Deal policy is participation. Democracy, of course, is all about participation, of, for, and by the people. This requires a passion on the part of citizens everywhere to get involved in global affairs and governance. And it depends on the rise of global institutions that recognize the sovereignty of the people on a world scale and provide channels for their will to be expressed and heeded.

An undeniable passion for participation ignited the raucous protests that rocked the WTO meetings at Seattle and all the successive trade summits. The signs waved on the streets proclaimed "No globalization without representation." Protesters wanted to tell the new architects of the world order that monumental decisions about how to run the world cannot be made behind closed doors. The protesters subjected themselves to tear gas and beatings to insist that they, along with other ordinary citizens, deserved a seat at the table.

The WTO, IMF, and related bodies are, in fact, shadow governments lacking the transparency and popular participation essential to democracy. The respected financial policy analyst and author, Howard Wachtel, writes that the WTO "has no written bylaws . . . holds no public hearings and in fact has never opened its processes to the public. Its meeting rooms do not even have a section for the public to observe its activities." The reasoning behind the decisions of WTO judicial tribunals are not publicly disclosed and public interest groups or ordinary citizens have no legal standing to present arguments to any WTO decision-making council. For a body that has effective power to overrule the environmental, health, and safety tax, or trade laws of any nation, this creates what some political scientists call politely a serious global "democratic deficit."[17]

Because the governing authority of the WTO, IMF, and related bodies are councils of representatives from member states, one might argue that the people's interests are safeguarded despite lack of public access. But each nation's representatives to the WTO are appointed by the national executive and are not elected or usually even known to the public. The people's own representatives in the legislative branch, in the U.S. Congress, for example, are themselves in the dark about the deliberations that take place. Fast-track trade authority in the United States sought by all recent U.S. presidents gives members of Congress only the authority to vote final trade agreements up and down, with no prior consultation and no power to amend.

Thus even national legislators are doubly excluded, first from any direct representation in the WTO or IMF and second from the right to participate in molding global rules within their own home nation's parliament or Congress. This has provoked a furious response among American Senators and Representatives to recent proposed trade agreements, such as the Multilateral Agreement on Investment (the MAI), a major financial liberalization program for the world. The MAI negotiations fell apart in 1999, after several years of secret drafting begun in 1995, partly because many American Congressional representatives were outraged that they were never informed about the very existence of the talks. One angry group of American legislators wrote a public letter noting that the MAI "would require significant limitations on U.S. laws and policy concerning federal, state, and local regulation of investment." They questioned why "would the U.S. willingly cede sovereign immunity" in a treaty that would allow foreign corporations to sue the American government for damages "if we take any action that would restrain 'enjoyment' of an investment." Despite legislators' deep concerns about sovereignty and participation, major provisions of the MAI, as noted in Chapter 5, have been incorporated into financial liberalization measures imposed by the IMF and integrated into new, ambitious financial liberalization agreements under consideration at this writing at the WTO.[18]

The growing public outrage about secrecy has led the WTO to promise greater transparency and to establish consultations with environmental, labor, and other public interest groups. But these reforms do little to alleviate the fundamental crisis of participation at the heart of the organization. Ordinary citizens of every nation and their elected representations still have no formal decision-making authority in the WTO, nor do they have legal standing in the proceedings of the tribunals wielding global sovereign power. In contrast, corporations have long been official advisers and inside players. The U.S. Council on International Business participated in every MAI negotiating session as official advisers and actually wrote the initial draft of the agreement, and corporate groups routinely serve as official advisers to WTO panels. Ordinary people and their elected representatives enjoy nothing remotely comparable to such institutionalized participation. There is little in the history and constitutionalism of the WTO or IMF and World Bank to suggest that they can ever be reformed to ensure genuine public participation and accountability.

The participation crisis exists in virtually every global authority, including the UN itself. The UN is a huge insular bureaucracy. At the top sits the Secretary General, who is subject to the Security Council, itself made up of official representatives of powerful nations who are appointed rather than elected officials. Poor nations and public interest groups have more access and influence in the UN than at the WTO or IMF, but ordinary citizens have a negligible involvement in the UN and little formal participation beyond that of their government's official delegates.

The most noticeable change in UN practice over the last decade has been the institutionalization of official consultation and cooperation between the UN and global business. As two political scientists observe, "Secretary-General (Kofi) Annan has made 'partnering' with the business community a major hallmark of his leadership. The United Nations has now established a formal business advisory council to formalize a permanent relationship between the corporate community and the UN." Annan has become a regular participant in the Davos, Switzerland, meetings of the World Economic Forum, the most important annual meeting of global corporate economic elites. And he has established a new UN-certified code of global corporate conduct that creates voluntary standards largely developed by the companies themselves, reflecting a new disturbing trend to increase corporate participation and influence at the UN without subjecting them to UN regulation or enforcement.[19]

But in contrast to the WTO or IMF, the UN has also expanded the participation of ordinary citizens through nongovernmental organizations (NGOs). These are nonprofits and public interest groups such as Amnesty International, Greenpeace, and Oxfam. The UN has identified over three thousand such groups and while some of them have become large bureaucracies themselves, they are an extremely important and rapidly growing expression of popular global will and participation. Since the early 1990s, they have played a heightened role in critical UN-sponsored conferences on the environment, women's rights, racism, and development. Significant NGO participation began to grow even earlier, in the early 1980s global negotiations over the atmospheric ozone crisis. At the Rio 1992 UN Framework Convention on Climate Control, NGO participation played a major role, arguably a turning point in opening the UN to serious participation by grassroots groups representing an aroused global citizenry.

Since then, popular participation through NGOs has increased in many UN-sponsored global agreements, including the Kyoto protocol, the 1998 convention outlawing landmines, and the 1998 creation of the International Criminal Court. A global coalition of NGOs won a Nobel Prize for their influential participation in securing the Oslo ban on landmines, and 136 allied NGOs gained official UN observer status in Rome at the conference creating the International Court. The NGOs have powerfully mobilized world public opinion, successfully lobbied governments in support of the UN agreements, and played an increasingly influential role in bringing in experts who can help draft the actual documents in the public interest.[20]

At the Millennium NGO Forum held at the UN in May 2000, Secretary General Annon invited 1,400 people representing NGOs to speak on critical issues, including citizen participation in global decision-making. The conference led to an agreement to establish a permanent assembly of NGOs, to meet every few years before UN General Assembly meetings. While this has not yet been implemented at this writing, it hints at a great leap forward in global democracy. It not only institutionalizes direct popular participation outside of official government channels but creates a model of representation based not on the sovereignty of the nation-state but of the world's people themselves.[21]

Political scientists Richard Falk and Andrew Strauss argue that the new NGO assembly is "a preliminary step toward creating a global parliament." Such a parliament, which they call a *Global People's Assembly* (GPA), could ultimately transform the UN into a world government that more fully embodies the principles of global democracy. Unlike the UN, it would not represent nation-states but the world's peoples in their new identity as global citizens. This is rooted in "contemporary sovereignty," a vision that views the people rather than states as the ultimate locus of authority.[22]

Democratization of the UN is crucial, since its influence will expand dramatically with the abolition of the Bretton Woods institutions. The new order will only be as democratic as the UN itself. As the UN is now accountable only to nation-states, many of which are themselves nondemocratic. Moreover the Security Council structure vests overwhelming power in the dominant nations, especially the U.S. While the UN is thus beholden to both the Great Powers and antidemocratic national governments, the GPA, since it is based on direct election by ordinary global citizens and not based on state representation, could be a far more credible and effective advocate of democracy and human rights.

While their proposal may sound unrealistic, Falk and Strauss note that the European Parliament is a practical model of such direct popular governance. In 1979, Europeans gained the right to elect their own representatives to the Parliament who would speak for them as European citizens rather than as citizens of France, Germany, or whatever nation they lived in. While the Parliament was originally very weak relative to the European Council and the European Commission, the other major governing authorities of the European Union, it has gradually assumed more influence. The 1993 Maastricht Treaty vested the Parliament with "codecision" authority shared with the European Council, including the power "to amend or veto legislation in specified legislative areas such as education, cultural affairs, and public health." The rising power of the Parliament has been a response to public anger at remote EU bureaucrats in Brussels who seem cut off from ordinary people.[23]

The General People's Assembly could emerge in similar fashion at a global level, starting as a pure advisory body to the UN. Its powers could grow in much the same way as the European Parliament, as the world's citizens and grassroots groups became frustrated with the bureaucratic inertia, Great Power influence, or growing corporate voice in the UN. It might begin without formal state or UN sanction, through the cooperation of the many influential civil society groups already participating in the 2000 UN Millennium Forum. By speaking out for popular labor, environmental, or human rights concerns that neither governments nor the UN supported, it could gain increasing public visibility and support. Eventually, a coalition of NGOs, sympathetic governments and even socially oriented businesses could draft a treaty establishing the Parliament as a formal body. They would then seek public participation to pressure governments to sign. It would not have to replace the UN, and more likely would develop a close relation with it, perhaps as a partner with the UN General Assembly in a new "bicameral world legislature."

Ultimately, its role would be to help transform the UN into a model of global citizenship, public accountability, and democracy, the precondition of the democratization of the world economy after the fall of the Bretton Woods triumverate.[24]

All of this will evolve slowly and ultimately depends on the passion of the world's citizens to participate. If the new global justice movements are any indication, that passion could spread as fast as globalization itself.

In February 2002, about thirty labor organizers, religious activists, student leaders, and policy experts met on St. Simon's Island in George to launch a campaign to end global sweatshops. The group asked this: If we protect the Disney or Nike labels worldwide with international patents, why shouldn't we have laws protecting the 16-year-old workers in every country who makes the product? The organizers agreed to draft a petition, to be signed by millions of people, that calls for the abolition of sweatshops and new globally enforceable worker rights.

In Chapter 5, we saw that business had to create a new constitution for the world economy based on property rights and enforced by the WTO. A global New Deal and post–Bretton Woods order requires its own new global constitution that will not abolish global property rights but offer equal protection for the global rights of workers, children, women, and nature. Interestingly, this does not require a new utopian experiment based on visionary international law. The world already has embraced a splendid set of human and worker rights, enshrined originally in the 1948 UN Declaration of Human Rights. These rights, later expanded in numerous UN Conventions dealing with children, women, and the environment, include nearly two-hundred worker rights propounded by the International Labor Organization (ILO) and ratified by most nations. To create the new globalization, we can move a long way by arming these existing rights with teeth. The idea of globally enforceable human and worker rights was the core vision of Citizens' Globalism at the end of World War II and the founding of the UN, and it has resurfaced as the great challenge of the coming century.

A key aim of a post-Bretton Woods global order order is to expand and enforce these rights. Some global democrats look to the UN's International Labor Organization since its historical mission has been to protect workers and to create agreements enshrining their rights. The ILO does not penalize transgressors although it can theoretically expel them or encourage other countries to not trade or invest in them, as it recently did unsuccessfully in Burma, an egregious human rights violator. But while many see the ILO as a paper tiger today, it could conceivably do the job tomorrow if citizens of the world created the pressure to make it happen.

The historic toothlessness of the ILO has led many to conclude that we must create an entirely new UN body. Like the ILO, its mission would be to affirm and protect the rights of all workers around the world. But, unlike the ILO, a new Worker Rights Authority (WRA) would be designed specifically as an enforcer with the judicial powers to judge and penalize offenses. Its authority would have to be as least as potent as that of today's WTO and its sanctions would include empowering workers or citizens to sue corporations that abuse workers or fire union organizers. The new authority would be empowered to levy fines or other sanctions against rogue companies as well as possibly devise penalties against countries that encourage corporate abuse or turn a blind eye. Such a new agency would have to be totally democratic in spirit and practice, modeling the transparency and public participation that we do not see at either the WTO or ILO.

As Europe economically integrated in recent decades, the European Union passed a Social Charter and Generalized System of Preferences that guaranteed basic worker and social rights enforceable in all European nations. This successfully reduced corporate incentives to flee from France or Germany or Sweden to poorer European nations such as Portugal or Greece. The Europeans started with a small number of simple and easily enforceable worker rights that could expand over time. Global democrats propose a similar model on a worldwide scale, starting with a core set of global worker rights that have been ratified by almost all nations and by the International Confederation of Free Trade Unions. Referred to as the "social clause," these worker rights include the right to associate (ILO Convention 87), the right to organize and bargain collectively (ILO Convention 98), the prohibition of forced labor (ILO Conventions 29 and 105), and the prohibition of child labor (ILO Convention 138). Some propose also adding minimum health and safety standards and a minimal wage adapted to the living standards of each country. Trade unions in Latin America have already argued that the social clause should be at the heart of trade agreements in the Americas, going well beyond the labor and environmental side-agreements to the North American Free Trade Agreement (NAFTA) that have proved ineffective.[25]

All global democrats understand that global constitutional rights will remain nothing but paper documents unless enforcement becomes a primary focus of worldwide social movements. It will take a campaign far more ambitious than that to eliminate global landmines or even global debt. A more apt analogy is a global civil rights movement that sees securing the rights of the world's workers as the great moral struggle of the new century. The movement to abolish sweatshops, launched by the thirty activists in Georgia, could be the spearhead of a new civil rights struggle to guarantee worker and human rights everywhere.

Global human rights are critical but they are simply one piece of a new post–Bretton Woods global constitutional order and the global justice movement necessary to create it. Human rights need to be struggled for and enforced at every level of government and community, as part of a broader struggle for deep systemic change in the world economy. A new global government will craft the new post–Bretton Woods system, but most of the real work to get there and make it work has to be done through national state and local governments working with aroused civic associations, unions, and grassroots movements.

The labor and social movements are key and the vision of global rights is a crucial new arrow in their quiver. But their burning daily challenges remain tangible and local, in campaigns, for example, to force Wal-Marts to pay its workers a few pennies more per hour and allow independent unions. The fight for global rights will materialize in thousands of such local power struggles in workplaces and communities everyday around the world. And as workers form unions to defend their lives, they will see that dignity and rights can be won in one country only when they are guaranteed everywhere, leaving corporations no place to flee. Global rights and local struggles against corporate power are the twin faces of the new globalization we need.

CHAPTER 8

PEOPLE POWER

Those who expect to reap the benefits of freedom, must, like men, undergo the fatigue of supporting it.

TOM PAINE

A nation of sheep will beget a government of wolves.

EDWARD R. MURROW

G LOBAL GOVERNMENT WILL LOOM LARGE IN THE DEMOCRATIC FUTURE but it will take a long time to create and it will always be a decentralized, federal structure limited in power. Countering the risk of global Big Brother that many rightly fear and preserving the democratic spirit that must infuse any international sovereign authority requires a democratic revival in more familiar terrains, including national governments, the business world, and local communities. Building global government is only the first of five essentials in the global democratic agenda. The four others, democratizing of nation-states, democratizing global business, reviving local democratic community, and creating collective security are equally important.

During the 2002 upheavals in Argentina, citizens poured into the streets and scrawled this grafitti warning on the sidewalk across from the Casa Rosada, the presidential palace. "We are going to keep on coming. Signed, the People."[1]

Ordinary citizens taking control of their own national governments is a key to a global democratic future. While this has an idealistic tone, it has been very real for people not just in Argentina, but the Philippines, Poland, Brazil, and Indonesia. All have had "people power" movements in recent years that have helped to overthrow repressive governments and restore faith in the democratic ideal. Nations around the world have seen an aroused people demanding popular control of government and a commitment to constitutional democratic ideals. Cynics about national democracy are ignoring one of the most powerful and importance forces in the age of globalization.

National democracy is central because the policies of national government still largely determine the fate of the poor and middle classes. Poverty relief and social welfare, whether in First or Third World countries, still depend on commitments by national leaders and governments. And the leaders will not raise up the wretched of their countries or serve their middle classes without sustained pressure from aroused citizens.

The problem of creating a meaningful and robust national democracy obviously looks very different in El Salvador or Pakistan than in Washington or London, but remains a challenge everywhere. There remain key areas of the world where military dictatorships and monarchies or sham democracies (authoritarian regimes with staged elections) retain the power they have had for centuries. Other nations, such as Brazil and the Philippines, have new and more promising democracies that are exceedingly fragile and have their own unique problems connected to ethnic divisions and weak civil societies, as well as external control wielded by global financial markets or the IMF. The democratic crisis in countries such as the United States, long blessed with constitutional democratic systems, is a third form, linked to the problem shared by all nations of creating popular control in a national politics saturated with global money and big business.

In all three contexts, new democracies, old democracies, and traditional dictatorships or sham democracies, the shared imperative is to create political systems and leaders truly responsive and accountable. And the shared obstacle to the "people power" movements, in addition to unique problems of corruption, illiteracy, overpopulation, and ethnic wars, is the power of global markets and corporations to dictate national agendas. The severity of the internal crises within nations is not to be dismissed.

As Robert Kaplan has shown powerfully in his book, *The Coming Anarchy*, many Third World countries have only the façade of government, dominated by warlords who rule fiefdoms only nominally knitted into nations. Such countries are constantly vulnerable to social breakdown, and democracy will be difficult or impossible before the conditions of order and unity essential to a viable government have been created.[2] But global businesses, often working closely with the United States, have functioned even within such anarchistic states by wedding themselves with warlords or national authoritarian leaders. Think only of Shell in Nigeria and the diamond and mining companies in the Congo and Sierra Leone. I have shown throughout this book that globalization has created a new crisis of legitimacy for all nation states, whether democratic, dictatorial, or anarchistic. It increasingly weds national leaders to the lucrative deals offered by global business rather than to the local aspirations of their own people, whatever the state of anarchy in the country. National democracy can only be achieved by breaking the marriage vows binding global corporations with authoritarian national leaders and creating a new marriage between popular leaders and their own people that can create the foundations of order and sustainable government.[3]

The democratic challenge is complicated further by the need of virtually all nations to attract money and jobs. It is hard to take on the global corporate Goliath when you desperately need his resources. And global companies or investors exact a price for their presence, a huge stake in the running of your government to assure that their stay will be profitable. So choosing national democracy over the global corpocracy may appear to come at the cost of bankrupting your country. This has been the chronic problem haunting nations such as Argentina, whose leaders wedded themselves to neoliberal global policy while alienating themselves from their people *and* eventually leading their nation into bankruptcy.

Despite the immense challenges of implementation, globalization itself has made the rhetoric of democracy the only acceptable global discourse and global businesses themselves have a stake in the transparency, stability and legitimacy that democracy brings. The idea of limiting the role of money in politics and making governments more accountable to people is already on the national agenda in countries around the world. There is no lack of ideas about specific electoral reforms and other concrete proposals to reduce corporate influence and deepen democracy. The challenge in both Western and Third World countries is to create a new comprehensive vision of national democracy and mobilize the political will to get the job done in an economically viable way.

Global desperation has turned the question of national democracy into an explosive popular cause. I talked at length with a middle-class Argentinian couple living in Buenos Aires shortly after their country's financial meltdown in late 2001. They were deeply upset; the husband had learned he might be losing his computer job and they were afraid that they could not get by even though they were living with his parents. His wife cried as she talked about their desire to get Italian or Spanish passports and live abroad, despite their love of their country. But they saw one silver lining. For the first time in their lifetimes, people in Argentina were rising up and demanding political accountability from their leaders. Ordinary Argentinians were rushing out on the streets, banging pots and pans. Some were raiding shops and breaking windows in government buildings but others were *waving the Constitution* in front of TV cameras. New democratic movements were sprouting up, challenging the established parties. Constitutions in hand, they were seizing a constitutional moment, demanding accountability to the democratic ideals so often preached and little respected.

Buenos Aires Congresswoman Elisa Carrio said the Argentine people, including an angry middle class, were going to go back constantly into the streets until real democracy was created. "People have seen that they can topple one President after another. They will not stop," she said, until their democratic dreams were realized. And leaders were beginning to respond, as successive presidents began to challenge the IMF and global neo-liberal orthodoxy, while promising to stop lining their own pockets and respond finally to the desperate needs of workers and the poor.[4]

The politics of national democratization is ever more linked with the politics of globalization. Global democracy will require alliances or coalitions of national democratic movements in every country. They will have to work in concert to create the global as well as local conditions supportive of the democratic path. What globalization has done is make national democratic struggles inseparable from global ones. As long as the global economy and the WTO and IMF operate on neoliberal rules dictated by global business, replacing corporate sovereignty in a single state becomes nearly impossible. Popular national democratic movements in every part of the world will have to unite in the service of new global constitutional rules for all nations and global firms. All national democratic movements will need to challenge global neoliberal constitutionalism and support the democratic alternative.[5]

Your problem, if you are American, is probably imagining Washington or other national governments serving the people again. Remembering Enron or the political scandals of the Clinton administration will likely increase your skepticism. Money and global companies, you will say, are simply too powerful. Presidents, national political parties, and the entire government apparatus are in the grip of the global markets, transnational business, and the "special interests." Re-inventing government has become a buzzword for talking about how to make government more lean and mean, as efficient as a business. But while efficiency is immensely important, the real task in the age of globalization is not how to make the American or other national governments look and act more like a corporation. It is how to protect national governments from becoming subsidiaries of the largest global companies.[6]

This is not a problem that can be solved through piecemeal reforms. We need a systemic challenge to the corporate/government incest that lies at the very root of today's globalization system, as discussed in Chapter 3. Rebuilding a fire wall between business and government requires cutting off the rights of corporations to political citizenship and outlawing the cozy cronyism that helped give rise to the Enron crisis in the United States. These involve constitutional changes in both the state and the corporation, reversing the corporate conquest of government that is arguably the great business revolution of the twentieth century.

By revoking the political citizenship of corporations, I mean abolishing the right secured by corporations during the Robber Baron era in the United States to be defined as legal persons with all the constitutional and political privileges of flesh and blood citizens. I expand on this in my discussion of corporate charters, but the key concept is that corporations larger than most countries snuff out democracy when empowered to use their money and influence for political ends. The solution is to restructure political systems to get corporations out of politics both globally and nationally. At the national level, this involves comprehensive campaign finance reform, including total public financing of elections. But we also need to curb corporate lobbying, outlaw use of shareholder funds for political causes, drastically limit corporate ownership of schools and media, reverse the current alarming trend to protect commercial speech under the First Amendment, rescind the "investor rights" clauses of NAFTA and the WTO that allow foreign corporations to sue governments for passing labor or environmental laws reducing profits, and criminalize threats by corporate officials to influence the vote of employees.[7]

Rebuilding a fire wall for democracy also means cutting off corporations from the illicit flow of public monies into subsidies, tax breaks, and other giveaways to giant global corporations. Conservative organizations such as the Cato Institute suggest that the scale of corporate welfare in the United States each year is larger than the entire government budget of many countries, amounting to hundreds of billions of dollars. Corporate critic and accountant Ralph Estes, taking into account all forms of government policies benefiting corporations, estimates that the annual amount in the United States alone was worth more than two trillion dollars in 1994. Some forms of public subsidies for business are necessary to support public interests such as saving jobs or training workers, but most of the money dispensed by politicians is pork, paying off the very businesses that forked up the money to elect them. This form of "crony capitalism"—made transparent to Americans during the Enron debacle—has a self-reinforcing character. As corporations gain more influence by flooding government with money, they get policy agendas tailored to maximize their profits as well as subsidies and tax breaks swelling their coffers, that in turn increase the amount they can afford to pour back into politics and campaigns. Americans have been spectators to this fantastic deformation of democracy in the Bush administration, where big energy companies such as Enron help elect Bush and then are rewarded access, insider influence, and giant subsidies. When Vice President Cheney refused to hand over the names of people who helped craft the Bush energy policy, he was making a futile effort to conceal the unholy marriage between the administration and the industry that spawned it. But his cover-up will help spur the social movement needed to break up the corporate/government monolith.[8]

I often ask public audiences what would happen if a fully enlightened being, say Buddha or Jesus, was the CEO of a major global corporation like Nike. Would such enlightened and saintly leaders, I ask, lead the company to end sweatshops or commit their profits to the development of the impoverished countries in which they operate? Few people have thought about the question but it can help us understand what is involved in democratizing business, a step as important as and closely connected to democratizing government.

After a little conversation, most people come to the conclusion that even Buddha and Jesus would likely fail to change corporate policy. U.S. corporations are legally obligated to pay off the shareholders with maximum return. Jesus or Buddha in the saintly CEO role would end up in court, sued by their own shareholders, if they lowered profits to help the poor of the world. And this is just one of many ways that global financial markets and firms are wired by their inner programming to put profit above people.

Many corporate leaders would like to "do the right thing" and "do well while doing good." But they are hemmed in by stockholder laws and financial markets demanding higher short-run returns. Even as the rhetoric about corporate responsibility escalates, the global race to the bottom intensifies. In the same companies that commit to innovative worker participation and community development programs, such as GM, we see massive domestic layoffs and cuts in core employee and community benefits. Leaders in corporate responsibility, such as Stride Rite and Levi Strauss, have seen some of their most ambitious social programs go up in smoke. Stride Rite abandoned the Boston inner city that it invested in for years, and Levi Strauss, after ironclad commitments to domestic employees, went to China for some of the world's cheapest labor. None of this implies personal bad faith on the part of corporate leaders but points to the hard realities of the larger system that inevitably turn corporations, whatever the personal values of their leaders, into cash registers.[9]

It is a major challenge to global democrats to re-invent the system wiring of global business. Can we realistically picture another kind of business system in a global age? One of three essential systemic transformations has been advanced by economic localists: break up global corporations and cut them down to human scale, in the process changing their basic nature. Informed corporate critics such as David Korten want business rooted in or actually owned by the community itself. And it is certainly the case that one strategy to create global economic democracy involves dismantling huge global corporations such as GM or Sony or Shell (all of them larger than most countries) and shrinking them radically. Many localists such as Korten envisage shifting business to a community institution that cannot prioritize the needs of global investors over the needs of the community itself. Global democrats of all stripes seek more nimble and human-size business players, big enough to compete efficiently but small enough to be controlled by citizens and their governments. In the United States, new alliances of consumer groups, local business, and civic groups and state governments are already mobilizing to help break up big monopolies such as Microsoft and keep giants such as Wal-Mart out of the local community.[10]

The notion of community-based business may seem quaint in the current age, but the Fortune 500 global corporations, while hogging about one-quarter of the world's income, employ less than 1 percent of the world's workers. In other words, small community-oriented businesses—whether partnerships, family operations, cooperatives, or single entrepreneurs—remain the most common type of business in the world, and economic theory suggests they have many competitive advantages over giant firms. Close to their customers, they have what Korten calls "engaged stakeholders," meaning workers, suppliers, consumers, and local governments who know and depend on one another. Ownership by community members enhances loyalty and productivity. Giant corporations dominated by absentee owners cannot deliver the loyalty or work ethos of the engaged worker, let alone sustainable community that promotes political democracy. This suggests that government should provide tax incentives for community-based enterprise, redirecting some of the billions of corporate welfare dollars now lavished on the Fortune 500.[11]

Even if economies of scale prevent many corporations from achieving the human-scale embraced by localists, there is an overwhelming case for breaking up the few hundred largest global corporations that choke democracy in both large and small nations. The global economy has become a playfield of monopolists and oligopolists, with virtually every industry dominated by two or three leviathans. Boeing and Airbus are the only two commercial aircraft producers in the world; Microsoft and Intel both control more than 80 percent of their global industries.

This makes a mockery of the capitalist concept of competitive markets. Not only global democrats but capitalists who believe in markets rather than centrally planned corporate kingdoms should embrace an assault on corporate concentration. The UN agencies succeeding the Bretton Woods trimuverate should require that every global industry have a robust number of players consistent with the preservation of both competition and democracy. Every nation should enforce its own constitutional limits on concentration, relying on enforcement through aggressive antitrust prosecution.

The second prong of a systemic agenda to democratize global business involves rewriting the corporate constitution: its charter. Remember that corporations are legal entities whose purposes are authorized by the government and laid out in the incorporating laws or charters that it creates. In the United States, both in the pre–Civil War age and the robber baron era, when the majority of Americans became concerned about excessive corporate power, corporate charters became subjects of intense public interest. Today, this interest is being awakened by a new generation of post-Enron activists who recognize that if you want a new business bottom line, you have to write it into the charter.[12]

The modern charter defines the corporation as a sacred free contract among private parties that neither government nor citizens have any constitutional authority to question.[13] Corporate critics such as Ralph Nader and Richard Grossman have long advocated a new federal charter. It would eliminate the debilitating competition among states and create a new uniform democratic charter for every corporation in the nation. The idea of such constitutional corporate reform, which would reverse the current protection of the corporation as a private "citizen" under the Bill of Rights and resurrect the early idea of the corporation as created to serve the public interest, would be a major step. As Thom Hartmann, a legal theorist, points out, the new charter would endow the corporation the ability to engage in enforceable contracts (a condition of creating any business entity beyond the individual), but it would not vest the corporate legal personality with the political and other rights of real persons. The new charter would make clear that commercial speech is not protected under the First Amendment and that corporate political contributions are not a form of protected speech either. It would also eliminate the current rights of corporations to sue governments in venues such as NAFTA or WTO tribunals. The notion that governments can be viewed as infringing on corporate "due process" rights by passing labor or environmental laws would become a relic, since corporations would no longer be protected under the Fourteenth Amendment when stripped in their charter of the fiction of legal personhood. This is hardly a radical proposition, since Justice William O. Douglas wrote in 1946 that there was no constitutional justification for viewing corporations as "legal persons." Current polls in the United States show that more than 80 percent of Americans reject the idea that a corporation, government, or international tribunal should have the power to overturn environmental or labor laws passed by other governments, whether on due process or any other grounds.[14]

The new form of business would be constitutionally mandated to serve the global common good or face being de-chartered. Charter activists in Pennsylvania have already called for state corporate charters to be limited to thirty years, and renewal could occur only after the corporation had demonstrated its service to the public good through a statutorily determined public review process. This could build on labor and environmental audits that some corporations have begun to initiate to satisfy concerned investors, but charter reform would turn the social performance audit into a system of genuine public accountability.[15]

The new charter would strip the corporation of legal personhood and citizenship rights, as noted above, a key step in moving from corporate sovereignty to democracy. But, in addition, we need to rethink the limited liability laws that protect investors from harm when their corporations engage in the kind of malfeasance shown by Enron and Anderson. If the charter were to hold shareholders to a new standard of liability, they would be motivated to review the legal, ethical, and social performance of the company. This would become feasible only with new reporting standards and the presence of public representatives on the board who could help investors access and understand relevant information, a step long discussed in Europe.

A new vision of chartering could easily be transferred to the international stage. Each nation will certainly want to put its own natural philosophical and cultural imprint on corporations headquartered on its territory. But just as the integration of the European market has led the EU to create European-wide corporate law, the new global era requires that every corporation in the world be bound by a democratic charter and live up to certain fundamentals of democracy and human rights. A baby step in this direction—which actually bears little relation to global democracy but hints at the possibility of global chartering—is the new UN Global Compact set up by Secretary General Kofi Annan. It invites major global corporations to embrace a global code of conduct in relation to worker and the environment consistent with the UN Declaration of Rights. Since there is currently no enforcement capability, this is a purely symbolic move, and many critics call it "blue-washing." Skeptics are rightfully concerned about a UN-corporate partnership that could make the UN itself a dupe certifying corporate conduct that is neither publicly monitored nor enforced. But a UN agency charted to monitor compliance with a global democratic corporate charter with enforcement powers and the ability to de-charter corporations that violated basic labor or human rights would be a step toward creating a constitutionally democratic global business.[16]

A third systemic transformation involves changes in corporate governance away from the shareholder as the only stakeholder vested with the vote and the only constituency to whom the corporation owes fiduciary obligation. The notion that only shareholders bear the risk entitling them to control has been decisively refuted by economists and legal theorists who demonstrate that workers bear their own form of risk by investing the firm-specific human capital they have in the firm. These arguments prove the obvious point that there is no compelling logic why investors who have never stepped into the company should be legally enfranchised while the worker who spends most of his years there has no legal voice or vote in company affairs. Some corporate leaders are themselves questioning this model, believing that corporations will function more profitably if they disenfranchise very short-term investors (who would be viewed as "guest-owner" without the vote rather than true owners) and enfranchise the worker and other stakeholders, including consumers, host communities, and the public itself. More than thirty states in the United States have already passed "stakeholder laws" that permit boards of directors to take into account the interests of worker and other stakeholders without violating their fiduciary obligation to shareholders. And European companies already work under stakeholder systems that vest workers with voting power at the highest level of corporate governance. The German co-determination model requires that one-half of the members of the board of directors of large German companies be elected by the workers. The workers do not necessarily own stock but are given the vote because they are viewed as members of the corporate community who bear risk, as the investors do, and whose commitment is essential to success.[17]

The European approach begins to redefine the corporation as a public enterprise with fiduciary obligation to multiple social communities, one way to end the legal fiction of the global corporation as private enterprise. Defining the corporation as "private" seems an absurd notion in the face of corporate dependency on massive public subsidy and corporate exercise of enormous public quasi-governmental power. The Enron debacle makes clear that the current closed, almost monarchic, governance system of the corporation is dangerous to investors as well as to the general public. Preventing future Enrons will require more than accounting reforms, and rooting out the systemic conflicts of interest in the current order will require a new public transparency and accountability enfranchising multiple stakeholders and the public itself.

The shift from shareholder to stakeholder governance has become part of the global debate, particularly given the history of more democratic corporate governance in Europe and many Third World nations now being pressured to embrace the U.S. model. For three decades, Europe has embraced forms of co-determination that are constitutionally significant because they repudiate the American concept that ownership rights should be restricted to investors. Beyond the legal extension of ownership to workers, there has been a robust European discussion about representation of the broader public on boards of directors. The recent spectacular failures of government regulation in the United States dramatized so vividly by Enron, Anderson, and WorldCom suggest the need for a new vision of ownership that brings public accountability right into the boardroom. There is every reason to believe that democratic ownership—rooted in the concept that workers and the larger public have ownership claims and the right to representation on the board—can enhance the efficiency and productivity of the enterprise. Germany and other European nations, while imperfect and far from fully developed models, show that more democratic governance systems are viable. The European economies have struggled with high unemployment but maintained strong productivity and growth, at minimum comparable to those in the United States. It should be noted that this approach to democratization and public accountability is quite different than government ownership of business, that has been plagued by bureacratic, command-style hierarchy, even though government ownership may be appropriate in many industries that are natural monopolies or are in sectors such as health care or education that should not be left to business on political and social grounds.[18]

The European experience suggests that change will happen only through labor movements with a broad social justice agenda. This will be different from labor movements in the pre-globalization era. It will have to be a movement for the protection of all members of society, a social safety net for all, rather than just union members. It will have to emphasize democracy since in so many countries even the most elementary rights to organize are brutally denied. And most of all it will have to be global, since the mobility of corporations makes it impossible for unions in one country to win strong agreements.

The obstacles are daunting, since global companies are so much richer and more mobile than struggling labor movements. Nonetheless, globalization cuts both ways. Precisely because corporations have globalized, so too a new transnational labor movement is slowly emerging. Unions in the United States have had a revolutionary change in the last two decades of globalization, seeing that their own success is tied to the success of unions in other countries. You simply can't raise wages and labor standards here if they are collapsing in other countries. The fact that the American labor movement has now recognized this is a sign of a sea-change in global labor politics and vision. The American AFL-CIO president, John Sweeney, has taken an explicitly internationalist position of solidarity with Mexican and other national unions, supporting organizing drives in Central American sweatshops with both U.S. organizers and AFL-CIO funds. While this change is new and still in its early stages, it is enormously important. American unions were among the most xenophobic sectors of the U.S. political community for most of the Cold War, railing against foreigners and immigrant workers. The Sweeney turnabout is one of the most remarkable developments in the American labor movement in decades and perhaps the most hopeful.[19]

While there are many reasons to be skeptical about the prospects of global labor movements, I regard their prospects as bright in the long term. They are the only vehicle to empower the billions who work in global sweatshops and whose plight will inevitably claim the moral attention of the world. Deepening global recession will strengthen labor globally as the Great Depression did in this country. Creating global labor rights in a world of sweatshops is going to become the new civil rights movement of the coming century.

What symbolizes true democracy to you? I would not be surprised if you said the New England town meeting. Two hundred years ago, Americans made history by gathering local citizens in a community hall to govern themselves. And they seemed to be following in the footsteps of Athenian democrats two thousand years ago, whose own town meetings helped define democracy for Western civilization.

Even outside the West, democracy seems to be connected to local community and small face-to-face gatherings. Tribal councils have brought together indigenous people from the Americas to Africa in local deliberative bodies. Even in war-torn Afghanistan, as we learned during the recent war, tribal congresses come together to talk and build consensus. As in the New England town meetings, through much of the world democracy seems inseparable from the process of face-to-face conversation among people and their leaders who know each other and work together to govern their own communities. Renewing local community is another key step in building global democracy,

Town meetings, though, seem almost quaint, if not totally obsolete now. When mom and pop stores are swallowed by Home Depots or Wal-Marts and local governments are overwhelmed by giant global businesses and the huge governments behind them, how can town meetings have any relevance today? And as we all become migrants surfing the planet and following jobs wherever they lead, do we really have any intact local communities any more anyway?

But don't put these questions skeptically to the many community activists around the world. They will tell you that the crisis of globalization is precisely that the footloose companies and global markets are trying to make local communities obsolete. And as we have seen in the last chapter, they will fiercely defend the view that the only way to create a democratic world is to re-localize it.

I started with my own serious skepticism about the passionate localist spirit energizing much of the antiglobalization movements. I was surprised to see its intensity especially among young people who have been raised on a diet of global corporate logos and the Internet. But there can be little question that the "small is beautiful" idea and the dream of self-governing communities sprouting up like colorful wildflowers on an Alpen field quickens the pulse of the new activists. Globalization has created a generation of avid global consumers but also of dissenters who crave attachment to land or place, and who destest the globalized, homogenized Gap and McDonald's culture.[20]

The history of local community has not been one of undiluted democracy or often of democracy at all. Many of the young U.S. activists do not remember that it took the federal government to eliminate segregation in closely knit Mississippi or Alabama towns and to give women the vote. We have seen too much romanticizing of community-based traditionalism that was often just plain local tyranny. Those who know some history will not be nostalgic for the "good old days" when racism, sexism, religious fundamentalism or local business elites dominated the life of villages and local culture.

Nonetheless, the new movements are helping skeptics gain new appreciation of the importance of local community. Democracy is not just a system of constitutional laws and rights. The legal skeleton has to be filled with living, breathing spirits who have taken the idea of public conversation and civic participation to heart. As political scientist Benjamin Barber has reminded us, democracy is a culture that has to be internalized in each citizen. And it has to be institutionalized through richly intertwined community and civic associations, the kind that de Tocqueville marveled about as the backbone of American democracy.[21]

The effort to create democracies has proved staggeringly difficult from Romania to Bulgaria to Russia, all countries where Stalinist regimes had destroyed autonomous civic associations and self-governing localities. And even in a country like the United States, the erosion of democracy, if we are to believe Harvard's Robert Putnam, is tied to our new condition of "bowling alone," with our bowling leagues, PTAs, and local neighborhood associations all losing members as people cocoon at home in front of their televisions.[22]

Global democracy, just like democracy within a country, simply cannot work without the revival of local democracy. And this requires revival of bowling leagues as Putnam suggests, as well as the forms of civic participation and citizenship that Barber praises. But today we need a new vision of local democracy that goes beyond these ideas and explicitly moves us toward a novel and organic connection of local and global citizenship.[23] The bumper sticker that I see often in Boston is "Think globally, act locally." It begins to get at the idea that we can no longer separate the local and the global. Globalization has globalized communities, incorporating them into worldwide economies, political systems and ideologies. The localist democratic goal is not to cut the ties between community and these global systems. It is to ensure that power flows upward from newly revived communities that gain a new measure of autonomy and self-governance while helping govern the world order.

The post-Seattle global justice movements have already begun to "localize." The activists who poured into the streets of Seattle are now increasingly engaging in local community activism and working to empower local unions, schools, and neighborhood associations. But they are not abandoning their global concerns. Instead, they have seen that the crises in their communities have roots in the global economy and culture, and that saving their community require a new activism focused on global as well as local policies. A new group of labor and community activists in New England have formed a "Northeast Labor Committee for Global Justice." They have an activist agenda on issues of "job loss, outsourcing and privatization, downward wage pressures, and immigration" that they explicitly link to problems of "corporate globalization." The title of their recent broadside, "Coming to a Town Near You: Corporate Globalization and Its Impact on Massachusetts Workers" seeks explicitly to educate and organize local workers on how their own problems intersect with global issues and what they can do about it.[24]

Connecting the local and the global and rebuilding local community in the new global context has to occur in three familiar arenas: the economy, politics, and culture. Democratic economic localism seeks to revive local business where possible, giving financial, technical, and customer support to small farmer coops and worker-owned cooperatives, community-owned businesses, and new associations of small family farms and mom and pop stores. Locally rooted businesses and farms remain the most sustainable and important sector of all economies. Global justice activists have focused especially on the crisis created by global agribusiness and trade liberalization in Third World nations and the desperate need to rebuild local farm economies. Billions of endangered peasants are being pushed off their land and those who remain cannot compete with the subsidized cheap agricultural exports flooding in from the United States and Europe. Only a relocalized farm economy based on fairer trade policy in food, land reform, and micro-credit programs can save the global poor.[25]

Communities in the United States are learning too that a local economy dominated by global leviathans such as Wal-Mart or McDonald's are exceedingly vulnerable. The local economy can collapse when the global giants decide to move. And since big discount firms such as Wal-Marts tend to use predatory pricing strategies to squeeze out local firms, they can extort communities even when they stay by raising prices once they have become local monopolies.[26]

The crises in local jobs, schools, housing and welfare, painfully obvious in the United States following the collapse of the high-tech economy, the end of the stock market bubble, and the arrival of the new recession, show the new connection between local and global realities. As communities have come to be dominated by giant firms and financial markets, global conditions increasingly shape the fate of all local communities. The millions of layoffs in the United States since the year 2000, devastating local communities and their workers, all reflect not just U.S. companies fleeing abroad but the intertwined deterioration of the American and global economies. And the bitter neoliberal medicine that the United States has long imposed through the IMF and World Bank on desperate Third World nations is now being turned on Americans themselves. In 2001 and 2002, local U.S. government services in schools, health care, and job training were all savagely cut. While the U.S. government is bailing out one industry after another, from airlines to insurance to agriculture, it is cutting back on virtually all social spending and giving precious little for local revenue sharing. In Buffalo, New York, a sorry symbol of the crisis spreading through U.S. poor cities, one-tenth of the city's teachers were laid off in the fall of 2001, in a school system already badly understaffed. One leader said, "It is frightening. They are talking about closing schools. School superintendent Marion Canedo described the situation as "just totally, totally horrendously difficult," speaking of a kind of terror in Buffalo about the collapse of city services.[27]

This points to the acute need for connection between local and global economic activism. Community activists, like the Northeast Labor Committee discussed above are seeking to save jobs, local education, and health services by challenging national and global policies. Buffalo is reeling from IMF-type policies, involving privatization and cuts in social spending, now being administered through Washington against its own citizens. Buffalo shares economic and political problems with Buenos Aires and Manila and needs to act globally as well as locally.

The political lesson is that we need to revive local democracy but there are no local politics today that can be separated from national or global politics. A community activist who does not have his eye on the global political scene will be fighting in the dark. He will not see the larger forces that shape his community's future and even if he gets himself on the city council, he will be relatively powerless to shape his community's destiny.

Global policies are increasingly constraining what state and local governments do. When Massachusetts tried to keep out companies that did business with the dictatorship of Burma, the Supreme Court and WTO both threatened to intervene. WTO policies now threaten the right of local governments to require that businesses hire a percentage of local residents, a critical way that cities have tried to boost employment and keep outside firms accountable. Companies now sue city governments in WTO panels where any such local preference in hiring is branded a mortal sin.[28]

The great challenge in the coming era is finding tangible ways to connect local and global citizenship. A young inner city Afro-American man, out of prison for a few years and now an activist in his community, came to a Boston conference and listened to talks on global poverty and global wars. He got up to say that he and his friends are busy just trying to find food and work as they walk through their own neighborhoods. It was hard to think about the larger world. But he came to the conference because he sensed that his community's fate was now all wrapped up with the larger world. He spoke eloquently about the connection between global terrorism and long-standing economic and physical terror on his own streets. He wanted to attack the roots of both kinds of violence. Only by helping nurture this glimmering recognition of the connection between the local and the global can we create viable local *and* global communities.

Global democracy requires a redefinition of community itself that this young man is beginning to articulate. We are all now part local, part global. The two parts meld in new and intricate ways and redefine who we are and what our community is. Pure localists are harkening back to an obsolete model of community just as pure globalists have lost their local footing. We are entering a new cultural era in which the idea of community is being revolutionized, wedding together local and global identities.

Sociologists have long distinguished between "locals" and "cosmopolitans," people who define themselves through their local connections and others through broader, typically national associations. Globalization seems to be eroding both forms of identities as we increasingly "bowl alone," defining ourselves as freelancers out to make our own way. Global democrats will have to lead the way beyond the new lone ranger or lone bowler toward the "local cosmopolitan," the new citizen who builds her local community and citizenship through an ever closer identification with the planetary community of global democrats and citizens like herself.[29]

I do not mean a complete melding of local and global culture. The events of September 11 have made clear that local communities, and vastly different regions across the planet, value the uniqueness of their own religions and cultures. They will not readily submit to a homogenized culture of the global marketplace and they are right not to do so, although terror and violence are hardly the ways to assert one's own autonomy or deepest values. Nonetheless, global democracy can survive only by respecting and nurturing diverse local cultures that are not printed off the same global corporate template and giving them the autonomy to support their own way of life. The barbershoppers deserve the last word on this subject. Their passionate commitment to local diversity and community is not only essential for global democracy but for world peace.

Have you read this bumper sticker? "Behind Every McDonald's lies a McDonnell Douglas." I have seen it on more than a few cars around Boston. Do you know what it means? You should, because connecting the overwhelming U.S. military force represented by McDonnell Douglas with the symbol of global commercial success, the Golden Arches, is vital to understanding globalization and the guns that back it up. More to the point in this section, it hints at the vast imbalance between the politico/military power of the United States and that of all other nations. To create global democracy, we must rectify that imbalance as fast as we can.

Put simply, we cannot have global democracy in a world so thoroughly dominated by the United States. Democracy means sharing power, and the United States wields far more power than any nation in history. As discussed in Chapter 4, U.S. power has been the driving force behind globalization, and nations who have resisted American prescriptions of open markets and neoliberal financial reform risk the economic and military wrath of the American government. In the name of fighting Communism, the United States has ousted democracies in Guatemala and Iran who challenged American economic interests or Bretton Woods policy. It has also supported numerous dictatorial regimes—think only of Duvalier in Haiti, Somoza in Nicaragua, Marcos in the Philippines, Sukarno and Suharto in Indonesia, Pinochet in Chile, and numerous others—who have rolled out the welcome mat to United States and other foreign corporations on Bretton Woods terms. The quick U.S. embrace of the temporary ouster of democratically elected Venezuelan President Hugo Chavez in 2002 was a reminder that the United States remains prepared to sacrifice democracies abroad when they threaten U.S. economic interests or mount a challenge to the Bretton Woods global order. U.S. political and military hyperpower—currently being massively increased and extended in the name of a global war on terror—remains a critical underpinning of today's globalization system.

While limiting American power will seem threatening to many Americans in the short run, it will be in the long-term interest of the United States itself to help create a new collective security system that better represents the democratic will of all nations. Even many in the American defense and security community are warning of the need for a change. Joseph Nye, now dean of Harvard's Kennedy School of Government, and former assistant secretary of defense, has warned of a new American hubris and unilateralism. We have become "arrogant about our power, arguing that we do not need to heed other nations," he writes. We have come to think of ourselves as "both invincible and invulnerable." But September 11 began to change that perception and help Americans realize the dangers of "going it alone." Condoleeza Rice, the national security advisor of the Bush II administration, argues that the United States must "proceed from the firm ground of national interest and not from the interest of an illusory international community." Nye counters that the international community is now very real and that America can ignore it only at its great peril. Respecting the international community's interest, he says, has become a vital American national interest.[30]

Collective security has many potential flaws, and the world

will have to move in incremental stages to get it right. We are seeing early signs of a renewed importance of the UN, multi-lateral peacekeeping, regional security bodies, and international law. At the same time, the United States, like other great powers past and present, reserves the right to use its vast power as it sees fit. But if the United States does not embrace the rise of a new collective security order, and accepts the associated risks of shared power, it is likely to incur greater risks of increased violence and terrorism from growing numbers of America-haters around the world. In a tour of the Middle East almost six months after the Trade Tower attacks, Thomas Friedman reported that "bin Laden touches something deep in the Arab-Muslim soul, even among those who condemn his murders. They still root for him as the one man who was not intimidated by America's overweening power."[31]

The American Head Umpire, in fact, has not abandoned the dream of Empire. That U.S. dream, with roots as early as the Monroe Doctrine and Spanish-American War of the nineteenth century, was inflamed by the collapse of the European colonial Empires after World II and the rise of the United States as the only survivor powerful enough to rule the world. During the Cold War, U.S. leaders propounded the view that any erosion of American power would open the world to dangerous Soviet expansionism. After the collapse of the Soviet Union in 1991, U.S. leaders asserted that rogue states, ethnic wars, Islamic radicalism, and drugs posed massive new threats. In his 2002 State of the Union message, President George W. Bush asserted the right of unilateral American intervention anywhere in the world to counter the new terrorist threat. "Some governments will be timid in the face of terror. And make no mistake," the president thundered, "if they do not act, America will." American leaders from Nixon to Clinton to Bush have insisted that vital American interests associated with the expansion of the global economy and protection of vital resources such as Middle Eastern oil require the world's sole superpower to intervene wherever it deems necessary.[32]

The view of globalization as a polite name for a new U.S. Empire is, as already noted, widely held in much of Africa, Asia,

Latin America, and the Middle East. While the terrorist attacks have muted their tone, Europeans have also become vocal in their condemnation of the American "hyper-power," their own polite term for an American global Empire. Friedman is just one of many observers who report that Arabs in the Middle East are loath to believe "anything good about the America," in part because of the perception of overwhelming and abusive U.S. power.[33]

Global democracy depends on restraining the power of any single nation, whatever its virtues. As discussed in Chapter 5, we already have a powerful historical model of how to proceed. The UN was established to create a collective security system as part of a new global democracy. Its ultimate challenge was to remove war from the might or whim of the most powerful country and vest security matters in the community of nations as a whole. This would require limiting the sovereign right and power of any nation—even one as politically and militarily dominant as the United States—and more evenly balancing power between the United States and the rest of the world.[34]

Collective security are perhaps the two most important words in the global democrat's lexicon. They imply replacing the anarchy of the world order with a system of international law and multilateral peacekeeping. Even though most nations are jealous of their own sovereignty in practice, collective security has been embraced in principle by all countries that have joined the United Nations and signed on to the core principles of its charter. Today, the United States increasingly seeks UN authorization for its military interventions, though it is very explicit about its right, as cited above by President Bush, his national security advisor Condoleeza Rice and many other United States officials, to take whatever actions it deems necessary to protect national interests.

We saw in Chapter 5 that the U.S. government and global financial leaders saw a very minimal role for the UN during the Cold War and have since resisted new forms of global governance and collective security. But the world is moving in this direction without us. Although the United States refused to join the Kyoto talks on global warming, all other major nations went ahead and signed the treaty themselves. The same was true of the International Criminal Court, which now exists and has been recognized by most countries despite the American failure to get on board. And the same has been true of various global agreements and UN conventions regarding labor, children's and women's rights, as well as regulation of chemical and nuclear weapons.

This rejectionism is not simply an idiosyncracy of the Bush administration. While the United States did sign on to the 1948 UN Declaration of Human Rights, it alone vetoed the Declaration of the Right to Development in 1990. This Declaration helped spell out the core vision of "positive rights" to food, housing, education, work, health care, and social services that were initially established in Article 25 of the 1948 Declaration. U.S. ambassador to the UN Jeane Kirkpatrick described such rights as a "letter to Santa Claus." Floyd Abram, U.S. Representative to the UN Commission on Human Rights, declared that "development is not a right," thus essentially repudiating Article 25.[35]

In an astonishing chronicle of American votes on UN General Assembly and Security Council resolutions, journalist William Blum documents that "Washington has found itself—often alone, sometimes joined by one or two other countries—standing in opposition to peace, nuclear disarmament, economic justice," and other human rights and development questions. Blum lists over 150 votes in the General Assembly during the period 1978 through 1987 in which the United States was either the sole "no" vote or one of two or three dissenters. Examples include the following. The United States was the sole "no" vote (132 nations voted yes) on Resolution 37/199 in 1982, that declared education, work, health care, proper nourishment, and national development as human rights. On November 22, 1983, the United States was the sole "no" vote on Resolution 38/25 (131 nations voted yes) that declared "the right of every state to chose its economic and social system in accord with the will of its people, without outside interference in whatever form it takes." On December 20, 1983, the United States was the sole "no" vote (98 yes votes) on Resolution 38/187A that urged "intensification of negotiations to achieve an accord on a prohibition of chemical and bacteriological weapons." On December 12, 1984, the United States was the sole "no" vote (84 yes votes) on Resolution 39/65 to prohibit chemical and bacteriological weapons. On December 13, 1985, the United States was the sole "no" vote (134 yes votes) on a Resolution 40/114 declaring "the indivisibility of economic, social, cultural, civil and political rights." On December 7, 1987, the United States was one of only two nations that did not support Resolution 42/101 calling for a convention on the rights of children. On December 4, 1987, the United States was one of only two nations voting against Resolution 41/92 calling for "a comprehensive system of international peace and security."[36]

Third World nations that have historically championed the UN and collective security, have now taken the lead in challenging U.S. rejectionism and unilateralism not only in the General Assembly but at the WTO and IMF. At the November 2001, WTO meetings in Quatar, poor nations launched a vigorous campaign to void corporate patents on pharmaceutical drugs for AIDS and other epidemics creating medical emergencies. They also challenged antidumping rules long promoted by the United States to protect inefficient U.S. industries. And they began a campaign to end the hypocrisy of the entire trade regime, which has forced poor nations to open their markets to U.S. agricultural exports while allowing the United States and other rich nations to protect textiles and many other of their own domestic industries. This has the makings of a potential revolution against the entire neoliberal regime and hints at an erosion of the long U.S. monopoly over WTO and IMF policy.

We are witnessing the dawn of a struggle by nearly the entire world to restrain United States power, partly in pursuit of a new collective security order. This new resistance is not obvious in the aftermath of the events of September 11, where the world seems to have initially, at least, embraced U.S. military and political leadership in the face of terrorism. And many nations do not want the United States to retreat into isolationism. But this should not disguise the rising tide around the world, even among America's allies and friends, challenging U.S. hyper-power and moving the globe toward more democratic arrangements.

While these pressures from the rest of the world will seem like just a new form of anti-Americanism to many of our citizens, the United States has much to gain by supporting this great transformation of global power. Empire, and the role of Head Umpire as well, is costly. It brings crushing economic burdens tied to military entanglements. From the Roman to the British Empires, global hegemony has eventually turned into a recipe for what Yale historian Paul Kennedy has called "imperial over-stretch." It can bring down even the most powerful of nations and bankrupt the wealthiest.[37]

As the United States faces intensifying economic troubles at home, Americans will have to choose between expensive imperial projects and their own domestic needs. Sharing global power frees up resources for desperate healing on the home front. It reduces the growing security costs that face any hegemon seeking to preserve its own global dominance. More broadly, it would permit the United States to redirect its huge military budget toward social ends: better job training, education, health care, child care, and social security. None of this would come at the expense of continued American involvement with the world. It would just make it far safer and less expensive.

The United States has been the leader in promoting the WTO, IMF, and other "world governments" that move the world beyond the rule of any one nation. While it has been able to largely dominate these new institutions, they are the core of a new order beyond the power of any one nation. U.S. hegemony and globalization have developed together. But U.S. unilateralism now threatens the very globalization that it has long championed. Ironically, if it wants to see some form of globalization retain legitimacy in the eyes of the world, the United States will have to take a deep breath and change direction. It will finally have to abandon all dreams of Empire and share power in a collective security system. It will have to end its long struggle against the UN and work globally toward the democratic ideals that it has long taught its own citizens to revere. It won't be easy but the alternative, pursuing global power at all costs, will be harder and, in the new era of terror, far more dangerous.

CHAPTER 9

SLEEPLESS IN SEATTLE

I like a little rebellion now and then. It is like a storm in the atmosphere.
THOMAS JEFFERSON

It is sobering that one of the best ways to get yourself a reputation as a dangerous citizen these days is to go about repeating the very phrases which our founding fathers used in the struggle for independence.
CHARLES BEARD

A T THE BATTLE OF SEATTLE, I WALKED THROUGH THE TEARGASSED streets with a cellphone. Every block or so, I got a call from another radio or newspaper reporter with more questions. One talk-show host even caught me at dinner and wouldn't let me finish my meal until I had answered his questions.

As Bob Dylan wrote in one of his famous songs, "Something's happening here but you don't know what it is." Well, that was how people all over the country seemed to feel about the protests in Seattle. Something very new had burst on the scene, and Mr. and Mrs. Jones didn't quite understand what it was. But they definitely wanted to find out.

With a new Seattle exploding every time the WTO, G8, IMF, or other globalization body calls a meeting, the public's curiosity kept growing. In the years following Seattle, I have received numerous invitations to talk about what it meant. And I have ended up going to speak to civic groups in the community, to the protesters themselves, and perhaps most surprising to me, to many corporations and other business groups. All were eager to understand this new movement and decide what they should think or do about it.

Since September 11, the movement has been forced to reflect

and regroup. Its future is up for grabs. Nonetheless, it is important to understand what this movement has been and how it will function in the new environment. It has challenged the global mystique in a dramatic fashion, and it is the beginning of a new movement for global democracy. It has brought to the world's attention the need for deep changes in globalization and for a shift from corporate to democratic priorities. It has sent alarm signals flashing through the corridors of power and has already triggered major new public debates about current global policy of the United States, the WTO, the IMF, and the World Bank. In this chapter, I've pulled together the most frequently asked questions about the post-Seattle legions. I hope my answers help you understand these movements better, as well as how they might play a new role in the looming debates about globalization and global democracy still to come.

Beyond the Seattle movements, there are, of course, also the indigenous movements, like the Mexican Zapatistas, the workers in Argentina rallying against the latest IMF edict, and the sweatshop labor organizers in Indonesia and Bangladesh. They are the core of the larger movement that will lead global democracy and justice struggles in the future, and I reflect here on their connections to the Seattle legions. While the Seattle-type mass protests could flame out, and while they will take a new form after September 11, the movement toward global democracy that they are building with global allies will be around for a long time to come. The speading global justice movements are the most important new grassroots political force in a generation, and they are the best hope on the horizon for a better world.

Q: *JUST WHO WERE ALL THOSE PEOPLE OUT IN THE STREETS OF SEATTLE, QUEBEC, WASHINGTON, AND GENOA?*

In the streets of Seattle, this was one of the first questions I asked myself. I was astonished to see so many thousands of people lining up for the big march and to discover they weren't just the usual suspects. The colorful posters made clear that there were almost as many political points of view as there were people. The variety was intoxicating.

In the lobby of my hotel there was a group of fifteen or so union members from a GE plant in Lynn, Massachusetts. We began a friendly conversation once they learned I was from the Boston area too. They looked and sounded a lot more like mainstream America than did some of the younger protesters who were bare-breasted or sported orange hair. The union folk were part of a much larger contingent of labor activists, including a big contingent from the local Boeing plant. The labor turnout of thirty thousand, addressed by AFL-CIO president John Sweeney, led the media to dub this the gathering of "teamsters and turtles."[1]

The turtles, environmental activists from large mainstream groups like the Sierra Club and smaller ecoactivist communities, were also out in force. The coming together of the labor and environmental movements, historically often at each other's throats, was only one part of the spectacular panorama of protesters. There were religious communities, women's groups, and students from universities around the country. There were animal rights groups and small business associations. There were Marxists and anarchists, Democrats and Republicans, internationalists and bioregionalists, liberals and conservatives, white-collar and blue-collar, gays and straights. There were people from rich and poor countries around the world. Even some U.S. political officials like Massachusetts congressman Barney Frank turned up.[2]

The spanning of generations was especially noteworthy and, to me, deeply heartening. Over recent decades, it has been rare to see young and old marching together or talking politics in the same room. But in Seattle there were people of all ages. This was a sign of a universal concern close to the human heart.

On the other hand, there were still underrepresented groups. Most important, Seattle—and Quebec, Prague, Melbourne, Washington, and Genoa too—were mainly gatherings of white people. The small percentage of African Americans belies the whole idea of diversity and multiculturalism. It has been a matter of much concern in the movement.

Seattle was mainly a group of white folks. Yet, and this was very important, there were people from India, Mexico, the Philippines, and Indonesia. They represented influential groups and millions of people who had protested on their own streets but couldn't come to Seattle. So if one looks at the larger movement and the swelling of the ranks of globalization activists around the world, one would have to conclude that this is a crossnational movement and very possibly the first truly global movement.

I have witnessed numerous larger protests. I remember a rally against the Vietnam war in Manhattan with almost a million people. But I have never seen anything approximating the vast spectrum in the Seattle streets. This strange and unexpected community of communities had never been together on the block before.

Q: *WHY HAS GLOBALIZATION BEGUN TO BRING SUCH DIVERSE OPPOSITION MOVEMENTS TOGETHER?*

Any observer of protest politics in this country over the last few decades has been struck by the fragmentation of movements. Most American protest groups look like they have been run through a homogenizing machine. Few men volunteer or are welcomed to join women's groups, and they don't typically show up at feminist demonstrations. I remember being at one political concert organized by feminists in which I was virtually the only man in an audience of five hundred people. And how many whites or women were there in the African American Million Man march?

Minorities organize themselves and march in their own separate movements of color. There is an environmental movement to save nature, and a labor movement to save jobs. There is gay liberation for gays, and "abling" movements of the disabled. All these movements have developed powerful constituencies and voices but have kept their distance from one another. Only globalization has begun to reverse this balkanization process. Suddenly we find groups coming together and speaking with something resembling a common voice.

Globalization affects everyone in all sectors within and across societies. While some get rich and others lose their jobs or home, nearly all of us feel vulnerable to big systemic changes out of our control. Each of the social movements is getting whipsawed in its own way by the globalization hurricane. Workers in rich countries know that they face their greatest crisis in a century as globalization brings them into direct competition with workers in poorer nations. Feminists increasingly recognize that the plight of young women in the global factory is now one of the great feminist issues of the coming century. Environmentalists see that the global factory is polluting on a new global scale, ferociously spewing out carbon dioxide and mowing down rain forests to help trigger the global warming crisis. Christian, Jewish, and Muslim groups see that they cannot speak about faith without talking about the agony of the global poor. And the new movements concerned about war and terrorism recognize that they have to address the problems of global injustice if they want a lasting peace. All the different movements are being forced to confront globalization as critically important to their concerns and to recognize that other communities and movements are in the same boat.

Q: *DOES THIS MEAN THAT GLOBALIZATION IS CREATING—OR WILL CREATE—A NEW POLITICS?*

The excitement of Seattle was the subliminal sense that a new opposition, and perhaps a whole new kind of politics, was being born, both in the United States and the world at large. If we look back on the history of dissent in the United States since World War II, the antiglobalization movement was a "third wave" of protest, representing a new kind of American opposition politics. The first wave mushroomed in the 1960s in the landmark civil rights movement and the antiwar movement. It proclaimed universal truths of peace and justice and took them seriously. The first wave transformed the consciousness of a whole generation, ended legal segregation in the South, and helped end the war, but it was finally impaled on the sharp edges of its own contradictions. White male students in top universities imposed their own leadership and worldview on the movement in its post–civil rights, antiwar phase. They made people who were not like themselves, whether women, African Americans, or the working class, feel marginalized and betrayed.[3]

This gave birth to the second wave in the 1970s. Women, minorities, and gays developed an acute consciousness of their own separate identities. Being victimized by a great (first wave) movement for social justice created a tipping point. These communities each built their own separate freedom movements, which created pride in their differences, told their own stories, and fought for their own liberation. The second wave is what sociologists call the "new social movements," also dubbed "identity politics," and has proved to be one of the great political and cultural revolutions of the twentieth century. Philosophically, it repudiated the idea of universal truth (accepted uncritically by the first wave) and embraced the postmodern vision of multiple, socially constructed truths. This led to multiple opposition movements (rather than the unitary movement of the first wave) and to astonishing changes in the consciousness and rights of women, minorities, and gays.[4]

By design, identity movements in the United States remained relatively isolated from each other. Postmodernism led the second wave away from any solid basis for common cause, contributing to the growth of strong political communities of women, minority groups, and gays but also showing the limits of second-wave politics. It failed to gain political control in the country or prevent the rise of deeply conservative movements that have taken over both the Democratic and Republican parties. The Reagan revolution and the politics of globalization consolidated corporate power over the country and the world at large. Identity movements lacked either the vision or organizational capacity to unify and resist.

Enter Seattle. The third wave burst on the scene unpredicted, like most revolutions in politics, but in retrospect it was not surprising. The limits of second-wave, or identity, politics made a new politics inevitable. No single identity movement or new social movement was big enough or strong enough to cope with globalization on its own. And all the identity movements together were not equipped ideologically to create a coherent intellectual analysis of globalization and its alternatives.

The third wave emerged as the first movement explicitly organized to challenge globalization and to envision an alternative to a corporate-dominated world system. Third-wavers think globally about markets, democracy, and social justice while also newly linking global and local politics. And their rising movement has been founded on models of organization never seen before but necessary to sustain cooperation among thousands of different groups and communities within the United States and across the world.

While the third wave has begun serious new political thinking about global alternatives, it is basically antidoctrinal, in contrast to both the first and second waves. This reflects the huge variety of global constituencies and the need to accommodate their many issues and points of view. Resisting a "party line" has kept the movement together as a global coalition and reflects its open, skeptical, and youthful spirit. It prevents different groups from feeling that others are stealing the agenda because each can participate while holding on to its own goals. But it also creates confusion because many different agendas get mixed together and lead the media and the public to ask, "What do these people really want?"

The third wave wants the participatory democracy of the first wave and the liberation of women, people of color, and gays sought by the second wave. But it also clearly wants something new: a marriage of different movements to create a less market-driven and more democratic world. It wants first-wavers and second-wavers to think more globally, both across single nations and single issues. And it wants them to figure out how to act more locally on global issues and globally on local issues.

Third-wavers have rejected the first-wave universalism that tried to build a new society on Western Enlightenment ideals. While resonant with the first-wave focus on participatory democracy, the third wave rejects the Western Enlightenment or any other single tradition as a basis for a global alternative. This sounds closer to second-wave postmodernism, but it is different. The third wave has been a coming together of groups and movements that do not want to lose their separate identities but also want to find common ground in struggles around globalization. They are united by their rejection of cowboy capitalism and by their commitment to global democracy and justice for the global poor. Divisive issues of race, gender, and ethnicity are being overcome by the shared urgency of creating a more democratic world empowering ordinary people. They all believe that human need should trump money and that we need new rules putting jobs, health, and human rights over property rights. With the coming of the new American and global recession, the idea of replacing neoliberalism with a new "new deal" has far greater chance of winning mainstream support.

Q: *CAN YOU TALK MORE ABOUT THE MOVEMENT'S ORGANIZATION—OR DISORGANIZATION?*

The third wave has pioneered the rise of the new organizational model that some call "the network" and others "the swarm." The network idea hints that the new movement is organized like the Internet. Thousands of different groups in the global network converge and swarm like bees around particular targets and then disperse back to their home bases until their next raid. The global network as organizational model and the swarm as tactic will probably be seen by historians as the defining mark of the third wave.[5]

The anarchistic streak in the third wave is very strong, creating the sense of a movement opposed to any organization at all. Third-wavers don't want leaders who tell them what to do, and they aren't even close to thinking about forming a political party or even a membership organization in the United States. This has been a movement of small affinity groups, traveling theater companies, spontaneous "convergence centers," impromptu organizing communities, and sites that magically appear, network, and then disappear overnight. Because these are all so ephemeral, I can see why some have seen the Seattle movements as the impulse of people without any idea of what to do on the streets except act like a mob. This mob image was never accurate, but the third wave has walked a thin line between artful organization and chaos.[6]

Many see the third-wavers as political groupies who follow financial and political elites from city to city the way addicted fans follow rock stars. Except these groupies hate the stars and want to shut down their concert. But they seem to be having a great party when they get together, and it is not clear to many that they should be taken seriously.

The groupie image unfairly trivializes third-wavers as people just out to have a good time—or worse, get drunk and begin throwing rocks. From my own acquaintance with many protesters, this image is way off the mark. Most protesters have been repelled by the violence and are introspective and reflective about their politics. Many are young and still learning about the complexities of globalization, but they are hungry for ideas and take issues of social justice and spirituality to heart. Perhaps they are *too* serious. At my university, the students who have gone to Seattle, Quebec, or Washington are the ones who spend their summers on Jesuit immersion projects in El Salvador or Mexico and their spring vacations building homes for the poor in Appalachia.

Nonetheless, the groupie image does capture something important about the third wave. The movement rediscovers itself at each new globalization "concert" (the latest meeting of the global elites) and runs the danger of losing itself when no concert is playing. Many movement activists worry that protesters will eventually stop showing up. People tire of just getting on the bus to the next protest. When protests do not create major change, many stop coming because they feel they are wasting time. I believe that the third wave suffered from a crisis of sustainability even before September 11 and needed to find new organizational forms.

There are other problems with a purely protest-driven movement, even if the third wave rediscovers its footing and mobilizes new and essential mass protests. When you spend all your time planning protests, you get sucked into tactical issues and can lose sight of the large ideas and global alternatives you are proposing. The real task of building a sustainable and effective movement occurs through the education and political work that happens in and between protests. This is the work that allows unionists, environmentalists, students, feminists, religious communities, small business groups, and immigrants to build ties, learn from one another, become more sophisticated about alternative global policies, and create networks that can influence business and governments.

The marvel of the Internet is that it allows groups from all over the world to communicate on a continuing basis, making the network potentially sustainable on a global basis. Even when there are no trade-summit protests being planned, activists from labor, environmental groups, and Third World countries are constantly logging on to each other's listservs, learning about each other's issues, and building a dialogue. I have seen this on issues like global sweatshops, where the Internet is buzzing every day with communication among labor organizers, environmentalists, student activists, human rights advocates, and others with listservs and information and projects to share. All this continued on-line after the terrorist attacks. Nonetheless, it all remains at an early stage, and the movement will have to institutionalize itself off-line and off the streets (as well as on them) if it hopes to survive.[7]

None of this should be read as a call to end mass protests.

They have been remarkably effective in galvanizing public attention and stirring up a new public debate. And despite the big chill immediately after September 11, there are signs of a revival of mass demonstrations continuing around the world. In February 2002, for a second year in a row, global democrats convened an alternative World Social Forum in Pôrto Alegre, Brazil, to protest the World Economic Forum that typically meets in Davos, Switzerland. A total of forty thousand people turned out in Pôrto Alegre, four times the number in 2001. Five thousand workshops dealt with issues of wealth, power, debt, and democracy in the global economy. This people's summit included East African farmers, Thai trade unionists, and American students, and was hosted by the mass Brazilian movements led by the Central Union of Workers and the Landless Workers' Movement.[8]

Q: *CAN THE THIRD WAVE SUSTAIN ITSELF?*

If the third-wave movement is to gain influence, it will have to sustain itself as a coordinating tool for mass protests while building a more solid alliance of policy-oriented activist organizations. The biggest challenge has always been to connect the street protests with institutionalized advocates and power brokers, both in the community and global power centers. Protests raise consciousness and spark new thinking about issues. But the new awareness has to be translated into specific political and policy agendas pushed by organizations with real clout, such as, the national AFL-CIO, the Sierra Club, the NAACP, and NOW (and similar organizations in other countries).

Many activists will see this advice as heresy. Institutionalize the movement, and you will kill off its free spirit. I agree that the impulse to preserve diversity, spontaneity, and local autonomy needs to be prized. The third wave is a movement that wants to put more life, humanity, and joy back into the world, not more bureaucracy or politics as usual. But politics, especially in the age of globalization, is about huge concentrated power that can only be fought with an equally huge countervailing force. So the third wave will have to join the real world with more than verve. Yes, small affinity groups, convergence centers, and the Internet networks are essential to keep the spirit of the movement intact. And the mass protests are very important. But these have to be joined with old-time political organization and institutionalized clout if the third wave is going to change the world.

A model that American activists might look at is in France, where the antiglobalization movement has become very powerful. It is led by an organization called ATTAC, formed in the late 1990s, that has thousands of members. ATTAC sees itself as a new kind of movement organization bringing together civic associations to defend society itself against the "economic horror" and antidemocratic assault of global finance. It sees globalization as an attack by the markets on democratic politics.[9]

ATTAC is charismatic, street-savvy, and committed to action. One local ATTAC chapter recently mobilized the folks in Brest, Brittany, to prevent the opening of a McDonald's. But while it turns people out for the big globalization protests, it also brings together established groups, educators and intellectuals, unions, farmer groups, and politicians (125 deputies in the French National Assembly are ATTAC members). ATTAC blends street politics with an institutionalized network that has the clout to promote a serious political agenda. Its founding policy aim was a variant of the famous "Tobin tax" that levies a small tax on all international financial transactions and would raise millions for education, health, and economic development in poor nations.

ATTAC is spontaneously developing as a worldwide organization. It has "sister organizations" in over twenty countries, including Argentina, Russia, Senegal, Sweden, Cameroon, and Ireland. Reflecting the spirit of globalism, its leaders dismiss the idea that ATTAC should become a global model, arguing that conditions are different in every part of the world and that "the French model is not exportable." ATTAC wants to link up, though, with activist civic associations across the world that share its desire to tame the global markets and agree, as ATTAC's president Bernard Cassen wrote, that "it is democracy itself that is the prime victim of free trade and globalization."[10]

France is hardly the only country where the new charismatic movement has connected with large institutional political players, especially trade unions. Since May 2000, unions, in association with smaller third-wave antiglobalization groups, have successfully mobilized "general strikes" of millions of people in India (20 million), Argentina (12 million), and South Korea (4 million), as well as in South Africa, Indonesia, and Uruguay. These were all directed against the IMF and World Bank policies of privatization, sliced wages, or lost jobs, and cuts in social services. The protests were explicitly attacking globalization as a "sacrifice of sovereignty" to global markets—and networked powerful political players to demand a new national budget, trade, and development policy. They prove that the third wave is capable of bringing together policy-oriented institutional players without giving up its spontaneity.[11]

The third wave will sometimes be able to bring nation-states themselves into its network. Brazil and South Africa have explicitly challenged WTO property and patent rules around AIDS drugs. In 2001, Brazil announced it would start manufacturing a generic version of Viracept, one of twelve drugs in the AIDS cocktail, made by the pharmaceutical giant Roche. While Brazil risks retaliation from the United States and the WTO, its action builds on an intense global third-wave campaign to challenge the morality of WTO patent law when millions are being denied medicine and will die. The third-wave network can embrace Brazil as a model of AIDS policy and work with José Serra, the country's health minister, to frame policies undermining the WTO rules and creating patent law respectful of human life.

As will be discussed in the next chapter, the climate after the terrorist attacks offers surprising new opportunities for such third-wave challenges. When the anthrax attacks began, and people desperately called their pharmacists for Cipro, the antibiotic made by Bayer, they were shocked to learn the high price of the pills. The Canadian government almost immediately announced it was going to make available generic low-cost versions of the drug—in direct violation of Bayer's patent. The U.S. government also negotiated with Bayer for a drastic reduction in Cipro's price.

The Canadian and American leaders who had denounced Brazil and South Africa for breaking patents suddenly followed their lead. This astonishing shift, followed by the modest success of Third World nations at the 2001 WTO meetings in Qatar to allow any country facing a medical epidemic to break patents, shows the unpredictable ways in which September 11 is shifting the debate. In Qatar, the poor nations did not win the great victory reported in the press; they only achieved a reaffirmation of the status quo while the United States was pressing for even more restrictive drug patents. But the new government activism of the Bush administration against terrorism weakens the neoliberal orthodoxy about privatization, patents, and free trade. It gives third-wavers a new opportunity to make the case that if terrorized Americans should have their health prioritized over corporate profit, so should Africans infected with AIDS.[12]

Q: *HOW DO YOU SEE THE ROLE OF VIOLENCE IN THE MOVEMENT, PARTICULARLY IN THE AFTERMATH OF SEPTEMBER 11?*

I remember walking through the streets of Seattle on the evening of the first day. The smell of tear gas and pepper spray hung heavy in the air. I saw some masked protesters overturning news kiosks and setting them afire. I saw others throwing rocks and breaking windows at McDonald's and Niketown. On some blocks it seemed as if nearly every store had been defaced with painted slogans or chalked obscenities.[13]

But when I came back on the same streets the next day, I saw a large group of protesters with buckets, soapy water, and brushes. They were vigorously washing away all the grafitti and obscenities. They were doing their best to clean up the litter and repair the damage. There was real despair about the destruction among a majority of protesters, who saw nonviolence as what they were all about.

The Black Bloc—protesters who are highly confrontational and sometimes engage in violence—have attracted a huge amount of media attention. These are often masked groups, some wearing scary military-type gear and others painted clown faces, who call themselves anarchists and make for good photo-ops. Typically, they are only a few hundred out of many thousands of protesters, but they can change the whole tone of a demonstration very quickly. In the first few sunlit hours of Seattle, the protest was a festival of celebratory marchers singing and walking peacefully. Only a few hours later, however, after the Black Bloc had torched kiosks and stores, there was a funereal tone, as the sunlight was poisoned with pepper spray and tear gas and people were grieving about the blood of fellow protesters pouring over the pavement.[14]

Third-wavers argue that only a small percentage of protesters want violence and that most of the violence has been triggered by the police. The savage police violence in Genoa led to the first death of a third-wave protester and to the unrestrained clubbing, kicking, and gassing of hundreds of other peaceful participants. Third-wavers are accurate in their claims that they have mainly been the victims rather than the perpetrators of violence. Too many peaceful protesters have been kicked in the kidneys or gouged in the eye or gassed. And they are being truthful when most say they are deeply nonviolent and horrified by the actions of both the police and the protesters who start throwing rocks through store windows or attacking police.[15]

But the truth is that the third wave before the terrorist attacks was somewhat ambivalent about the role of violence in the movement. This is to be expected from a movement centered on mass street protests. The main purpose of these demonstrations is to attract media attention and thereby engage the public with their issues. But the media is mainly drawn by the sensationalism of violence itself, and third-wavers know that the more violence there is, the more likely that they will get airtime on CNN. I am not implying the movement has been responsible for or tacitly collaborating with the Black Bloc's violence. But as in war itself, protesters can get caught up in the thrills and dangers of violent confrontation. War stories become standard fare on the bus rides home from each new demonstration.

The media focus on violence becomes so intense that Mary and John Q. Public can read one story after another in their morning newspaper and have no idea what the protesters want. They come to associate globalization rallies with violence and nothing more. The protesters themselves often lose sight of their original concerns. The war stories crowd out the issues about the WTO or neoliberal policy. Even when the media do ask them about the issues, many protesters often go back to protest tactics. A friend described radio interviews she heard with leaders of the 2001 demonstration against the IMF in Washington. National media were giving them the opportunity to talk about IMF policy, but the leaders were focused only on the denial of their constitutional right to protest. This is very important, but it does not educate the public about globalization.

Most third-wavers understand that the Black Bloc could become a serious liability to the protests. Any hint that global justice activists acquiesce in throwing rocks or attacking police who are trying to defend the population against terrorism could be counterproductive for the larger movement. If the movement returns to mass protests, and there are encouraging signs that it will, it will be faced with the daunting challenge of restraining the small number of militants bent on property destruction or police provocation.

I am not trying to discourage the militant expression of outrage against the horrific disenfranchisement and exploitation that brings the protesters into the streets in the first place. Nor am I in any position to dictate to small farmers brutally repressed in Guatemala, sweatshop workers ruthlessly exploited in Indonesia or Mexico, people who have lost everything in Argentina, or fellow protesters in the United States the appropriate form of their response. There are times when people abroad will take to the streets to overthrow their governments or drive out foreign companies, and they will be justified in doing so. Should they face violent repression, as they have for so many years, they will have to defend themselves, and I hope that activists in the United States and Europe will be vocal and militant in supporting them.

Q: *WHAT IS MOST INTERESTING AND VALUABLE ABOUT THE NEW MOVE-MENT—AND IS THERE REASON TO BELIEVE IT WILL FIND NEW LIFE AFTER THE TERRORIST ERUPTION?*

The very existence of the third wave is something to marvel about. All pundits were predicting that globalization represented the "end of ideology." Most of the public were said to be converts to TINA (there is no alternative). Common sense said that the whole world was buying into American-style, free-market capitalism. Instead, globalization has triggered one of the most radical new political oppositions that we have seen for a long time.

We have to go back to the idea of a Constitutional Moment to understand why radical thinking exists at all in the age of globalization. The very nature of a Constitutional Moment is to stir up questions about the fundamentals in people's lives. A Constitutional Moment buries the old rules and begins to put new ones into place. It is only when the rules have been suspended or put in play that most people are forced to think about what the rules are and what they should be.

Globalization encourages everyone to question their own lives, their own societies, and the world as a whole. It leads protesters and many in the public to ask fundamental questions. Is democracy still possible in a corporate-dominated world? Do I want to live in a world run by the market? Do I believe in the U.S. role in promoting global business? What is the responsibility of the U.S. government for the agony of the global poor, and what should it do to help? What is real democracy in the world today? Can we save nature without ending industrialism and consumerism? What is the meaning of my life? That is why the movement can seem so naive to experts who have already made the transition in their minds to globalization's new rules. The experts have moved from questioning the new rules to implementing them.

In Genoa, one British protester told a *New York Times* reporter that he "really didn't care about globalization." He meant that the whole capitalist system and way of life were in question for him. Globalization can seem an abstract idea when you are trying to figure out your own life and what you believe in. In this sense, the new movement has an existential quality. Many of my own students have been swept up in the globalization movement, and I sense that they are not only questioning the world but their own purpose on the planet. While many have come from comfortable suburbs, they are suddenly wrestling with whether they believe in the system that produced their affluence and whether they believe in the values and way of life of their own country and families.

This is reminiscent of the political concern in the sixties with personal authenticity (the first wave). Students came to political meetings throwing in guilt money to atone for the sins of their corporate fathers. They read the philosopher Herbert Marcuse's *One-Dimensional Man*, the famous book arguing that people were shedding their humanity and subjecting themselves to "surplus exploitation" to get the goodies of a material order. And they agreed with the Berkeley firebrand, Mario Savio, who said it was time to throw a monkey wrench in the machine. These all seem consistent with the spirit of today's new movement.[16]

Yet the new opposition today seems less intellectual and more visceral, less ideological and more artistic. The new activists are interested in ideas, and they sit for hours at each big protest to take in marathon, two-day teach-ins. But they seem more driven by passion in the heart and trouble in the spirit. That may be why the new protests seem more raw and often more disorderly than earlier ones.[17]

Nonetheless, the movement has moved beyond gut-level reaction toward an educated analysis of the global system. I never thought that so many people in the United States or the rest of the world would be asking serious questions about the world economic order and how global corporations and labor markets operate. Or that they would take an interest in in who runs the WTO and IMF, or in how the new system of international trade laws affects democracy. I certainly never thought that these would become common subjects in the media or that I would be spending a lot of time talking about them to reporters and civic groups.

This new public interest in world affairs and how to promote global democracy will mushroom. People will be asking new questions about the roots of terrorism and the role of the United States in the world. They will want to know why so many people hate the United States and whether this has anything to do with globalization and global injustice. They will want to know why the United States is supporting undemocratic regimes in the Middle East and whether this is related to the issues of globalization and poverty in the region. They will ask whether religious fundamentalists such as bin Laden are exploiting the sense of illegitimacy of Middle East governments getting rich from oil but not offering their own citizens ways to express their grievances.

September 11 temporarily slowed the momentum of the globalization movement. But in the longer term, the attacks will open a much broader, mainstream conversation about the way the world works and the role of the United States in both globalization and geopolitics. In addition, the new American and global recession, with vast new layoffs and unemployment, is undermining traditional free-market nostrums and opening the door to new thinking about the role of government and business. The third wave will find a far larger and more passionately interested public urgently wanting to find answers.

Q: *Is this a movement that can connect with the mainstream of the public, particularly after September 11?*

The public shares a lot of the third wave's values and concerns about globalization. Americans (60%) and, to a lesser degree, Europeans (e.g., 53% in France) have a positive response to the word *globalization*. But when you get more concrete, a different picture emerges. A 1999 U.S. poll showed that between 60 and 80 percent of ordinary Americans think that the architects of globalization in Washington and other capitals are taking into account the interests of big business and ignoring the needs of workers and ordinary citizens. And almost 90 percent say that globalization should be based on values other than free trade, including protection of workers, the environment, and human rights. In France, clear popular majorities in recent polls support robust government regulation of trade, global companies, and the financial markets as well as the provision of extensive social welfare and income floors.[18]

The third wave's focus on corporate power and the corruption of democracy definitely rings the public's bell. A *Business Week* cover story in 2000, well before the Enron crisis, reported a detailed survey showing that 72 percent of Americans thought that big multinational corporations wielded too much power, 75 percent explicitly said that big business had too much power over politicians in Washington, and 84 percent said that campaign contributions by big corporations were excessive. A total of 95 percent of respondents said that the entire economic system was too focused on profit and that corporations should balance their obligations to shareholders with equally strong commitments to their workers, host communities, and the environment. After the huge Enron scandal in 2002, concerns mushroomed among ordinary Americans about corporate power, greed, and the corrupting influence of big business in Washington.[19]

Whether Democratic or Republic, liberal or conservative, Americans are overwhelmingly distrustful of big corporations and their globalization agenda. Many see globalization as corporations trolling abroad for sweatshop labor without any sense of loyalty to their own workers. In a class I taught to managers in large companies, the students told me there was nothing that a corporation could say that would make them believers in corporate responsibility. They had seen too much downsizing, outsourcing, and blatant greed in their own companies to have any faith in the conscience of business. Europeans have long had a far more regulated economic system, and by huge majorities they reject the U.S. model, believing that they have a more humane recipe for the rest of the world.

Thus, a large chunk of the public in both the United States and Europe is in a sense already converted to third-wave thinking. Peoria is as concerned about a corporate-dominated world as are the protesters in Seattle. Americans and Europeans have strong moral concerns about sweatshops and global poverty, and Americans are worried that globalization may steal their jobs and undermine their American dream. Europeans worry that globalization could turn them into *les Americains sauvages* (savage Americans), stripped of their generous welfare state. And the concerns of people in the Third World are far more intense because so many are at the edge of starvation while IMF policies tear apart their fragile safety nets.

This is far from ensuring that the third wave will win the global public's confidence. The movement is sometimes prone to demonizing both globalization and the corporation, a powerful way to mobilize the converted but also a way to lose support of the unpersuaded. The public has deep concerns, but it sees many hopeful possibilities in globalization, and it does not want to give up the goodies that the corporate system has delivered. Moreover, the majority of people do not currently see any realistic alternatives and are not interested in betting the ranch on utopian experiments.

I see several implications for the new movement. One, paradoxically, is that it should not compromise its radicalism, because people in a global Constitutional Moment are receptive to rethinking the basic rules of the game. While most do not see clear alternatives, they are most intrigued by root questions about what the corporation is for, whether it is compatible with democracy, what has happened to the idea of "we the people," and whether money should trump human rights or erase national boundaries and local cultures. The third wave should persist in raising the most basic root questions about globalization.

But this is not the same as trashing the corporate system or globalization. This often turns the public off because most people believe that global corporations bring benefits as well as abuse and exploitation. They need to hear a radical message and will listen, as long as it thoughtful and respectful of the complexities and contradictions. But that means the third wave has to own up to the attractions of global capitalism in the large parts of the planet trapped in feudal poverty. And that it must also take seriously the goods that global corporations have already delivered to many people in both the First and Third Worlds.[20]

In the wake of the September 11 attacks, the opportunity to raise basic questions in the United States will change over time. In the short term, people will be focused on their own safety and war in the Middle East. Anything sounding like an attack on the United States or its economic system could be branded as unpatriotic or even treasonous, although this is hardly a reason to restrain dissent and should actually encourage people to raise dissenting views. In the longer term, people will want to link their understanding of Islamic radicalism and Middle East politics with larger issues about the global order and globalization itself. This opens a very broad new conversation that can connect with the general public about globalization, global justice, and geopolitics and American foreign policy, and that needs to go forward urgently.

This is tied to a second issue of style. As I view it, outrage and militancy seasoned with humor is an effective strategy widely used in the movements. I have even seen rich Republicans chuckle appreciatively at signs waved by tuxedo-garbed Seattle protesters inviting them to join the Billionaires for Bush club. Some ask whether millionaires are eligible to join, and the humorous interchange melts defensive armor. The implications for the third wave is that it can engage a far larger part of the public by infusing its moral outrage with wit and ribald political thea-tre.[21]

A third implication is the need to be positive and explicit about concrete alternatives. The public is very pragmatic, and while it is hungry for the real story about globalization it will not risk change without some credible options. The third wave has begun what will be a long process of thinking about a big-picture alternative and has also advanced many specific proposals, from easing the debt crushing poor nations, to taxing global specu-lators, to raising global labor and environmental standards. These are the kinds of practical steps that when explained clearly will make a difference. If the movement can show how its proposals will help the personal situation of John and Mary Q. Public, both in the rich and poor nations, it will move people from their cur-rent passive cynicism into live third-wave recruits. And if it can show that its policies will play even a small role in reducing global violence, millions of people will perk up and pay attention.

Q: *IS THERE A PLACE FOR BUSINESSPEOPLE IN THIS MOVEMENT?*

The third wave is all about limiting corporate power, but it is not antibusiness. The respect for small business is very strong in sectors of the movement. Even the Black Bloc tried not to break windows or scrawl grafitti on local Seattle businesses, and there was a great deal of effort by many protesters to protect such businesses from damage. Many see the third wave as an effort to sustain or create new forms of community-based business, from family farms and local farmer's markets to the mom-and-pop hardware store that used to thrive before Home Depot came along. There were many Seattle protesters from cooperatives and from worker-owned and community-owned businesses, the forms of small business that have the most obvious political af-finity with the movement.[22]

Those who stress localism are working hard to build alliances with small and independent business associations as well as create these businesses themselves. The third wave publishes much of its educational material through the independent press and depends for its public relations on the alternative community-based media. Many activists are involved in alliances with small business groups in their community. A good deal of both the writing and activism of third-wavers is aimed at new thinking about how to encourage what some call the "hometown advantage," the economic and social advantages of local business.[23]

The more surprising issue, though, has to do with large global corporations. While the movement is unified in its attack on global corporate power and the need for fundamental corporate restructuring, many big companies are wrestling with new thoughts about the social mission of global business. Partly in response to the protest movement itself as well as the fear of terrorism against the companies themselves, there is a growing sense that the corporate world has to restructure itself to maintain legitimacy for its operations, reduce security costs, and ultimately increase profits. Some companies and corporate leaders are on a mission to create a new vision of "global citizenship," and the most visionary talk about enforceable measures of global corporate accountability, especially after Enron. While much of this is pure public relations, the relation between the third-wave movement and serious reformers within the corporation may prove important to the success of both groups.

In 1968, anti–Vietnam War protesters found allies on Wall Street who told President Lyndon Johnson that the war was no longer affordable economically. The crack in the elites, who had become divided about the war, together with the persistent wave of protest, forced Johnson's hand. Alignment between a sector of the elites and a large popular movement is typically the brew required to create societal transformation. Social change involves the knack of linking influential insiders with determined outsiders at the right moments, although grassroots social movements are by far the most important force in creating systemic change.

We are already beginning to see limited collaboration between third-wave groups and global companies. Global Exchange, one of the most militant of the third-wave NGOs, has recently worked together with Levi Strauss on issues of labor standards and human rights in China. Global companies need to work with NGOs and critics outside the business world to maintain credibility with consumers, and the critics often depend on information and resources from the companies to force real change.[24] Most third-wavers reject "global citizenship" as just the newest wave of corporate PR. But while such skepticism is often entirely justified, globalization, pushed along now by fears of terrorism, is helping to catalyze parts of the corporate community toward a more systemic way of thinking about corporate responsibility. "Corporate responsibility" started as charity pure and simple a hundred years ago when robber barons like John D. Rockefeller were being pilloried for their greed and power and so started giving away millions in philanthropy to save their reputations and weaken the antitrust movement. In the 1920s, American corporations devised the American Plan, a largely paternalistic vision of corporate medical plans and housing, to prevent unions. In the turbulent 1960s, a third wave of corporate responsibility began to redefine workers, communities, and consumers as corporate stakeholders who had to be treated with dignity and granted new forms of decision making. The movement toward a new stakeholder vision of business was far more important than any of the earlier social-responsibility movements, because it created a new social vision of business and began to extend power to workers and the community as a core part of business strategy. But it remained a corporate-designed affair that did not aim to change the larger economic system; it also created no public accountability and was far too small-scale to impact the issues created by globalization.

Nonetheless, globalization has catalyzed a new school of business thinking about global corporate accountability that is moving sectors of global business into dialogue with third-wave concerns. In Europe, influential corporate associations, as well as business visionaries such as Body Shop founders Anita and Gordon Roddick, are dialoguing with European political leaders about how global corporations can join with government and NGOs to move the Kyoto treaty forward and create a sustainable global economy. The Fair Labor Association (FLA), the apparel partnership brokered by the Clinton White House to address sweatshop issues by the companies, labor, and human rights, is only one of many new global industrywide initiatives. The FLA has proved deeply flawed, and many labor and religious groups have abandoned it, as it has prevented adequate public monitoring and disclosure. But such initiatives represent a new model that emphasizes industrywide initiatives for systemic global change designed and carried out by business, government, labor, and grassroots groups. There are serious risks in this approach, but the intersectoral conversations can at minimum give activists more access to useful information and are one of many potential steps toward more comprehensive systems of democratic accountability.

The third-wave movement will rightly remain a severe critic of global corporate power and seek yet more radical changes. These include fundamental changes in corporate charters making global firms accountable to the public and governed by their own workers and communities. It will involve breaking up the largest firms; returning privatized enterprise in medicine, education, and social services back to government; and democratizing the corporation in a way that will change its basic identity. But inevitably the real-world process of creating global alternatives will bring third-wavers and corporate reformers into limited but important forms of collaboration.[26]

My guess is that terrorism and the Enron crisis will intensify the conversation in the business world about global accountability and crack open the door to reforms. The threat to global business is now on a different scale. Business also now relies on government for huge new bailout as well as security measures that no company or industry can afford on its own. At home, business will become a more open supplicant for public spending and corporate subsidies. In the process it will weaken its traditional case against regulation, social accountability, and worker ownership or other forms of economic democracy.

Abroad, companies will depend on the goodwill and support of both governments and host communities. The costs of fortress globalization will force companies to take more seriously their pledges to be responsible. In the wake of September 11, businesses may develop a different mind-set about accountability to the community and concern with local poverty and grievances. In the short run, they will focus on security, and they may even shut down plants abroad in large numbers to avoid attacks and new fortress costs. But in the longer term, the same incentives for operating globally will reassert themselves; however, they will only make sense when combined with a legally enforced commitment to the dual bottom line of "doing good and doing well."

Q: *Is a truly global social movement possible?*

I have a student named David who has been very active on my campus in the campaign against sweatshops. He wants to track down where Boston College caps and T-shirts are manufactured. David is one of thousands of students across the country who are trying to force their universities to develop corporate codes of conduct and full disclosure. He won't stop until he is sure that Boston College logos are not being sewn on garments made in sweatshops.

David's work led him to Indonesia for a summer where he spent a lot of time talking to students and young workers. He saw at close quarters how teenage Indonesians are piled up ten to a small room in factory dorms. He saw global poverty up close and learned what Indonesians think about globalization (most see it as Americanization with a strong racialized dose of "white is beautiful"). He also developed strong friendships with many Indonesians.

Since his return, David keeps in contact by e-mail with his Indonesian friends, helping him stay close to the people he wants to help. And it allows coordination between the U.S.

sweatshop movement and Third World labor organizers in campaigns against global giants like Nike or Wal-Mart.

Our third-wave David is learning that to fight Goliath he has to imitate him and globalize in a rush. A David that is not global has no chance against a global Goliath. So the Davids are connecting with their counterparts around the world, using the same Internet that Goliath has capitalized on for his own globalization agenda.

But globalizing a movement is much more difficult than globalizing a bank or corporation. Money is rootless, mobile, and unburdened by feelings of loyalty. And while corporations have the money and political influence to go where they want, workers and activists can run into denied visa applications, barbed wire, or armed patrols when they try to cross national borders.

As a result, the third wave simply has not been able to keep up the globalization pace of business. In fact, the main charge levied against the third wave is that it is not really global at all, but rather a First World movement pretending to speak in the name of the Third World. Free-traders argue that the third wave is really just a shotgun wedding of First World workers who want to protect their jobs and First World students who naively believe that shutting down Third World sweatshops will help the workers.

This is a powerful tactic to discredit the new movement and a serious charge. It falsely argues that the Third World is the greatest supporter of globalization and that the global poor have the most to gain. We have already seen that many Third World leaders see globalization as a new colonialism and that many of the world's poor have in fact gotten poorer. But the question of whether the third wave really speaks for the global poor is not a trivial issue. The third wave needs to take this issue very, very seriously. The Hippocratic oath should be the first credo of the movement. Do no harm, especially to the people you are trying to help.

The third wave is, in fact, overwhelmingly First World, at least if you count the people protesting on the streets of the great cities in the United States, Canada, and Europe. And this is of concern because the Davids of the First World can unwittingly mimic the imperialism of First World Goliaths and impose their own views on Third World people they want to help. Moreover, there are real conflicts of interest between workers in rich and poor nations (most obviously, a job that moves from Knoxville to Jakarta hurts the Knoxville worker and may well help the Jakarta one). Well-intended reforms that the third wave proposes could potentially eliminate desperately needed jobs in Jakarta.[27]

The most critical thing is to develop a truly global agenda designed in large part by Third World people themselves. The Third World has to guide the movement because poor nations are four-fifths of the world's population, and they face emergencies of mass starvation and disease reminiscent of the fourteenth-century European black plague. After five centuries of colonialism, the only way a globalized movement makes sense is if it helps redistribute power, money, and respect to the global poor. This has to start within the third wave itself.

The only way to make this happen is to work tirelessly to build a genuine political community between third-wavers in the First and Third Worlds. As globalization accelerates, so does immigration and Internet communication. The globalization of business makes contact across borders for workers and citizens more and more routine. As globalization erases national boundaries, it creates ripe conditions for the globalization of the third-wave movement itself.

While it has a long way to go, the movement is globalizing at an extraordinary rate. A 2001 campaign by Bangladesh human rights and union activists against thousands of sweatshops in their country began a month after the New York and Washington terrorist attacks. The Bangladeshis, with American and European financial support, traveled to El Salvador and Honduras to meet with organizers there, learn from their experience, and coordinate strategy. Then, they came to the United States to meet with students, workers, and civic groups. They are developing alliances with Latin Americans, North Americans, and Europeans.[28]

This is an example of a third-wave campaign led by a Third World group as part of a global labor and human rights struggle. If the U.S. trade office says, well, the Bangladeshis really want these sweatshops (and they do want to keep the jobs in Bangladesh, but are passionately organizing to make the factories respect international and Bangledeshi labor law), they will have to have that conversation with Bangladeshis. U.S. activists are involved, but they are taking their lead from the Bangladeshis and not speaking for them. This not only protects them from criticism that they are misrepresenting the desires of Third World people, but it also creates the foundation for dialogue in which Third and First World activists come to understand each other and find genuine common ground.

Such new globalized activism is emerging as the most important feature of the third wave. A group of Third and First World thinkers and writers, called the International Forum on Globalization, has mounted the marathon teach-ins educating the activists at Seattle, Quebec, and other third-wave protest sites. Through years of scholarly exchange, they offer an intellectual vision that is led by Third World scholars such as the Filipino sociologist Walden Bello, the Indian scientist Vandana Shiva, and the Malaysian thinker Martin Khor. So the third wave is being educated increasingly by the Third World itself.

Similarly, the movement toward international solidarity by the AFL-CIO is incredibly important. President John Sweeney has begun to see foreign workers as fellow members of a global labor struggle. Sweeney has gone a long way in moving the labor movement away from its earlier protectionist xenophobia to the view that raising Third World labor standards and organizing Third World workers are key to helping American workers win their struggles. The AFL-CIO and textile unions are putting money and organizers into cross-border organizing to help Mexican, Salvadoran, and union organizers throughout Central America and other parts of the world. Transnational unions are just emerging, but they will help make sure that the First World labor movement does not revert to its traditional protectionism and will propel Third World labor organizers into leadership positions in the antiglobalization movement. No voice can be more important or credible in ensuring that the new movement keeps the interests and views of Third World workers at the forefront of its agenda.[29]

Another key way to globalize the third wave comes from expanding the movement's base at home to include more immigrants and people of color. They are crucial participants in the third wave, and the movement is trying to build ties with African American, Hispanic, and other groups around trade, migration, employment, and civil rights issues. African Americans have taken their own initiatives to challenge neoliberal trade agreements with Africa, and Jesse Jackson, Jr., sponsored his own Hope for Africa trade and development alternative. Moreover, the domestic movement for economic justice led by African American civil rights groups and churches is essentially a struggle against neoliberalism at home. No one knows better than African Americans how globalization and neoliberalisn can undermine the fragile economy of the poor and dismantle their safety nets.

U.S. minorities and immigrants are among the groups most seriously impacted by the loss of jobs overseas and government cutbacks in social spending similar to the IMF cuts devastating Third World workers and poor people. The Bush administration budget is essentially a structural adjustment program, a very cold bath, for African Americans and other minorities. In the context of recession, it cuts very deep and draws unacceptable blood. Globalization starts at home, and the American third wave is increasingly joining with African Americans on domestic struggles to sustain a living wage and social safety net. And as the third wave establishes ties to immigrant groups, they can connect with immigrant networks linking people here with their native countries. Immigrants will play a crucial role in bridging First and Third World communities and ensuring that the voices of people of color help guide the movement.

Q: *HOW DOES RECESSION OR ENRON-RELATED ECONOMIC TURBULENCE IN THE UNITED STATES, TIED TO A SEVERE GLOBAL ECONOMIC CRISIS, AFFECT THE PROSPECTS OF THE GLOBAL JUSTICE MOVEMENTS?*

Politics is full of strange twists. President Nixon went to China. President Clinton ended the welfare state. President Bush could preside over the death of Reaganomics and the revival of a new global attitude toward markets and governments.

If this were to happen, it would not be because Bush intended it. Bush is a conservative Republican and is governing by the Reagan playbook. He is cutting taxes on the rich and corporations, flooding money into the military to stimulate the economy, and squeezing spending on every social program but education. Like Reagan's, Bush's vision of government seems to be police, surveillance, and the military—with huge subsidies for big business and some education spending thrown in. Reagan's rhetoric was antigovernment, but his practice was to build the national security state, a blueprint that seems to guide and energize the Bush team.

But U.S. recession and post-Enron financial crises, global economic turbulence, and continuing uncertainty due to war could lead the nation in unexpected directions. A tottering economy could end the blind faith in markets and create a large public constituency for government activism. This will not happen without public mobilization, but it represents a window of opportunity that global justice movements cannot ignore. The new circumstances in the U.S. economy make possible a dramatic shift in the reigning economic orthodoxy that could support a new deal for both the United States and the world at large.

Within three months of September 11, almost a million additional workers in the United States were laid off. The American economy, already going south before the terrorist attacks, raced into a full-scale recession and the Enron crisis. Forecasts for the global economy were even more dire, with countries like Argentina teetering on bankruptcy and entire regions like sub-Saharan Africa and central Asia in a state of near total collapse.

The shifting economic tides in the United States reflected the confluence of faltering economic fundamentals and the new uncertainties of a terrorized world. As Bush entered office, the stock-market bubble burst, and the fizz of the new economy was drying up. "Irrational exuberance" could not power the economy forever. The Clinton boom faded well before September 11, with a 30 percent decline in the financial markets, huge layoffs in the two years preceding the terrorist attacks, mounting consumer debt, growing overproduction and corporate inventory, and finally serious erosion in consumer confidence and demand. The World Trade Center attacks and the Enron crisis added severe new shocks to the U.S. system, leading even the most seasoned economic observers to hedge their bets about the future.

After the attacks, airlines, insurance companies, hotels, and other major industries edged toward the brink. In aviation alone, more than a hundred thousand jobs were lost within two months. The loss of a million new jobs by January 2002, followed by new mounting personal and corporate bankruptcies after Enron and the 2002 market collapse, created the specter of a potentially long-lasting recession and prolonged turbulence.

The Bush administration, despite its antigovernment rhetoric, created a new agenda of government activism on four fronts. First, it mobilized the entire government and spent added billions to fight terrorism. Second, it created a new activist agenda of "homeland security," investing billions more in internal security programs. Third, it spent billions bailing out the airlines and other failing industries. And, fourth, it called for a government stimulus program and new corporate accounting regulations.[30]

Simultaneously, pollsters picked up an immediate shift in public attitudes toward government. In a dramatic change, the U.S. public said they now looked to government as the solution to the pressing problems of the day, expecting government to protect them and keep them safe. They also wanted public leaders to get the economy going again and to create new jobs for them. And, most dramatic of all, they expressed new trust in government to achieve these ends. Confidence levels in government, the president, and the Congress (before Enron) shot up from about 20 percent who said they trusted government to do the job to more than 60 percent, a thirty-year record high.[31] Since Reagan, government had been defined as "the enemy," and Americans had trusted the market as the solution to their own problems and those of the nation. The new polls showed a watershed transformation. The Reagan religion had finally crashed on the rocks of recession and fears about personal safety that no free-market ideologue could answer.[32]

The Bush form of government activism seemed a success on the military front after the initial quick apparent victories in Afghanistan and against Al Qaeda. But precisely because of Bush's early success, Americans began to raise their expectations about what government should do. They saw some initial progress on the security front, but there was far less confidence about jobs and the economy. Ordinary Americans noticed that while Bush invested $20 billion to bail out the airlines, he gave not a red penny to help laid-off airline workers. They saw that Bush's idea of government stimulus was to cut corporate taxes, and increase subsidies to agribusiness, and that his idea of regulation after Enron was to preach ethics to his corporate friends.[33]

The Bush administration was exposing the contradictions in the reigning free-market ideology and opening up a potentially explosive window of opportunity for national and global justice activists. A conservative Republican was selectively increasing government spending and intervention in the economy, transparently showing that the markets and corporations ultimately turn to the government when the going gets tough. But the bailouts and welfare that Bush readily handed big business were not matched by a corresponding concern with workers and the poor. The free-market rules applied to the people, while welfare seemed an entitlement of the rich.[34]

On the trade front, the Bush administration was displaying other contradictions. Bush kept pushing "free trade" as the centerpiece of an antiterrorist agenda binding nations together. But he raised protection on textiles, steel, and other U.S. products that were severely threatened by cheap imports. Again, the deeds conflicted with the free-market rhetoric.[35]

Such contradictions, tied to a national or global economy that remains turbulent or depressed, could blow apart the global religion of neoliberal economics. If the United States were brazenly seen to be violating its own prescriptions at home, as well as contradicting its own stated trade policy, it would discredit the constitutional ideology at the core of both the American market order and globalization itself. If the global justice movements were able to educate the public about the hypocrisy at the heart of neoliberalism, while simultaneously offering a credible alternative policy, it could have a huge impact. In a deep recession, with millions more workers laid off, Americans would eventually demand that the governments act aggressively to create jobs as well as ensure public safety. A new deal could become politically possible for the first time in fifty years.

None of this is foreordained, and much will depend on both the trajectory of the economy as well as the skill of national and global justice movements in making the case for a new way of thinking. But one thing is certain. If the conversation in the United States were to shift away from the old-time market religion to a new economic vision, it would have an instant and profound effect on the global debate. The United States has been the messiah converting the world to the religion of free trade and free markets. If this messiah were to become widely seen as a heretic to its own preaching, the entire ideological foundation of globalization as we know it would crumble.

The challenge for the global justice movement is to advance a coherent and pragmatic new vision at the very moment that millions more Americans need jobs, health care, retirement security, and financial stability. More than one-third of Americans, even before the recession, were only a few paychecks away from bankruptcy. Should the downturn continue, and economic terror rise along with other forms, Americans will be ready to hear new ideas. At a minimum, the movement will enjoy a "teachable moment," and its long-term success will depend on teaching well.

CHAPTER 10

GLOBAL DEMOCRACY AS ANTITERRORISM

I don't know how World War Three will be fought but World War Four will be fought with sticks and stones.

ALBERT EINSTEIN

O N A RECENT VISIT TO MY MOTHER, ABOUT THREE MONTHS AFTER September 11, we watched a lot of evening television. We clicked back and forth between CNN news channels and action films on other cable channels. On nearly every click, we saw men in military fatigues and semi-automatic machine guns going after the enemy. We sat upright as bombs exploded and buildings and people were blown sky high. Fires raged and wounded or dead people were everywhere.

The interesting thing is that we could never tell right away whether we were watching the news or Hollywood dramas. Bombs and blood filled the CNN reports and the movies. The blurring of media images and life was dramatic, and the common thread was sickening violence in a world of spies, war, and terror.

Even before September 11, violence was everywhere. I wrote a book several years ago, *The Wilding of America,* all about violence here at home. I had to write a new edition of that book even before the Trade Tower attacks, just to record the new forms of mayhem, such as hockey fathers killing coaches, Columbine kids machine gunning fellow students, and laid-off workers shooting up their offices.[1]

September 11 showed America's vulnerability to a new kind of terrifying global violence—and could be a tipping point in our focus on hate and violence in the larger world. We have always known the world is a violent place but we have felt protected. Now we know that we are vulnerable—and may be becoming a leading target. This has led many Americans to think more about world affairs and the roots of terrorism. As I noted in the last chapter, this creates a major new window of opportunity for the global justice movements. A growing public interest in the roots of anti-Americanism and violence will inevitably lead to a focus on issues about power, democracy, and poverty at the center of the globalization debates, especially as they are now being played out in the Middle East.

Terror—and violence in general—arise from widely shared grievances and hate that have become staples of both Middle East politics and the broader global landscape. Because terrorism has roots does not justify it. I do not believe that the deliberate killing of innocent civilians is justified even if the cause is just. But if we don't deal with the underlying government policies and global conditions giving rise to terror and other globalized violence, we won't stop it.

Not everyone believes that we should explore the grievances and conditions creating hate. My dental hygienist, while cleaning my teeth, made it clear that she was worried about Americans, not foreigners. Friends of her husband were killed in the Trade Towers. Her view was that a lot of innocent civilians in the Middle East would have to die in our war against terror but that was inevitable and necessary. And she said she really didn't care because her loyalty was to Americans and that she would be prepared to nuke the entire Middle East if it was necessary to eliminate the terrorists.

I recently heard Bibi Netanyahu, the former hard-line leader of Israel, offer a similar analysis. There was no point, he said, in trying to understand terrorists and their sympathizers or responding to their grievances. The only antiterrorist strategy that works is "victory, victory, victory." Israeli Prime Minister Sharon executed Bibi's plan ruthlessly and unsparingly in ordering the 2002 Israeli invasion of the West Bank after Palestinian suicide bombings, killing hundreds of innocent noncombatants and terrorizing nearly the entire civilian Palestinian population.

But even Israeli officials acknowledged that the attacks on Jenin and other West Bank cities would not stop terrorism and might increase suicide bombing and other violence against Israel. This is not just because of the hate sowed by the killing of Palestinian civilians and mass demolition of their homes and cities, but the deliberate destruction of any Palestinian state authority that could negotiate a political settlement to the problems underlying the conflict. Israel's application of Bibi's principle over many years has only escalated the terrorism and hatred against it, substituting a military response for a political solution to the underlying Palestinian grievances.

As in the Middle East, a global program to counter terror has to attack root causes. I do not argue in this book that globalization is the primary cause of the September 11 attacks or of terrorism in general. Noam Chomsky has written that "as for the bin Laden network, they have as little concern for globalization and cultural hegemony as they do for the poor and oppressed people of the Middle East who they have been severely harming for years. . . . Bin Laden himself probably never even heard of 'globalization.' Those who have interviewed him in depth, like Robert Fisk, report that he knows virtually nothing of the world, and doesn't care to."[2]

A focus on globalization as the cause of Islamic terrorism can easily obscure the central role of U.S. foreign policy in helping giving rise to the crisis. The U.S. position on the Israeli/Palestinian conflict is probably the single most important factor breeding hatred of America in the Arab world. Changing U.S. policy to do all in its power to bring about a viable Palestinian state would lessen Islamic terrorism faster than anything else that America can do. Other changes in U.S. foreign policy, including ending American support of dictators, monarchs, and other repressive regimes in the Middle East; removing U.S. troops from Saudi Arabia; and refraining from military intervention against Iraq or other regimes we find distasteful, would also drastically reduce

Islamic terrorism. Hatred of America and Islamic terrorism against the U.S. will grow as long as we are not prepared to reexamine the imperial dimensions of our presence in the region and transform our foreign policy to help create a new regional order free of any external domination.

But, beyond the need to rethink both U.S. foreign policy and the war on terrorism in the region, I want to persuade you in this chapter that my five-point agenda for global democracy could jump-start a powerful strategy to help reduce terrorism and end global violence in all its forms, and well beyond the Middle East. I have shown that globalization does not fulfill the happy promises of its mystique. Almost half of the world continues to live in wretched conditions, like the garbage towns surrounding Manila, where people crawl through smoking heaps of rubble to find crumbs to eat or burnt metal to sell. We have seen that three billion people live under the poverty line in their countries and that the gap between the global rich and poor has mushroomed. We have also seen that most of these people—even those living in countries with elections—have no real political voice. This is because the elections are rigged or nonexistent, the politicians and generals corrupted (often by their ties to the Pentagon), the governments too hemmed in by global markets and the IMF, or the state simply too weak, unstable, and poor to implement a development strategy. Whatever the reason, the lack of any political nonviolent channels for the 3 billion people living on fewer daily calories than our own household pets vastly increases their receptivity to calls for violence or terror against America by extremists.

In Chapters 7 and 8, I have already outlined the five prongs of a global democratic agenda. In the rest of this chapter, I return to each of them, but with a specific focus on how they can help to attack the roots of terror and other global violence. I will be mainly focused here on the Middle East and how they might help counter Islamic terrorism. But I hope also to show that the democratic agenda will reduce anger toward America among millions around the world who are not Muslim or Middle Eastern but may be receptive to violence against the United States and Western business.

I need to add one extremely important caution about the use of the term *terrorism*. There is no solid consensus in the world about how to define and distinguish terrorism from other forms of violence, including war. Terrorists in the eyes of one group are viewed as freedom fighters by others. Palestinian suicide bombers are freedom fighters to many Palestinians and Arabs throughout the Middle East but are defined by the Israeli government as terrorists. When Israeli operatives assassinate Palestinian militants or bulldoze homes in the Gaza Strip, Palestinians call it terrorism but Israelis call it self-defense. Indians call Kashmiri militants terrorists, but many Pakistanis and Kashmiris see them as fighters for national liberation. In Columbia, peasants see paramilitary groups and death squads as terrorists but many Columbian elites see them as defenders of the nation.

Terror, like war, is the use of violence for political ends, although it explicitly targets noncombatants while leaders of warring states often define the inevitable death of noncombatants as "collateral damage." Whether killing of noncombatants is defined as terrorism or freedom-fighting or a struggle for national self-determination is shaped by the ideology and interests of the parties involved. Powerful states have resources to spread successfully their own labels of who are terrorists, particularly among their own citizens. But they do not necessarily persuade other groups. For example, a recent poll showed that 95 percent of educated Saudis support bin Laden as a freedom fighter for Islamic ideals, even though he is almost universally seen as a murderous terrorist in the United States.

The problem is complicated by the global proliferation of "low-intensity" violence, which does not rise to traditional definitions of war but does not constitute peace either. Such violence often erupts between conflicting parties within states, as in Rwanda or Kosovo, or between a state and nonstate actor, as between India and Kashmiri groups or between Israel and Palestinian militants. Such violence can be deadly, but is often carried out by small groups, sometimes connected with official armies or internal security forces of states. Sorting out the forms of such low-intensity violence that are terrorist from other forms can be maddeningly difficult, since nearly all have political aims and involve killing of noncombatants.

This does not imply that the world cannot reach a more consensual definition of terrorism but it has not done so thus far. A definition on which all nations could agree and international law could codify would be an enormous step forward. Whether the U.S. "war on terrorism" or UN efforts in its wake will help to create a clearer international understanding remains unclear. What many Americans view as necessary violence in the war against terrorism will be seen as terrorism itself by many in the Middle East and elsewhere. For example, should the United States intervene unilaterally to overthrow the governments of Iraq or Iran as terrorist states, such actions will almost certainly be defined as terrorist by many in the Arab world and probably in many other nations. A war against terrorism—when the word is so ideologically fraught—can thus increase global violence and trigger more terrorism.

As noted in the Introduction, I cannot attempt a systematic conceptual definition or analysis of terrorism here, but need to caution that any use of the term is ideologically explosive. Since there is no firm global agreement on what constitutes terrorism, either theoretically or in practical application, inevitably many around the world will disagree with how any particular analyst uses the word. This suggests enormous caution in using the term, and I use it with these caveats in mind. Whenever possible, I refer to specific events, such as September 11, and I also try to specify ways in which global democracy can be an antidote to all forms of global violence, not just acts defined in the United States as terrorist.

Each year in a course I teach on war, I ask undergraduate students what they think is the best way to end global violence and terror. The most popular answer is to somehow end the anarchy of the nation-state system and create a collective security order based on new models of democratic world government. They see all the problems of the UN, including the difficulties in getting countries to relinquish sovereignty over military affairs and the controlling power of the United States and other rich nations in the Security Council. They also see the limits of international law and global government in an anarchistic world without a common sense of shared values or a culture of global citizenship. But they think that we are going to need an international legal order backed by a stronger UN to create a more peaceful world.

My students have a point. Global bodies operating in and around the UN—that give poor nations a voice—are essential to creating a more democratic community of nations and limiting the overwhelming power wielded by the United States. They know that as long as the United States dominates the world on its current scale, there will be "blowback," a CIA term for the unintended consequences of the exercise of great and often exploitative power. Terror is, they believe in part, a global blowback against U.S. hyperpower. But limiting U.S. power and the creation of collective security as an antiterror strategy is a matter I flesh out in my fifth and final point.[3]

When my students raise the issue of world government, they believe its role is not only to provide global peace-keeping but to target the poverty that afflicts the majority of the world's people. They see global poverty as the deepest root of global violence. They see the potential of violent anti-Americanism when people like Nisran, the Asian sweatshop worker for U.S. retailers who is paid 17 cents an hour for her seventeen hour days, has no effective way to express her grievances within a union or the political process. This is a view now widely shared by world leaders. On February 1, 2002, Colin Powell told the World Economic Forum that terrorism spreads in "areas of poverty, despair, hopelessness where people see no future." We have to make sure that our military response, Powell argued, is matched by measures "to put hope back in the hearts of people."[4] Gloria Macapagal Arroyo, president of the Philippines, has argued repeatedly that the underpinning of terrorism is world poverty. Speaking also at the

2002 World Economic Forum, she said that military force should now be replaced by a war against "the handmaiden of terrorism, poverty." When the military operations are over, she said, the antiterrorism "coalition should stay on and fight against poverty."[5]

Shortly after 9-11, *The Boston Globe* ran a story about escalating terrorism in many parts of Africa. The terrorists were "home grown, the products of slums in Cape Town or Cairo." Islamic extremists are exploiting horrific African "poverty and anger" to recruit prospective terrorists across the continent and especially in sub-Saharan African, the most wretchedly poor part of the planet. Abdurahman Kahn, a Cape Town Muslim recruiting Africans to defend the Taliban and fight for bin Laden, said that "Recruitment is going well." We are taking only unemployed men. Already over one thousand have applied.[6]

Of course, there have always been billions of poor people in the world, and few have become terrorists in the past. Poor people in the Middle East become receptive to terrorism and other violence not just because they are poor but because they believe U.S. policy is brutally unjust in the Palestinian situation, Iraq, and throughout the region. The perception of U.S. foreign policy as imperialistic is widespread among both poor and prosperous people in the Middle East and breeds hatred of America throughout the entire population, not just the poor.

While we should not identify Middle East poverty, then, as the cause of Islamic terrorism, there is little question that poverty throughout the Middle East and Third World helps to breed hatred toward the United States and receptivity to violence. This is partly because poor people in the Mid-East and elsewhere see global economic policies—implemented by the IMF, the US, and big business—as helping perpetuate their poverty. The poor have more reasons to hate the United States than the rich, and they have less to lose if they risk violence against America.

Globalization contributes to violence against the United States wherever it locks people in poverty. But even in countries where it is not the cause of poverty, globalization has changed how people experience being poor in a new sociological sense that may make a violent response more likely. Even in the poorest streets of Cairo, Karachi, Manila, and Bangkok, one finds barefoot kids crowded around television sets gawking at the mansions of the rich and famous in the Western sitcoms. They are as bombarded as we are by glitzy advertisements for enticing goods that they know they will never be able to buy. Globalization has transformed poverty by making prosperity so visually vivid to the global poor. The global rich—who are symbolized by America and all its consumerist glitter—are now in their face in a new way. They look at how we live and wonder why their fate is so different, just as we may wonder and thank God that we are not in their miserable shoes.

Sociologists speak of relative deprivation. Poverty is more tolerable when everyone you know is poor. But as globalization—through television and other mass media—brings the global rich up close and personal to the poor, they experience their own poverty differently. They begin to measure their own well-being not against the poverty of their neighbor but the wealth of the people they see on TV or who employ them in their factory. Such relative deprivation hurts—and is far more likely to breed resentment, anger, and finally hatred and violence. Shortly after the September 11 attacks, President Thabo Mbecki of South Africa highlighted the relative deprivation of poor people as the main source of global violence. At the UN, he said that "the fundamental source of conflict in the world today is the socioeconomic deprivation of billions of people across the globe, co-existing with islands of enormous wealth and prosperity within and among countries."[7]

The Arab world is a cauldron of both absolute and relative deprivation. Some of the poorest countries in the world are in the region, including Bangladesh, whose wages make China's look good, and Afghanistan, where desperate indigents gingerly pick up fragments of bombs and land mines to sell as scrap metal. Core states such as Egypt and Pakistan, both operating under IMF Structural Adjustment Programs, are teeming with millions who live in rural huts without electricity or running water. Urban slums in Cairo or Karachi are some of the worst and most densely populated on the planet.

Relative deprivation in the Arab world arises from domestic and regional inequalities as well as comparisons with the West. Many Arab countries have fabulously rich ruling oil oligarchies, notably Saudi Arabia, which helps explain why they are hated by many of their own citizens who admire or support bin Laden. The gap between rich and poor is vast in most Arab nations. Much of the anger of Arabs in poor nations is directed against richer Arab countries that do not share their oil revenues. And relative deprivation helps breed intense anger toward the United States, both because of the omnipresent images of rich Americans permeating the media and the sense that Western wealth has been achieved through a colonial exploitation of the region for at least two or three centuries.

In Chapter 7, I argued that global government had to commit to a New Deal for the world. The U.S. New Deal became possible only because of the Great Depression and a 25 percent unemployment and poverty rate. But the depressive conditions of most Third World nations—now made even more acute by the severe global downturn—are on an entirely different scale. From Haiti to Zimbabwe to Indonesia, we see unemployment and poverty rates ranging from 50 to 90 percent. And the majority of these people have no opportunity to elect a leader like FDR who wants to address their problems.

Wahidullah Adel, 23, a tailor in Afghanistan, told a *New York Times* reporter as U.S. troops were circling Taliban forces in Khandahar, that the real problem for his country was its poverty, with his friends and millions of Afghans on the verge of starvation. He thought hatred of the West would persist after the Taliban unless there is "education for all, not just the elite. . . .We need a society of equality for all, rich and poor."[8]

Aimel Khan, 27, another Afghan sewing machine operator, made the connection between poverty and violence more explicitly. "We need roads and factories, because we have so many jobless youngsters. If they don't have work, they'll go for their guns."[9]

Afghanistan may get a Marshall-Plan type relief and recon-struction effort because of U.S. strategic concerns about post-Taliban terrorism in the region. The UN-led effort to create a new Kabul central government offers Afghan ethnic factions the promise of billions of dollars to rebuild the country and feed and educate its poor. The U.S. government has, at this writing, rhe-torically supported Afghan reconstruction as an antiterror stra-tegic agenda. Many world leaders seem to recognize that without addressing the emergency of poverty, the new government will not hold and more bin Ladens will appear.

But precisely the same strategic calculation relates to Pakistan, Aghanistan's nuclear armed impoverished neighbor, and more broadly to all countries in the region. Religious fanatics such as bin Laden, who are anything but poor, lead the jihad against the West, supported by the mullahs and clergy who teach radical Islamic doctrine. But the religious extremists can prosper only in the barren soil of nations like Afghanistan where young people with no hope for jobs or even their next meal see salvation in Islamic martyrdom. No matter what else we do, we need to mo-bilize international emergency reconstruction and development programs comparable to the one envisioned for Afghanistan throughout the region.

Ending global poverty is part of any long-term global anti-terror agenda—and it will have to be led by international bodies in and around the UN that allow the poor to speak for them-selves. We need a new global consciousness about the truth of the Great Depression that is breeding suffering everywhere in the Third World—and we need the global poor to educate the rest of us about their views of American and Western roles in helping them help themselves. If we don't listen or help, we will hear from them in less friendly ways.

International bodies—led by the UN—will have to lead this effort, with cooperation from the United States and other rich nations as well as aid from global corporations, who have their own interests in this matter as discussed shortly. A global economy redesigned around ending world poverty could become a key part of the solution of global violence. William Lederer, the author of *The Ugly American*, said it this way after September 11: "We're still fighting poor, hungry, angry people with bombs and tanks when what they would really respond to is food and water, good roads, health care, and a little respect for their religion and culture." The abolitionist movement of the twenty-first century—a key to creating a more peaceful world—is abolishing world poverty.[10]

Wahidullah Adel, the Afghan tailor quoted earlier, said this when asked what he wanted after the war. "I want a democracy, without people lording it over one another." It's a simple idea, expressed by a simple man. But it is probably the single most important way to end violence and terror in Afghanistan, the Middle East, and the rest of the world. Unfortunately, elites in most nations, while they may accept the tailor's wisdom in theory, reject it in practice.[11]

The second prong of my global democracy agenda is national democracy, and if we focus on the Middle East and Muslim nations more broadly, we do not see an encouraging picture. There are about fifty Muslim countries in the world. Only five— Turkey, Bangladesh, Senegal, Sierre Leone, and Suriname—are democracies. While they are the exception to the general pattern discussed below, they prove that Muslim nations today can be democratic. The idea of a fundamental incompatibility between Islam and democracy is misplaced, despite the historic tie between religion and the state in Islamic doctrine. Islamic scholar Shireen Hunter writes that "throughout history, religion has been . . . subordinated to politics and to its requirements." Karen Armstrong, the esteemed writer on Islam, rejects the idea that Islamic tradition and democracy are in necessary conflict. Western democracies have, themselves, not always separated church and state, and the Islamic tradition has long debated varying liberal and conservative versions of how secular the state can be. Benjamin Barber points out that Islamic ideas "of *umma* (community), *shura* (mutual consultation) and *al maslaha* (public interest)" are integral to the Koran and consistent with Western democratic notions of civic participation and democratic accountability of leaders.[12]

Nonetheless, most Islamic countries are authoritarian. Albania, Gambia, Indonesia, Lebanon, and Niger have emerging democratic, multiparty rule but are still very limited in popular participation. About twenty other nations have some form of indirect elections or participation but are run by military strongmen, including Algeria, Egypt, Uzbekistan, Turkmenistan and Yemen. Jordan, Kuwait, Malaysia, and Morocco are hereditary monarchies with elected parliaments exercising consultative functions. Bahrain, Brunei, Oman, Qatar, Saudi Arabia, and United Arab Emirates are monarchies with no elected parliamentary bodies. Iraq, Libya, and Syria are all run by military dictatorships and Iran is a theocracy. Kings, emirs, sheiks, sultans, and other military strongmen essentially run the region and democracy is scarcer than in any other part of the world.[13]

Many writers have observed that the Middle Eastern regimes are brutally repressive and unpopular among their own people—and have been the main targets of Islamic terrorist attacks. Bin Laden has sponsored terror against the Saudi royal family ruling his native country. He has found support among ordinary Saudis, Egyptians, and others who see their regimes as corrupt Western puppets or oil plutocrats willing to do anything to hold on to their wealth. Islamic extremists in Egypt assasinated Sadat, leading to twenty years of brutal Egyptian repression of Islamic groups that seems to have only spread their popularity.

But the idea that the way to help end terrorism is to democratize Middle Eastern and other Muslim nations is not high on the agenda of American leaders or the global oil giants who do business with repressive regimes. While there is some broad rhetoric about the importance of promoting democracy in the region, Western elites claim that democracy would bring Islamic extremists to power and likely increase rather than decrease terrorism. But they are afraid most of all that democratic governments would be less friendly to U.S. foreign policy and less generous to U.S. business than the repressive regimes in place.

Jean Charles Brisard, a French defense analyst, argues that "the American addiction to Saudi oil and arms money threatens to undermine national security in the West." He means that U.S. businesses are making so much money in oil and arms deals that they support the Saudi regime despite knowledge that its corruption, unpopularity, and sponsorship of the extremist Islamic school of Wahabbism is actually increasing terrorism in the region. The Saudi oil deals with six major U.S. energy corporations—ExxonMobil, Marathon, Conoco, Unocal, Amerada Hess, and Texaco—are yielding billions of dollars in profits every year. Unocal has a joint multibillion dollar venture with two Saudi firms to develop Azerbaijan's reserves. In 1998, Texaco joined with Nimir Petroleum to begin drilling in a 1.5-billion-barrel oil field. In 2001, the Saudi government signed a *$25 billion* deal with the biggest U.S. firms to develop Saudi Arabia's natural gas reserves. And the profits of U.S. military firms with the Saudi government are equally stupendous, with the Saudis paying U.S. arms makers more than $30 billion between 1990 and 1999 for everything from F-15 fighter aircraft to Apache attack helicopters. Other secretive private firms known as "spook outfits"—a few politically connected American firms working with the Saudi government to train its military, have earned "billions over the of dollars over the past decade alone, equipping, training and managing virtually all branches of the Saudi Arabian armed forces." U.S. leaders support the monarchy to keep the fabulous profits coming—even though democratization would lessen the growing Arab hatred of the regime and reduce risk of terrorism throughout the Middle East.[14]

Undoubtedly, there are real concerns that Middle Eastern democracies could turn more anti-American and more violent. And there is the possibility that in some Muslim countries, such as Algeria, the electorate might vote for Islamic fundamentalists who would abolish elections and parliaments and become new sponsors of state terror. While this is a frightening scenario and part of conventional wisdom, the probabilities are higher in most nations that a more democratic Middle East is much more likely to end terrorism and other violence.

This is partly because the majority of Middle Eastern peoples are not Islamic extremists. When free elections have been held in countries such as Pakistan, extremist parties have won less than 10 percent of the vote. Islamic extremism seems to spread only in countries where people don't have the opportunity to vote for alternatives. Democracy advocates in Pakistan have made this case forcefully, arguing that if the only choice you give people is between today's U.S.-allied dictators and Islamic fundamentalists, they will choose the fundamentalists. But if you give them a broader choice, they will elect more moderate Muslim parties who will help develop the nation and spend money on jobs and social services for the poor rather than on the fancy, expensive weapons bloating the current military regimes. If you are a poor Egyptian or Pakistani who has the opportunity to vote for a moderate Islamic political party that will spend public funds on food for your family, a job for you, and school for your kid, might you not want to give that party a chance? Might you not prefer that party to the dictator who spends on guns or the Islamic extremist who will spend on weapons and subject you to a new Taliban-style Department of Morals and Virtues?

Thomas Friedman argues correctly that when "Islam is imbedded in authoritarian societies it tends to become the vehicle of angry protest, because religion and the mosque are the only places where people can organize against autocratic leaders. And when these leaders are seen as being propped up by America, America also becomes the target of Muslim rage." Friedman notes that in democratic Islamic countries such as Bangladesh, Islamic extremism and anti-Americanism are low, while in authoritarian regimes like Pakistan and Egypt, fundamentalism and support for terrorism is mushrooming. Pakistan, he notes, is "trapped in the circle of bin Ladenism—military dictatorship, poverty and anti-modernist Islamic schools, all reinforcing each other"—and they are a deadly brew intensifying poverty and spawning violent anti-Americanism.[15]

Friedman summarizes his point vividly: "Hello? Hello? There's a message here. *It's democracy, stupid!* [Friedman's italics]. Those who argue," Friedman continues, "that we needn't press for democracy in Arab Muslim states, and can rely on repressive regimes, have it all wrong. If we cut off every other avenue for non-revolutionary social change, pressure for change will burst out anyway—as Muslim rage and anti-Americanism."[16]

Raja Mohan, editor of the *Hindu* newspaper, makes precisely the same argument for democracy as the best antiterrorist medicine in the Middle East. He writes that if the United States wants to weaken the appeal of bin Ladenism, "it needs to find role models that are succeeding as pluralistic, democratic, modernizing societies like India—which is constantly being challenged by religious extremists of all hues—and support them." In other words, the best way to diminish the appeal of Islamic fanatics is to let them compete with democratic alternatives—and the fastest way to spread their terrorist doctrine is to ban them or violently repress them through U.S.-armed military oligarchies. Anti-Americanism and Islamic fundamentalism, as noted above, have spread like wildfire in Egypt, as in Pakistan, paradoxically because a U.S.-armed authoritarian regime has used brutal violence to suppress the extremist movements.[17]

In the Cold War era, the United States used the threat of Communism to justify its support of military dictatorships like the Somozas in Nicaragua, the Duvaliers in Haiti, Marcos in the Philippines, the Shah in Iran, Sukarno in Indonesia, and Diem in Vietnam. The result was almost always disastrous, spreading anti-Americanism like smallpox among the people and brewing internal revolutions creating Islamic fundamentalist regimes in the Middle East, like that of the Ayatollah in Iran who overthrew the Shah.

The danger today is that under the rubric of antiterrorism, the United States will again seek to suppress democracy by supporting brutal dictatorships or authoritarian regimes. We see this clearly not only in Saudi Arabia, Pakistan, and Egypt but in strategic or oil-rich Asian countries like Uzbekistan, bordering Afghanistan. Uzbekistan allowed its air fields to be a staging base for U.S. military operations in Afghanistan during the war against the Taliban. The United States is giving strong new support to President Islam Karimov, who runs a brutal regime notorious for its use of torture, censorship and repression of any opposition parties. Karimov, a former Communist party boss, jails or kills nearly anyone who opposes his regime, calling them Islamic terrorists. There have been significant extremist Islamic movements in his country, but Karimov applies the same brutal tactics to democratic dissidents as he does to the extremist Islamic groups. Should we repeat the Cold War history of supporting tyrants like Karimov under the guise of antiterrorism, it will fan more acutely the global flames of anti-Americanism. And the consequence today may be even more tragic, especially for Americans themselves. What we need to do is take seriously our own cherished rhetoric of democracy—and make it the cornerstone of U.S. foreign policy—if we want to weaken the appeal of bin Ladenism anywhere in the world.

The image of the Gilded Age on a global scale began to haunt me after a recent trip to Thailand. I visited a coconut farm where a large foreign company was replacing workers with monkeys to scale the trees and harvest the fruit. When I asked why, a Thai raised four fingers signaling 4 reasons: "The monkeys don't ask for higher wages, they don't ask for vacations, they don't form unions and don't go out on strike."

Socially accountable business is the third prong of a global democratic antiterrorist agenda. Workers who are treated with dignity and feel a stake in their companies are not likely to hate their employers or use violence against them. But when the model of a good global worker is a monkey, we are asking for trouble. The Gilded Age robber barons treated their workers like animals and inspired violent protest by radical unions, anarchists, wobblies, and ordinary workers who couldn't take it anymore.

The titans of industry struck back with deadly force, turning factories into war zones. In the famous 1894 Homestead Steel strike, Carnegie responded to labor organizers as terrorists, employing his private security force to shoot to kill with help from the National Guard called out by the governor.

Today's global robber barons are following the same low road. I have already described the eighteen hour days, six to seven day weeks, 8 to 18 cents an hour wages, unpaid overtime, sexual harassment, and other poisonous conditions that Muslim workers in the Middle East and Central and Southeast Asia routinely suffer. The global sweatshop has become the symbol of the corporate low road in an age full of rhetoric about social responsibility and global corporate citizenship. Can anyone believe that such radical abuse practiced routinely by contractors for Wal-Mart, Nike, or the Gap against millions of workers like Nisran and Samima is not one of the root causes of anti-Americanism? Or that it is not a breeding ground for recruits to violent movements, even terrorism?

Just like domestic abuse, corporate abuse is an inspiration to hatred and violence. The victim of domestic abuse stays in relationship with her abusive partner because she feels she has no alternative, but she can ultimately end up killing her abuser out of desperation. Nisran and Samima have no options to quit, but their anger against the companies whom Samima says "has robbed us of our lives" runs deep. Their first response is not toward violence but to organize their fellow workers to speak up for such simple rights as a 34-cent hourly wage and trips to the bathroom without being beaten on the head by a supervisor. When Nisran is asked what her life goal is, she says, "I would like to devote my life to working for the welfare of the workers in Bangladesh . . . I want to spend my whole life helping the workers establish their rights."[18]

The movement for basic rights of Muslim and other global workers like Nisran and Samima is the great global civil rights struggle of the coming century. Like the civil rights movement of Afro-Americans in the United States led by Martin Luther King, it is a fundamentally nonviolent movement, full of hope and peace. But when organizers such as Nisran are fired, beaten up, or killed, the nonviolent spirit of the workers can turn into seething rage, violence and even terrorism.

Samima, says that when her bosses learn that she is helping organize workers, she "will be fired and blacklisted for certain. They could even send thugs to attack us." The truth is that without some protection from Western labor leaders who helped bring them to speak in the United States, Samima and Nisran could well be killed. Samima tells us that any form of organizing triggers repression: "When workers try to organize, supervisors follow the leaders to find out who is actually leading the effort. . . . Sometimes the bosses give them extra work. Then when they cannot complete the extra work, they are fired." This is actually one of the more benevolent responses to union organizers in export zones from El Salvador and Guatemala to Indonesia and the Philippines. The common fate of these organizers is far too often jail, torture, or murder by death squads, company goons, or state police and security forces.

The most important first step in a corporate antiviolence agenda is, then, quite simple: respect the right of workers to freely associate and organize. This is the most fundamental democratic right that a business must respect, and it is already enshrined in Article 23 of the 1948 UN Declaration as well as the International Labor Organization's agreements signed by most countries as well as written into most global corporate codes of conduct. But neither the companies nor countries go beyond lip service, and unions are crushed even in countries such as Bangladesh with strong labor laws on the books. When a Bangladeshi labor organizer is asked why the laws are not enforced she talks about the complicity between the U.S. companies, the Bangladeshi sweatshops, and the Bangladeshi government. "Bangladesh has good labor laws," she says. "But these laws are not obeyed because the owners are driven by greed and have no accountability to the state or to anyone. They are the powerful ones. They know that if they don't comply, there is no one to force them." She mentions that the sweatshop, owners are often the brothers or cousins of officials in Bangladeshi ruling political circles and that the foreign companies do not intervene to break this circle of corruption because they want to squeeze every last penny out of Nisran and her fellow workers.

Even when government officials want to enforce their labor laws, the U.S. and other multinational firms know they are in the driver's seat. Wal-Mart, Nike, or the Gap can simply threaten to go from Bangladesh to Vietnam or China. This "exit power" is central to the abuse they inflict and it functions very much like the power dynamics in abusive marriages. Abused wives stay because they feel they cannot leave for financial or emotional reasons, and the husbands have the power to inflict the abuse because they are the ones with the exit power and they know it allows them to perpetuate the abuse without losing their marriage.

A democratized and socially accountable global business regime must end this abuse—starting with finally putting an end to the humiliation of workers like Nisran—before it creates new violence in Muslim and other Third World countries. Creating the new regime will take the change laid out in Chapters 7 and 8: international rules in a post–Bretton Woods order to help limit corporate exit power, global labor, and consumer organizing to force the companies to be democratically governed on new ownership and chartering principles, and business itself taking what I described in the last chapter as a new wave of global corporate responsibility to support systemic change. Ultimately, doing the right thing is in the long-term interests of the businesses themselves because it will create greater buying power in the Third World, increase their brand reputation at home, and reduce violence or terror directed against them in their foreign operations.

The key way in the short-term that the firms can sustain global operations while helping end anti-Americanism is to negotiate in good faith with Third World labor movements and governments to respect basic rights and pay survivable wages. The demands of the Bangladeshi workers show how easy this would be for the companies. American audiences listening to Nisran and Samima told me how touched they were by how little these sweatshop workers were asking. They wanted a raise of a few pennies an hour that would give them enough to eat but would increase the cost of the product only about a tenth of 1 percent, hardly impacting corporate profit at all.

The workers want one day off a week. They ask to be paid for their overtime. They demand not to be beaten or sexually harassed. They seek the freedom to speak and organize, but only within the boundaries of the Bangladeshi labor law already passed.

Business leaders who accepted these modest demands would be setting the tone for a new global economy that rejected abuse based on exit power. This would be a patriotic service since it could dramatically reduce hatred of America in Muslim countries like Bangladesh and Pakistan and would be a potent antiterror strategy. But, you may say, it will never happen because business is either too greedy or too driven by the dictates of Wall Street for faster and higher profit.

Yet a new corporate accountability to workers and public needs is pragmatic even in business terms because, in the long run, it is consistent with the bottom line interests of the companies themselves. Even companies like Nike have begun to recognize the dangers of being identified as a symbol of sweatshops—and they recognize that their future profitability is tied to a perception by customers that the Swoosh is sweat-free. Moreover, the cost calculations in sweatshop operations favors paying marginally higher wages rather than the radically higher security costs in a world of terror and fortress globalization. Treating the workers more humanely and paying them a living wage will cost the companies less than the price they will pay for military protection in a regime perpetuated on abuse. And, in the last analysis, only an approach that gives workers dignity and enough wages to afford the necessities of life will create the global demand that will sustain global production.

Global overproduction and the current global recession point to the core business interest in seeing Third World consumers gain the purchasing power to buy the goods they produce. We should remember Henry Ford's rationale for his shocking proposal of paying workers what seemed a fortune of $5 a day in the 1914; the only way he would make Ford a mass consumer item was to pay his workers enough to buy the car. In today's terms, the Nikes and Wal-Marts would have to pay a lot less than $5 a day to make good on Ford's calculation while contributing to a peaceful and less violent world.[19]

In the 1960s, the Iranian writer Jalal Al-e Ahmad diagnosed what many Islam writers have now called "westoxication," a cultural illness striking at the heart of the Arab world. Inventing the word "gharbzadegi" to mean "West-strickenness," he denounced Arabs who rushed for their Coca-Cola or to see the latest Hollywood film. Since the 1960s, heated discussions about Western cultural imperialism and the dangers of westoxication have permeated nearly all nations in the region and become a staple of Arab culture.

Western culture comes to the Middle East courtesy of Disney, News Corp., AOL Time Warner, and the other mega media monopolies. Their magical appeal coexists uneasily with traditional religious sensibilities and pride in Arab cultures. Extremist movements, drawing on the broader Muslim intelligentsia critical of gharbzadegi, align themselves with nationalist cultural and political anxieties fueled by globalization and widely spread throughout the population.

In Chapter 7, I argued that the defense of "localism," including vibrant local communities and cultural diversity, seems a driving force behind global justice or antiglobalization movements everywhere—and a fourth key to both global democracy and a world free of terror. Nowhere does this seem more true than in the Middle East. In Egypt, where support for Islamic extremists run strong, even an antifundamentalist government official complains that Americans come here and "want us to be like them. They understand nothing of our values or our culture." And an Egyptian journalist adds, "We have a different background, a different history. Accordingly we have the right to a different future." Fatima Mernissi, a feminist Muslim writer, agrees that Western culture "is the source of all trouble. The West," she says, "alone decides if satellites will be used to educate Arabs or to drop bombs on them. It crushes our potentialities and invades our lives with its imported produces and televised movies that swamp the airwaves." And Shiek Ghanoushi, an influential cleric, writes that "the bottom line is that our societies are based on values other than those of the West."[20]

The idea that the Trade Tower attacks reflect ultimately a cultural war between globalization and all of Islam is very popular in the West but is extremely problematic. Shireen Hunter has correctly observed that "the largely unspoken and unacknowledged cause of the dichotomy between Islam and the West is the question of power." She says that the "balance of power, which is heavily weighted in the West's favor, gives the West a tremendous influence over the fate of the Muslim states and peoples . . . and a good deal of influence on the internal politics of Muslim countries." Graham Fuller adds that the Middle East crisis is really "a conflict between those who have power and those who do not, those who control the world's destiny and those who are subjects of control." A "civilizational clash," he concludes, is not so much over Jesus Christ, Confucius, or the Prophet Muhammad as it is over the unequal distribution of world power, wealth and influence." The roots of anti-Americanism and terror in the Islamic world have more to do with U.S. warplanes over Iraq and military support for Israel and the unpopular Saudi royal family than they do with the spread of Coca-Cola.[21]

But this does not negate the importance of the genuine cultural crisis in the Islamic world—and other far-flung regions—that globalization has helped create. The preservation of Islamic localism is vital to building a world free of terror. Chomsky comments about a *Wall Street Journal* report that anti-Americanism runs rampant among "rich and privileged Egyptians at a McDonald's restaurant wearing stylish American clothes," who are bitterly critical of the United States for what Chomsky calls "objective reasons of policy." Chomsky is absolutely correct that U.S. foreign policy drives the hatred of America in these elite Arab circles—and in much of the Arab street—rather than any rejection of McDonald's or blue jeans. But their very embrace of jeans can be seen as part of the cultural crisis of Islam today, that struggles between pride in Islamic tradition and the seductiveness of the American lifestyle as glamorized and spread through cultural globalization.[22]

Our basic values define who we are—and when any of us, whether Islamic or Western, feel that something threatens or is overwhelming our core culture, we will fight to defend who we are. Globalization has triggered a violent crisis of cultural identity not only among Egyptians and Saudis but among the French and other Europeans. Think of the antiglobalization French farmer Jose Bove, hardly a terrorist or fundamentalist but a very modern European so angry at the American-led cultural assault on French culture and social democracy that when he helped block construction of a McDonald's, he instantly became a national hero.

Benjamin Barber has argued that globalization—or "Mc-World"—helps inspire jihad by crushing any values systems other than Western secularism, materialism, and consumerism. He notes that Hasan al-Banna, founder of the extremist Egyptian Brotherhood, assailed Westerners for importing "their half-naked women into these regions, together with their liquors, their theaters, their dance halls, their amusements, their stories, their newspapers, their novels, their whims, their silly games, and their vices." Globalization's media empires, led by the likes of Rupert Murdoch and Barry Diller, Barber suggests, could bury Arab identity even "where colonial empires failed." This overstates the case, but makes clear that bin Ladenism finds fertile soil in a region that fears its young will abandon Islam entirely for what al-Banna called its "wave of atheism and lewdness."[23]

Samuel Huntington puts the cultural threat to Islamic peoples in stark terms. "The problem for Islam . . . is the West," he writes, "a different civilization whose people are convinced of the universality of their culture and believe that their superior, if declining, power imposes on them the obligation to extend that culture throughout the world." Like Barber, Huntington sees in American-led globalization a dangerous tendency to "universalize" Western values and impose them on every community across the planet. Persistence in such a missionary movement (i.e., cultural globalization) will create endless new recruits for bin Ladenism.[24]

One finds a loose parallel between the Islamic fear of westoxication and the antiglobalization Seattle legions who fear rampant global commercialism and seem so fiercely committed to localism and cultural diversity. I have often asked Seattle veterans and other globalization activists what personally motivates them. A story they have told me captures the spirit of their answer and both the localist and spiritual essence of their cause. A U.S. businessman goes on vacation to Mexico and notes an especially successful fisherman who catches enough in the morning to feed his family and spend the rest of the day on the beach enjoying himself. The businessman pitches an idea to the Mexican: "You and I could be rich! We should go into business together and grow this little business of yours into a multinational fishing conglomerate. We'll have to secure adequate venture capital to buy more boats, staff a crew, hire a management team, and develop an advertising scheme. Soon we'll be fishing fish from every ocean on the planet. We'll have to work all hours of the day to make it successful, but when we're sixty-five years old we can retire comfortably and spend the rest of our days relaxing on the beach."

The fisherman responded, "I already spend my days relaxing on the beach."

The new activists on many continents share the fisherman's sense—and perhaps of many Muslims in the Middle East—that globalization is "totally misaligned"—and that the "dominance of corporate power, materialism, and greed has confused our priorities." Many activists believe that globalization's ideology of consumerism is crushing the possibility of living a spiritually rich life in America, much as some Islamists see the West dooming their own spiritually. In the United States, as the global justice activists watch their classmates turning cartwheels to get that management degree that will get them stock options in some multinational corporation, they feel sadness and revulsion. They want something different that the new world of corporate greed could close off forever. Perhaps this is why so many of them read this generation's *Catcher in the Rye*—the book, *Tuesdays with Morrie*, that was a moral allegory about Morrie Schwartz, a dying sociology professor who preached the hollowness of material ambition to Mitch Albom, a young person like themselves. A generation raised in the malls is saying life has to be more than a cash register.[25]

The question, then, is whether there is any form of globalized world that can preserve Islamic traditions, local French cuisine, and vibrant local American communities rejecting values of the marketplace. Huntington's answer is that globalization will crash on its pretensions of cultural universality—and that not only Islamic civilization but the Chinese, Africans, Japanese, and other great historical civilizations will all successfully resist—violently if necessary—westoxification. But this will happen only with the collapse or extreme weakening of economic globalization, as civilizations tend to wall themselves off from any global order to defend their way of life.

Barber has a different and more hopeful answer: that localism and the creation of civil society is the only way to build a democratic global order. Democracy, he notes, is a habit of mind and a form of civic participation played out in the town square and local mosque, church, or synagogue as well as in the PTA, Kiwanis club, or their equivalents in countries around the world. Barber believes that it will not be international law or world government but the free association of local communities in what he calls "global confederalism" that will create the alternative world to globalization. He envisions a world that looks something like Switzerland in its earliest confederation—a nation of almost totally autonomous local cantons that associate together for mutual gain. And he points also to the ways in which the Committees of Correspondence in the American Revolution brought together patriots in different U.S. colonies into a voluntary loose federation in the late eighteenth century. Might we not internationalize civil society today, he suggests, through local virtually associated committees of correspondence from around the entire world on the Internet?[26]

Barber underestimates the importance of international law and world governments (whether the WTO or UN) that already are in formation. His confederation cannot end the global race to the bottom that helps create violence and anti-Americanism; I have already shown how that can be accomplished through other means. But by reminding us that democracy is always rooted in local participation and based on vibrant and diverse civic communities, he clarifies the essential role of localism in a democratic and peaceful global order. There can be no democracy in a world wiped clean of locality and cultural diversity, nor can there be peace in a global order that does not offer each citizen the means to participate through local community channels.

It will take a politically assertive localism to tame the cultural imperialism of McWorld and the arrogance of the West's messianic vision of universalizing its own values. One place to begin— and where nonviolent Western and Islamic activists may find common cause—is the breakup of the seven or eight global media empires. These include Disney, AOL Time Warner, News Corp., and others that beam globalization's commercial culture into every corner of the planet. The media monopolies are on the front line of the global cultural wars. If their power can be constrained by antitrust action in many different nations, a major step toward democratic localism of news and entertainment will be achieved. And that will play a major role in weakening extremism and violence among people who feel that a few Western companies are trampling their own media and threatening the survival of their own cultures.

While it may seem impossible to stem the tide toward media monopolization, it is interesting that during the months following September 11, far greater numbers of Americans began watching the BBC, shifting loyalties from Fox and CNN because they were seen as so partisan to the U.S. perspective. BBC news directors noted that their producers and journalists come from all over the world and thus offer a more diverse perspective than the U.S.-based networks. The rise of Al Jazeera, the Arab cable station as a global player, also shows how the Western media may be forced to share the airwaves with media representing entirely different cultural and political perspectives.

Global monopolies are crushing local community economics and cultural diversity in nearly every sector of the economy. Breaking up global corporate empires will have to emerge as a key regulatory feature of regional or global governing agencies— and we are already beginning to see some promising signs. European Union regulators have in recent years stopped key mergers and acquisitions, including one desperately sought by famed CEO Jack Welch of GE that was approved by more permissive U.S. regulators. This suggests that the Welch U.S. model of global dominance by one or two companies does not have to become the norm for the world. If national monopoly is destructive of democracy in a nation, global corporate monopoly is even more threatening to democracy in the world. It is the central threat to local community and cultural diversity and will stoke the flames of a violent localist reaction against both globalization and the West if other means do not succeed. The peaceful alternative involves regional and global governing bodies building a growing legal apparatus for international regulation to break up global monopolies and nurture smaller firms. Such policy to preserve economic localism and domestic businesses from being swallowed up by the global megafirms can also only be realized by discrediting the entire philosophy of neoliberal constitutionalism now governing the WTO and the world economy—and the enshrining of alternative rules already discussed in Chapter 7. When understood as essential to an antiterrorist agenda, it will gain growing support.

The preservation of localism and cultural diversity is part and parcel of the broader democratic assault on concentrated corporate and American power. The Middle East is reacting not just against modernity and Western cultural seductions but the broader forms of economic, political, and military power concentrated in the new Pax Americana. Ending terror requires moving beyond the relocalization and democratization of culture toward a new global political and security order better representing all the world's nations and citizens.

Omar Shelbaya, an importer in Cairo, called the September 11 attacks "insane" but said the United States had to "take 75 percent of the blame" because of its partisan support of Israel when it murdered Palestinian children. Another Egyptian wonders how "could Bush say that if you're not with us, you're against us? Did Bush stand with Arabs?" He and his friends are angriest about U.S. policy in the Israeli-Palestinian conflict, but they also hate U.S.-led sanctions in Iraq that led to the death of hundreds of thousands of children. And they are angry about Egypt itself where the United States gives $3 billion annually in mostly military aid to a strong-arm regime that is brutally cracking down on both extremist and moderate Islamists. Gamal Sultan, an Islamist Egyptian and founder of a new Reform party says that the purpose of the most recent crackdown "is to appease the American anger" after September 11. But "What is happening is the complete opposite of before September 11. If things continue as they are, a new generation of far more bloodthirsty people will arise."[27]

The "Arab street" (the widely used term for Arab public opinion) all over the Middle East is seething with anti-Americanism. "It's amazing," said Saud Alanezi, a Kuwaiti businessman and self-defined computer nerd educated in the United States. "No matter what the issue is these days, if the U.S. is on one side, everyone else wants to be on the other." He added this is true "even here in Kuwait," where only ten years ago the United States was seen as the great liberator from Iraqi aggression.[28]

The Arab street rages about Israel, Iraqi sanctions, and U.S.

troops in Saudi Arabia, but all these issues converge into a general fury about U.S. power sweeping over their region and the world as a whole. While it is difficult for Americans to understand or respect such feelings, they are so pervasive—from Egypt and Saudi Arabia to Pakistan and Indonesia—that we need to listen. A columnist in the respected Egyptian journal, *al Arabia*, writes after September 11: "For the first time in my life, I witness with my own eyes the defeat of American arrogance, tyranny, conceit and evil." A young Muslim tells an American journalist that after September 11, the attacks "are a sign of people who want to demonstrate to the world that they still have pride, that they don't want to give up and that they are able to resist violence." Another says bin Laden was wrong in his means but, "Yes, he was right politically." For him, bin Ladenism meant standing up to an America horrifically swollen with its own power and military prowess.[29]

I have argued that the fifth and final agenda of global democracy is moving beyond Pax Americana toward a system of collective security, a world where American unilateralism would be curbed and U.S. power more evenly balanced with that of other nations. This will inevitably weaken American dominance of globalization but it is in the nation's long-term economic interest, saving it the debilitating economic and military costs of Empire, as suggested in Chapter 8. It is the most important way to end terror and protect American lives—and also the most difficult for us to accept, even though the United States will remain the most powerful nation in the world. It is the only change that will finally end the anti-Americanism not just aflame on the Arab street but spreading like gangrene around the world.

After September 11, there was a great surge of sympathy for America in all parts of the world, and a rush to join the U.S. coalition against terror. But this support was tempered by almost universal concern—in regions far outside the Middle East—about the U.S. dominance of the globe. In France, for example, while public grieving about the Trade Tower attacks was deep and widespread, other conflicting feelings were evident. Alain Leforestier, a forty-four-year-old civil servant, is no anti-American, living near the Normandy beaches where U.S. troops helped liberate his country. But he is worried about unrestrained U.S. power and its tendency toward unilateralism. "If Bush decides to drop a thousand bombs on Kabul," he says a few weeks before the actual bombing, "do we have to follow you? It is not okay to do whatever just because Bush wants to do it." The same question was being asked in 2002 about the "regime change" in Iraq that President Bush unilaterally pledged to carry out.[30]

Le Forestier and his French compatriots echo a bit of the Arab street when he says, "America is expansionist. It is everywhere. It is the strongest. McDonald's are everywhere. . . . Then there are foreign policy issues like what happened in Chile with the military coup in 1973." He continues, "Now if you look at Africa and some of the other underdeveloped places and think of how they see you, how can they not want to knock you cold?" And he continues self-reflectively: "We (the French) have the same politics, the same capitalist economy. And we are even the ones selling them arms. We must all examine ourselves." Le Forestier is appalled by the attitude of many of his coworkers. They believe that the United States "deserved what it got for paying so little attention to the misery in the world" and for wielding power that helped create it. *Marianne*, a French political weekly, runs a banner headline typical in the French press asking "How far do we go in standing with America?"[31]

The refrains of the Arab street spread all the way to our neighbors in the Americas. President Vicente Fox expressed "unlimited" support for the United States after the September 11 attacks, but the Mexican public displayed its own ambivalence. Mexicans shared deep grief for the horrendous loss of innocent American lives but did not want their president to be a puppet of the Bush administration. Carlos Fuentes, the famed Mexican novelist, expressed the public's view when he said, "We are business partners with the United States, but in no way are we their lackeys." Felipe Arizmendi Esquival, the Catholic bishop of San Cristobal de las Casas, had an even harsher message. He told his parishoners that the United States "has generated so much violence to protect its economic interests, and now it is reaping what it has sowed." President Fox was forced to revise his earlier unconditional support, indicating that Mexico would do nothing to aid the war on terror that violated its own laws or "the pacific will of our nation."[32]

Such global concern about U.S. dominance reflects the fact that the United States is by far the most powerful nation in history. Oxford historian Niall Ferguson notes that "the US is vastly wealthier relative to the rest of the world than Britain ever was. In 1913, Britain's share of total world output was a shade over 8 percent; the equivalent figure for the United States in 1998 was just under 22 percent." And Ferguson, an American friend, argues that the United States is moving "from informal to formal imperialism. Since 1945," he argues, "the United States has been largely content to exercise power indirectly; exercising economic leverage through multinational corporations and international agencies like the International Monetary Fund and political power through 'friendly' indigenous regimes." Now, he argues, although "it has tended to do so behind a veil of multilateralism, acting in the name of the UN or NATO," the new situation hints of a more explicit U.S. colonialism. He finds himself "quoting Rudyard Kipling on 'the White Man's burden.' " He argues that the "precedents set in Bosnia and Kosovo are crucial. What happened in the 1990s was that those territories became a new kind of colony: international protectorates underwritten by U.S. military and monetary might." He sees the war on terrorism leading to U.S. military occupations veiled by multilateral agreements and terror labels being pinned on any anti-American group, used as a basis for U.S. military intervention and support of client states everywhere.[33]

Ironically, President Bush, himself, seemed to have some intimation of the dangers of these developments before he assumed office. In his debate with presidential candidate Al Gore focusing on U.S. foreign policy, he emphasized the need for a Great Power to be "humble." That profoundly important emphasis on humility is the first step in the shift toward a more democratic community of nations and creation of the collective security system that will weaken anti-Americanism and terrorism.

After September 11, Bush appeared to shift away from the unilateralism of the early months of his presidency. Before the Trade Tower attacks, he played John Wayne, as he pulled the United States out of the Kyoto treaty, the international criminal court, arms control agreements with the Russians, and biological weapons agreements. But following in his father's footsteps, he discovered after September 11 the need for a new multilateralism and a global coalition. Yet he has remained clear that the United States will act unilaterally to protect its own interests and will not allow concerns about global consensus to undermine "the mission." He has not moved toward his own aim of what might be called a humbler umpire.

Nonetheless, his rhetoric of globalism—and the moderating influence of Colin Powell—has permitted the beginnings of a far more important role for the UN in dealing with the political crises raging in the Arab world. This is a small but hopeful step in moving toward a new world of collective security. The UN brokered the Bonn talks, putting together the new interim government in Afghanistan following the collapse of the Taliban. The Security Council also authorized the new international force that would keep the peace there—although it would not be a force led by a UN command.

A growing role for the UN in other raging conflicts, notably the Israeli-Palestinian conflict and Iraq, may prove critical. Here, as in other parts of the Middle East, it is in America's own interest to see the UN and the larger international community play a far greater role in peace-keeping and shaping international policy and political solutions. It will save the lives of U.S. soldiers, reduce the huge economic costs of global policing, and weaken bin Ladenism.

Bush has repeatedly emphasized that global terrorism—in a world of nuclear, chemical, and biological weapons—is a "threat to civilization," and that all nations have a stake in ending it. But the implications are different than he recognizes. He sees the need for a global coalition, but one controlled by the United States. He does not acknowledge that terrorism can only be fought through global law-enforcement and collective security, combined with an end to unilateral American power and interventionism that he now wields in the name of antiterrorism. Great Powers have long justified their wars in universal or absolute values—often even invoking God on their side as they fought the evils of Nazi Germany or Soviet Communism. A unilateral war against terrorism as defined by Bush—even acting under the veil of multilateralism and nominal UN authorizations—will eventually be seen as just another American imperial venture, igniting more hatred of America. This will change only if the international community as a whole—acting through the UN, the international criminal court, and globalized policing and financial authorities—defines how terrorism should be defined and prosecuted.

The struggle against terrorism, even as Bush conceives it, must be more global and less warlike than any war before globalization. It requires enlisting all the nations of the world on a long-term coordinated effort against a common problem. Military action is now defined by the Bush administration itself as only one arm of the struggle, with a new emphasis on coordinated global political, financial, and international law enforcement activity. Military strikes and brute force dictated unilaterally by the United States contradict some of Bush's own framing of the problem. The new assault on terrorism—if the problem is truly a threat to all nations and an inherently global transnational problem—has to subordinate U.S. unilateralism to a broader vision of global sovereignty and law enforcement. It has to get serious about collective security.

Building a collective security system is obviously a long-term proposition, and the United States will resist because it would subject American policy to the same uncomfortable scrutiny faced by other nations. The United States is one of only two countries refusing to sign on to the international criminal court, precisely because U.S. leaders fear that they could themselves be held legally accountable for past policy. This includes American support for death squad regimes in Duvalier's Haiti, Duarte's El Salvador, Sukarno's Indonesia, or Marcos's Philippines. But if the United States is serious about ending terrorism, it obviously cannot hold itself exempt from the same standards of antiterrorism applied to every other nation.[34]

Creation of collective security will take years, but the first step is to ensure that any further military response to terrorism be authorized and controlled through the UN. Bush, as noted above, worked from the beginning to assemble a global coalition, relying on Secretary of State Colin Powell and others who had helped assemble his father's global alliance in the Gulf War. On September 29, only seventeen days after the New York attacks, the UN Security Council passed a U.S. resolution declaring the most sweeping declaration of war in its history. It called on all nations immediately to take actions to commit to the U.S. coalition. The UN mandated that every state "prevent and suppress the financing of terrorists," "freeze without delay" resources of terrorist organizations, "deny safe haven" to terrorist groups, "prevent terrorist movements" through border controls, and a host of other mandated strikes against terror.

The power of the United States in the UN cuts both ways in building collective security. On the one hand, it facilitates the turn toward the UN that we need by lessening the fear of American leaders. On the other hand, it drastically limits the autonomy of the UN and its capacity to create policy and institutions opposed by U.S. officials. This should not be viewed, though, as a death knell for the UN, that could become a more authentic expression of the will of the international community in ways discussed in Chapter 7.

Ironically, U.S.-led globalization has set in motion the paradoxical move toward world government and collective security necessary to end terrorism. Life is filled with unexpected consequences. In helping create a world safe for U.S. business, American leaders have laid the foundation of the new order that could eventually curb U.S. unilateralism. Happily, this change—that requires an end to U.S. domination of globalization and the world at large—will benefit Americans as well as the rest of the world and let us sleep more peacefully without basements stockpiled with gas masks or Cipro.

EPILOGUE

WHAT TO DO RIGHT NOW

WHEN I TALK TO PUBLIC AUDIENCES OR STUDENTS ABOUT THE IDEAS
in *People Before Profit,* many people are fired up and feel
something has to be done. But doubts and questions always
arise. People who are not already active in organizations or
movements, and some who are, often say, "I feel overwhelmed.
Changing the world is a tall order." And they ask, "Are there
really any useful things that I can do to make a difference?"

Here are my thoughts about what you can start to do today
if you are not already involved. I hope these proposals will offer
many readers a place to begin and provide those already active
with some new inspiration.

1. Be self-reflective. Reflect in a personal way about globalization. Your job, your clothes and food, your cable channel,
   and your investments all connect you with transnational
   firms and the global business order. What is your own small
   role in keeping the system going? Is it consistent with your
   values? What do you feel in your gut about the problems
   of globalization discussed in this book? Reflect often and
   deeply about your emotional reactions to what you have
   read here. Let your images, free associations, and feelings
   suggest the next step about what to do.

2. Educate yourself. Are you a captive of the globalization mystique? It will take more reading and discussion to make yourself aware of how you may buy into the myths of the age. Once you have read this book, read some related books, and get on an Internet listserv about globalization. Subscribe to a magazine based abroad to get a view of how those outside the United States see it. Or listen to a European, Latin American, or Middle East cable news channel.

3. Start a study and action group. You can't change the world alone—or even understand it all by yourself. I know churches and unions that have formed groups to study globalization. They read books together, bring in speakers, and create their own study guides. Very often, they move on to create projects in their community or help sister congregations, unions, and communities abroad. You can create a study group in your congregation, public library, local school system, or union, or at your place of business.

4. Travel. This is the fun part. I have found that students who are most energetic and hopeful about making a difference are those who have spent time on service projects in El Salvador, Guatemala, or another Central American country. Even as a tourist, you can get a new sense of how the global poor live if you venture out of the big Western hotel complexes. There is nothing quite like seeing up close and personal the latrines or huts in a poor country. It will change your views about yourself and—watch out! It is the thing most likely to turn you into a dedicated and activist citizen of the world.

5. Buy smart. We all buy things—it's almost a patriotic thing to do in the United States these days. But if we spend our consumer dollars wisely and strategically, we can move even big companies like Nike, McDonald's, or Disney. Catholic high-school students along with nuns in New York City boycotted a Niketown, demanding that the company live up to its own code of conduct in sweatshops. When the

store manager saw the nuns and neatly dressed kids, and the media they were attracting, he promised to get on the phone to corporate headquarters. Students at my own campus, Boston College, and many other universities around the country are pressing their university presidents to insist that the caps, sweatshirts, and polo shirts with their college logos be produced sweat-free. State employees or workers and managers in any company can insist that their employer only buy from vendors who respect global labor rights and environmental codes. Hook up with one of the many consumer groups in your community, including any of the Nader-inspired public-interest groups, that link concerns of consumers with issues of trade and corporate power.

6. Be a global feminist. Every time you look at your shoes or skirt or polo shirt, think about the hands and faces of those who stitched it together. I hope you will call to mind the images of the young Muslim Bangladeshi workers. They are the faces of the new global workforce—female and in trouble. If you care about your own wife, sister, daughter, or mother, remember that Nisran and Samima are also someone's daughter and sister. In the age of globalization, a feminist cannot think only about affirmative action and other protections for women in the United States. Most of the world's women live in poor countries and are begging for our help, and we can take up their cause, speaking about them to everyone we know, and petitioning our own governments and foreign governments to respect and enforce their rights. If you are already involved in feminist groups or action, make sure that you expand your agenda to support Nisran and Samima.

7. Think globally, act locally. This well-known bumper sticker has real implications. Global democracy begins at home. Think long and hard about how problems in your local community, from potholes to rotten schools to layoffs, are

related to the shifting tides of the global economy. And think of how social cutbacks in your community mirror the harsh neoliberal policies being imposed on neighborhoods in Argentina, Thailand, Mexico, and other poor countries. As you get together with your neighbors to get better schools or jobs in the community, keep thinking about people all over the world who are challenging the same system and working for the same goals. Then think about how you might be able to link up with them and help each other. After all, the big companies in your community are probably the same ones in their communities, and the policies dictated from Washington through the WTO and IMF are affecting all of us in similar ways. Link up with the community groups that are seeking to make connections between local and global issues. A good place to start would be the Nader-inspired network of public-interest groups operating in hundreds of cities across the country on everything from health care and electricity to gas rates and trade policy.

8. Make change from the inside. Social change happens when protesters banging on the outside door link up with insiders who share some of their values and concerns. There is no better place to start making change than right at your workstation or in your office. Get together with some fellow workers at lunch, and talk about how globalization affects your business and your job. Together, come up with answers and an action plan for the following questions. How could your company become a leader in helping enforce its own codes of conduct and thereby increase its brand reputation and bottom line? How could it be a leader in the industry to speak up for global labor rights and environmental standards? What can you personally take on as a project that would help put your company on the high road in your community and in global markets or export zones? Start a study group, work team, or personal project to get the plan going.

9. Unite! Unite is a coalition of global textile and apparel unions seeking to end sweatshops and defend the rights of workers like Nisran and Samima. They are part of the new civil rights struggle of the twenty-first century: to secure the rights of workers everywhere to organize for dignity and a living wage. Unions, labor rights, and organizing are all going global. Good jobs and working conditions at home now depend on good jobs and conditions abroad. If you are a member of a union, make sure that it supports sister unions in other countries. If you are not in a union, give money to help support sweatshop organizing, and petition foreign governments to enforce their own labor laws. And write your congressional representatives to penalize corporations who abuse workers or try to undermine unions either here or abroad. Ask your representatives to provide positive incentives for companies that cooperate fully with unions and help enforce global labor rights. Support the efforts of the National Labor Committee based in New York City, which has been a leader in exposing sweatshops, mounting corporate campaigns, and fighting for the rights of vulnerable workers.

10. Be a global green. Have you noticed that the winters are getting warmer than ever and the summers a lot hotter? Does the idea of global warming scare you? If so, you have no choice but to get up out of your chair, pick up the phone, and call one of the local or national environmental organizations you know about. It could be the Sierra Club or Greenpeace or a local group. The Greens have become leaders in the global justice movement and for good reason. We aren't going to have a world left to enjoy if we don't get behind sustainable development programs and support the environmental groups working for the Kyoto global convention and for global environmental standards. We all have to play our part, and you can do yours. Watch your own consumption patterns. Recycle your garbage,

and live ecologically yourself. Support companies known to observe global ecological practices. Become a member of one of the environmental groups pressuring our own government and others around the world to get serious about saving the earth.

11. Support a strong UN. It's not a question of whether some kind of world government should exist; it's what kind it will be. We already have the WTO and IMF as well as the UN. All these institutions are dominated by rich nations and corporations, but the UN has the best chance of becoming accountable to poor nations and ordinary citizens. You can support the UN by becoming a member, reading its publications, and joining the many U.S. advocacy groups that work to strengthen the UN. I'll bet there is one such group in your local community. Stage community, church, or workplace events that discuss how the UN can become a true global peacemaker while also helping to enforce labor rights and environmental standards through UN conventions. Write your congressional reps, and ask them to help get the United States to sign on to the International Criminal Court and UN labor and human rights agreements that Washington has refused to support.

12. Be a human rights activist. I bet you believe strongly in human rights. After all, they are the foundation of our own Constitution. You can make yourself and Thomas Jefferson feel good simply by mailing membership dues to Amnesty International, Human Rights Watch, or other human rights organizations. Following September 11, there is a real danger that our nation will support more dictatorships or monarchies that promise to combat terrorism against us. But these same nations often practice terrorism against their own people, violating their rights of free expression and association. So get on the phone to your congressional representatives and the White House, letting them know that antiterrorism is no excuse for supporting regimes that violate human rights. This is true at home as

well as overseas; we need to protect our own Constitution as our government contemplates crackdowns on dissent, new military tribunals, detention policies, and wiretapping or eavesdropping of suspects and their attorneys.

13. Protest! The globalization movements are spilling out into streets all over the world. They started in Seattle and just kept going at every new meeting of the financial elites. Is it time you joined them? This can be a great educational venture because there are usually huge teach-ins, with leading intellectuals discussing the financial and political policies that are ruining poor nations and hurting the poor in rich nations too. It is also a personal adventure, and will put you in touch with other people and groups concerned with workers, the environment, poverty, human rights, and global ethics. Protesting is the easiest way to express your views as a global citizen concerned with global justice and democracy. If you have never protested before, you may be surprised at how much you learn, how much fun you have, and how good you feel about yourself when you come home.

14. Get big money out of Washington. Think of Granny D. At age ninety, she got so upset about the plague of big money spoiling our democracy that she walked across the country to express her outrage and shame. I recently met Granny, and she is indeed an exceptional woman. If she can walk three thousand miles at her age, we can certainly get on the phone or in the car and link to local, state, and national groups fighting for campaign finance reform, clean elections, and control of corporate lobbyists. There are vigorous movements for clean elections in many different states as well as at the federal level—for example, Common Cause. Support candidates who pledge to support electoral and campaign finance reform, especially those who support public financing of all elections. The best way to bring democracy to the world is to make it real in the United States. In fact, this is the special opportunity and responsibility of Americans. We have dic-

tated free-market policy to the world, and if we can change our own model at home, the world will never be the same.

15. Be selective. Pick one global issue that inspires you with passion or anger or compassion. It could be AIDS in Africa, sweatshops, Third World debt, WTO policy, or global warming. Read as much as you can, and sign on to relevant Internet listservs and discussion groups. Join at least one organization that you respect for its educational work and activism on this issue. Commit at least a few hours a week to pitching in and helping them. Make a New Year's resolution to work on the issue for at least a year. Then, the following year, reevaluate, and see whether you want to continue to concentrate on this issue or expand into new ones.

16. Become an abolitionist. The great abolitionist campaign of the coming century is ending global poverty. The first step is abolishing the debt that is strangling countries from Argentina to South Africa to Pakistan. Jubilee 2000, Fifty Years Is Enough, and many other organizations are trying to get the United States and other rich countries to support abolition, especially for the world's poorest nations. Abolishing the debt is the first step for survival of many poor nations. You can help by making abolition a big issue in your community, on your campus, in your place of worship, or in your business or union. As for the larger issue of global poverty, there are hundreds of groups concerned with poverty and development in the Third World, and they are sure to exist in your community. Contact groups like Oxfam International or Caritas for more information on where to start. Many local groups start by adopting a sister neighborhood in a poor country like Haiti or El Salvador, collecting money, medical supplies, or textbooks to send for use in the adopted community.

17. Take on the iron triangle. The policies of the WTO, the IMF, and the World Bank are a global scandal. Ordinary

citizens, policy makers, and protesters are all concerned about the callousness of these institutions and their bailouts of the rich and cutbacks on the poor. Make your own voice heard in this debate. Join any of the hundreds of organizations trying to change the IMF's structural adjustment programs, boycott World Bank bonds and its massive development programs, and democratize or abolish the WTO. Get out to one of the many protests seeking to change or terminate the damaging policies of the Bretton Woods institutions. Write your congressional representative about your opposition to the current policies and these antidemocratic institutions. Get in touch with the national organization based in Washington, D.C., Public Citizen, or the San Francisco group, Global Exchange. Both have been leaders in national campaigns focused on the WTO, IMF, and World Bank.

18. Speak out against U.S. intervention and unilateralism. George W. Bush said in his campaign, during one of the presidential debates, that a Great Power should be more "humble." We need to hold him to his words. The United States should not act as global police, and it must reject unilateral interventionism, turning instead to multilateralism and collective security led by the UN and regional forces. Criticizing U.S. foreign policy can be difficult in the wake of September 11. But as more and more people ask why people hate the United States, in the Middle East and elsewhere, you should be prepared to offer answers. You can do this by reading more about American foreign policy in publications like *Z* magazine or the *Nation*, and by joining many of the peace groups critical of American unilateralism and seeking to build collective security. On nearly every foreign policy and military issue, from the Israeli-Palestinian question, to Columbia, to the U.S.-led sanctions against Iraq, there are many grassroots groups seeking to develop a different approach. You can find these groups easily by going onto the Web and looking

up listservs and chat groups on these issues. You can also go to a local university, church, or union to find people who can direct you to relevant groups. Organizations like the American Friends Service Committee have lists of groups and activities that can help you get going. Meanwhile, you can write letters to the editors about foreign policy issues you care about, and talk to all of your friends about them.

19. Close the global gap. United for a Fair Economy (UFE) is one of several important grassroots groups dedicated to public education and political activism about inequality, both at home and abroad. Based in Boston, UFE runs workshops all over the country teaching individuals how to lead popular workshops on the gap between rich and poor. The workshops are packed full of information and presented through exercises that involve all the participants. UFE also publishes a huge and entertaining set of brochures and pamphlets providing graphics and stunning visuals about inequality in the United States and the world. Members will come to your community to teach you skiils in popular education, and give you ideas about how to develop your own local activism on these issues. They have a very strong group focusing on issues of globalization and what ordinary people can do about it.

20. Take democracy seriously. Find out where your congressional representatives and senators stand on trade, aid, human rights, and other global issues. Don't let the big companies be the only constituents they hear from. Let them know very clearly about your own views. In fact, pepper them with letters, e-mails, information, and demands. Give your time, money, and vote only to candidates or elected officials who support human rights, democracy, trade reforms, and measures to alleviate debt and global poverty. Look into alternative parties or candidates who break from the official proglobalization positions of both the Republican and Democratic parties.

21. Bust the trust. Virtually every Top 200 company from Microsoft to Nike to Philip Morris is currently the target of global grassroots campaigns challenging their monopolies, political influence, global labor practices and even their charter or very existence. Don't stand on the sidelines. You might want to pick one company that gets you angry. Let members of your community know about abuses perpetrated by that corporation in your own community and in the larger world. Join local groups, including both labor and consumer groups, seeking to democratize the company and make it publicly accountable. Network with groups around the world through the Internet who are involved in campaigns against the same company in their own communities or nations. Companies care a lot about their reputations. They will pay a lot of attention if you have done your homework and collected information that can be documented. Even big companies such as Nike and Philip Morris have begun to change their policies in response to the committed work of activists around the world. In the United States, the movement for corporate accountability is growing after Enron. Now is the time to press for radical change, including public and worker representation on the board of directors, the abolition of corporate citizenship rights and of corporate protection under the Bill of Rights, and the democratization of corporate charters.

22. Bug the media. The broadcast media are legally obliged to serve the community because they use the public airwaves. And the print media are also subject to legislation requiring that they serve the public interest. Hold them accountable. Insist that they cover critical perspectives on global issues. Demand that they show protests and debates showcasing people with alternative perspectives. Write letters to local newspapers and to editors if you are bothered by the tendency of your local media to parrot official positions on global issues. Write about your own

point of view on these matters. Organize community meetings requiring media organizations to demonstrate how they are living up to the public-interest laws. And make them aware of the competition. Listen to and support alternative media. Join those trying to break the monopoly of global giants such as News Corp. or Aol Time Warner, and cut them down to size. Challenge in new corporate media monopoly as an unacceptable threat to democracy.

23. Have fun. Believe it or not, political activism can be a lot of fun. You meet interesting people and learn amazing facts. People stay committed to social activism that gives them pleasure. You have to like the people you work with. The organizations you support should feel like a community. Something is wrong if you don't feel that you are learning a lot and if you are not looking forward to planning your next project. If you are burning out, give yourself space to rest, reflect, and renew. And don't feel guilty about enjoying your activism—it is your reward for your good deeds.

24. Integrate your action into your work or profession. As a teacher and writer, it is easy for me to meld my professional activity with my social activism. I do it every day. It may be harder for you, but everyone can find a way. If you are a teacher, you can provide a curriculum on global matters to your students. If you are a college student, you have the luxury of taking courses on global issues and joining one of the many groups sure to exist on your campus about global justice. If you are a doctor, you can join one of the many socially activist medical groups trying to provide medical service abroad or change medical policy around the world, such as Doctors without Borders. If you are a manager or businessperson, link up with groups such as Business for Social Responsibility or more socially activist groups led by business leaders such as Ben and Jerry or the Body Shop's Anita Roddick. If you are a blue-collar worker, talk often with your union or fellow workers about

global issues and their relationship to your own work problems; also, strategize about how to join forces with fellow workers in other nations. If you are a journalist, take a risk by stepping out of the mainstream of your profession in your writing. If you are a lawyer, you can join with numerous groups concerned with civil liberties, constitutional rights, and representing the poor, giving as much of your own time as possible to relevant cases and clients. Your ability to use your work as a vehicle to get involved in social action is limited only by your imagination.

25. Live your values, walk your talk. Actions speak louder than words. The values that lead you to care about the issues discussed in this book are expressed in the way you relate to members of your family, your friends, and your community. If you believe in more equality and democracy, you should take these issues personally. By applying them to your own behavior, you will understand the complexities more and come to recognize the things you believe in. Ask people who know you how well you live up to or practice these values. Examine the social structures and inner limitations that keep you from living up fully to your own ideas. Analyze what keeps you from becoming more socially or politically active, and talk with people you trust and respect about how to move beyond these limits. Look closely at people who are practicing these values and integrating social activism into their lives. See what you can learn from their own successes, and let them inspire you.

NOTES

INTRODUCTION

1. "Employees in the Twin Towers," *New York Times*, September 16, 2001, p. 10.

2. Ibid.

3. The income data here are taken from data reported by the World Bank in its annual World Development Report, 2000.

4. Bill Clinton, "Clinton at Yale," October 14, 2001, cited in www.nytimes.com, p. 4.

5. "Attacks May Cost U.S. 1.8 Million Jobs," *New York Times*, January 13, 2002, p. 14.

6. Thomas L. Friedman, *The Lexus and the Olive Tree* (New York: Anchor, 2000), pp. 112–113.

7. Colin Powell, cited in Elizabeth Neuffer and Fred Kaplan, "Aid Poor to Beat Terror, Powell Says," *New York Times*, February 2, 2002, p. A6.

8. Tony Blair, Labour Party Conference at Brighton, U.K., cited in www.labour.org.uk.

9. I have changed the names of the workers to protect them from harm in their nation. The quotes from the Bangladeshi workers, here and throughout the book, are taken from personal conversation and from transcripts of their remarks sent to me by the sponsoring organization for their tour here in the United States. Again, I withhold the name of that organization to protect the workers involved.

10. Friedman, *The Lexus and the Olive Tree*, pp. xxii 104.

11. Richard Flacks, *Making History* (New York: Columbia University Press, 1988).

CHAPTER 1

1. For a discussion of the source of this and later quotations from the Bangladeshi workers, see footnote 9 in the introduction.

2. This is especially true in the Middle East, as documented in Chapter 9. See Shireen T. Hunter, *Clash of Civilizations or Peaceful Co-existence* (Westport, Conn.: Praeger, 1998).

3. A variant of this argument has been made by researchers working in the sociohistorical school known as world system theory, which I discuss more fully in Chapter 2. For an overview of world system thinking, see Immanuel Wallerstein, *The Essential Wallerstein* (New York: New Press, 2000).

4. For a biography, see Antony Thomas, *Rhodes: The Race for Africa* (New York: St. Martin's, 1997).

5. For a discussion of the relevance of the Gilded Age to the United States today, see my book, *Corporation Nation* (New York: St. Martin's, 2000).

6. For a biography of Rockefeller, see Ron Chernow, *Titan: The Life of John D. Rockefeller* (New York: Vintage, 1999). For a discussion of Gilded Age labor conditions, see Matthew Josephson, *The Robber Barons* (New York: Harvest Press, 1962).

7. For an excellent discussion of Gilded Age labor and politics, see Josephson, ibid.

8. Thomas L. Friedman, *The Lexus and the Olive Tree*, pp. 45–47.

9. Neil MacFarquhar, Bin Laden's Wildfire Threatens Might of Saudi Rulers, *New York Times*, November 6, 2001, pp. B1, B4.

10. Cited in "Cecil Rhodes: Low-Down Thief or Hero for the Nation?" Internet, Odyssey African Stage, 1999.

11. Ibid.

12. Ibid.

13. Rockefeller quote cited in Derber *Corporation Nation*, p. 27.

14. See Wendy Goldman Rohm, *Rupert Murdoch: The Digital Transformation of a Media Umpire* (New York: John Wiley, 2001).

CHAPTER 2

1. Paul Krugman, "Hearts and Heads," *New York Times*, April 22, 2001, p. A17.

2. Ricardo cited in Fernand Braudel, *The Perspective of the World*, Vol. 3 (Berkeley: University of California Press, 1992), p. 48.

3. For a readable introduction to Wallerstein's work, see Wallerstein, *The*

Essential Wallerstein. Wallerstein's most important and pioneering work on world system theory is his three-volume work, *Modern World System.* See especially the first volume, *The World System I: Capitalist Agriculture and the Origins of the European World-Economy in the Sixteenth Century* (New York: Academic, 1997). See also Wallerstein, *The Politics of the World Economy* (Cambridge: Cambridge University Press, 1984).

4. For a provocative development of these historical insights, see Christopher Chase-Dunn and Thomas D. Hall, *Core/Periphery Relations in Pre-Capitalist Worlds* (Boulder, Colo.: Westview, 1991).

5. The best discussion I have seen of the core/periphery distinction is in Chase-Dunn and Hall, ibid.

6. Ibid.

7. Ibid. See also Wallerstein, *The Essential Wallerstein.*

8. Documentation of this and all other quotations from Kernaghan can be found in reports issued by the National Labor Committee based in New York City. Go to their Web site for a list of all their publications.

9. Charles Kernaghan, *Made in China: Behind the Label* (New York: National Labor Committee, 2000).

10. Cited in Josephson, *The Robber Barons,* p. 371.

11. Sam Dillon, "Profits Raise Pressure on Border Factories," *New York Times,* February 15, pp. A1, A15.

12. For these and other dramatic data on inequality, both in the world and the United States, see Chuck Collins and Felice Yeskel, *Economic Apartheid in America* (New York: New Press, 2000).

13. These data are cited in Richard Abrams (ed.), *The Issues of the Populist and Progressive Eras* (Columbia: University of South Carolina Press, 1969), p. 33.

14. These data are drawn from the World Development Report published by the World Bank in 2000.

15. Cited in Colin Nickerson, "Melee Surrounds Trade Talks," *Boston Globe,* April 21, 2001, pp. 1, 10.

16. Quoted in ibid.

17. Cited in Howard Zinn, *A People's History of the United States* (New York: Harper and Row, 1980), p. 367.

18. See Derber, *Corporation Nation,* p. 25.

19. Josephson, *The Robber Barons,* p. 316.
20. Ralph Nader, Mark Green, and Joel Seligman, *Taming the Giant Corporation* (New York: Norton, 1976), pp. 44ff.
21. Ibid., p. 51.
22. Ibid., p. 50.
23. Richard Grossman has helped awaken us to this history. See Richard Grossman and Frank T. Adams, *Taking Care of Business* (Cambridge, Mass.: Charter Ink, 1993). See also Grossman's writings in Dean Ritz (ed.), *Defying Corporations, Defining Democracy* (New York: Apex, 2001).
24. Cited in Derber, *Corporation Nation,* p. 27.
25. Samuel Huntington, *Clash of Civilizations* (New York: Simon and Schuster, 1996.

CHAPTER 3

1. Robert Monks has used the term *corpocracy* in a different way, to describe corporations that have become unaccountable even to their own shareholders. As a shareholder activist, Monks is trying to create a corporation accountable not to citizens but investors. His usage differs from mine in being (1) a "micro" focus on corporate governance rather than societal governance and (2) a focus on empowering shareholders in the firm rather than citizens in society. See Robert Monks, "Growing Corporate Governance: From George III to George Bush," in Brenda Sutton (ed.), *The Legitimate Corporation* (Cambridge, Mass.: Basil Blackwell, 1993), pp. 165–177.
2. See Sarah Anderson and John Cavanagh, *The Top 200: The Rise of Corporate Power* (Washington, D.C.: Institute for Policy Studies, 2000). I have constructed these data from *Fortune,* "The World's Largest Corporations," July 24, 2000.
3. Ibid.
4. Scott Bowman, *The Modern Corporation and American Political Thought* (University Park, Pa.: Pennsylvania State Press), 1996.
5. I am much indebted to Gabriel Kolko's analysis of what he calls "political capitalism." His analysis of the relationship of government to business is mainly applied to the U.S. context, but it is extremely relevant to the global scene. Kolko's best work on the subject, focusing on the robber baron and Progressive eras, includes *The Triumph of Conservatism* New York: Free Press,

1963). See also *Main Currents in American History* (New York: Harper and Row, 1976).

6. See my discussion in Derber, *Corporation Nation*, pp. 129ff.

7. See Martin J. Sklar, *The Corporate Reconstruction of American Capitalism, 1890–1916* (Cambridge: Cambridge University Press, 1988). See also Derber, *Corporation Nation*, Chapters 6–8.

8. See Derber, *Corporation Nation*, ibid., especially Chapter 8 for a detailed discussion of the dependency of the corporation and all markets on public expenditures and government intervention.

9. For further discussion of the illusion, see Derber, *Corporation Nation*, ibid.

10. Sara Anderson and John Cavanagh with Thea Lee, *Field Guide to the Global Economy* (New York: New Press, 2000), pp. 16, 33. This is an invaluable and easily accessible guide to the way the global economy works. The last quote is drawn from Walden Bello, Nicola Bullard, and Kamal Malhotra, *Global Finance* (Dhaka: University Press in association with Zed Books, London, 2000), p. 5.

11. Thomas Friedman, *The Lexus and the Olive Tree*, pp. 105, 107.

12. The evidence about growth is reviewed in detail in the section on "Popeye Economics" in Chapter 4 (see p. 89).

13. Belloet al, Global Finance. Op. cit.

14. Ibid.

15. Anderson and Cavanagh, *The Top 200*. See also Anderson and Cavanagh, *Field Guide to the Global Economy*.

16. See Josh Karliner, *The Corporate Planet* (Sierra Club Books, 1997). See also David Korten, *When Corporations Rule the World*, 2nd ed. (San Francisco: Berrett Kohler, 2001).

17. Diane Vaughan, *Uncoupling* (New York: Vintage, 1990).

18. Leslie Sklair, *The Trans-National Capitalist Class*, Oxford: Blackwell, 2001), p. 75. This issue is explored richly throughout Sklair's work.

19. Ibid., p. 50.

20. Bennett Harrison, *Lean and Mean* (New York: Basic Book, 1994).

21. Mark A. Jamison, "Emerging Patterns in Global Telecommunications Alliances and Mergers," New York Law School Communications Media Center, 2000.

22. Harrison, *Lean and Mean*, especially pp. 136ff.

23. See also Derber, *Corporation Nation*, Chapter 2.

24. Ibid.

25. This is the theme of Thomas Frank's *One Market under God* (New York: Anchor, 2001).

CHAPTER 4

1. Such views about globalization as an American-led system of rich nations exploiting poor ones have been expressed routinely by leaders of poor nations in recent decades. The interesting new development after September 11 has been the rise of similar concerns in rich nations themselves. At the 2002 meetings of the Davos World Economic Forum, hardly a place where such views would be expected, many European leaders and even some American corporate leaders expressed concerns of this nature. A French scholar at the WEF meetings expressed some of the sentiment at a panel on "global anger." His studies suggested that global perception "is reducing the creation of good while creating private wealth: that the process is biased against the poor; and that this agenda is shaped by the United States . . . without any tolerance for alternative prescriptions." This and other perceptions of this nature, now spreading from the developing nations to the rich ones, are sometimes shared by business leaders themselves. In the same WEF meetings, Bill Gates said, "We need discussion about whether the rich world is giving back what it should in the developing world. I think there is a legitimate question whether we are." Reported in Serge Schemann, "Where McDonald's Sits Down with Arab Nationalists," *New York Times*, February 2, 2002, p. A8.

2. In most games, rules can be interpreted so that they apply differently to some players than to others. The "globalization game" falls on the far side of this spectrum, where the rules are fluid and manipulable. Double standards—where some play by one set of rules and some by others—are also part of the game. This reflects specific aspects of the globalization game: (1) those who make and interpret the rules are also players, (2) the game is new, and rules are thus not fully crystallized, (3) vast inequalities of power distinguish the various players, and (4) the technical rule-setting bodies, such as the WTO, are themselves subject to disproportionate influence by the most powerful players.

3. While I have coined the term *Popeye economics*, I am only paraphrasing

the story line of the prevailing defenders and ideologues of the current global economy, including those who have criticisms of the system. Thomas Friedman, for example, rests his whole argument for globalization on the premise of growth mediated through the Popeye model, though he recognizes there will be losers as well as winners. See Thomas L. Friedman, *The Lexus and the Olive Tree.*

4. I rely heavily on data drawn from the World Bank in this discussion, despite many criticisms of its methodology by analysts who dispute the Bank's approach. I am thus relying on conservative data sources, although I have also presented much of the counterargument and other interpretations of the data developed by the critics. See *The World Development Report, 2000/2001: Attacking Poverty* (New York: Oxford University Press, 2000), p. 64. See Chapters 4 and 5 for a discussion of the data presented here. See also the report prepared for the G8 summit on global poverty, which has useful global data on world poverty: "Global Poverty Report," G8 Okinawa Summit, July 2000, photocopy.

5. Mark Weisbrot, Robert Naimon, and Joyce Kim, "The Emperor Has No Growth: Declining Economic Growth Rates in the Era of Globalization," Center for Economic and Policy Research, Washington, D.C., Briefing Paper, September 26, 2000, especially pp. 9–12.

6. Scott draws much of the data in his tables from the World Bank and other official sources. For a discussion of these data, see Bruce Scott, "Sovereign but Unequal: The Great Divide in the Global Village" (unpublished manuscript). I want to thank Scott for providing me with his data, and for the personal communication we have had about it.

7. Ibid. See also Sarah Anderson, John Cavanagh, and Thea Lee, *Field Guide to the Global Economy* (New York: New Press, 2000). See also Jeff Faux and Larry Mishel, "Inequality and the Global Economy," in Will Hutton and Anthony Giddens (eds.), *Global Capitalism* (New York: New Press, 2000), pp. 93–111.

8. For a powerful argument elaborating the political and structural problems internal to poor countries—and one arguing that these are central to the growth problem, see David Easterly, *The Elusive Quest for Growth* (Cambridge, Mass.: MIT Press, 2001).

9. These arguments are made powerfully by researchers at the World Bank.

Contact David Dollar at the World Bank for some of the most cogent World Bank reports documenting these "success stories." See also the relevant discussions in *The World Development Report, 2000/2001*, Chapters 4 and 5.

10. David Sanger, *New York Times*, July 25, 2001, p. A6

11. For a discussion of the democratic crisis of corporate globalization, see William I. Robinson, *Promoting Polyarchy* (Cambridge: Cambridge University Press, 1996). See also Derber, *Corporation Nation*.

12. See Scott R. Bowman, *The Modern Corporation and American Political Thought* (University Park, Pa.: Penn State University, 1996).

13. Walden Bello is one of the most cogent Third World critics of globalization as an American-designed project. Bello has fired off a set of papers over recent years that have circulated on the Internet and helped inspire global justice activists. A full list of his publications can be found on the Web site of Focus on the Global South, the institute in Bangkok, Thailand, which he directs. His books include Walden Bello et al. (eds.) *Global Finance*, and Walden Bello and Anuradha Mittal (eds.), *The Future in the Balance* (San Francisco: Food First, 2001). See also Walden Bello et al. (eds.), *Dark Victory: The United States and Global Poverty* (San Francisco: Food First, 1999).

14. Bello and Mittal, *The Future in the Balance*. See also Bello et al., *Dark Victory*, and Walden Bello, "Blowback": A Review Essay on an Academic Defector's Guide to America's Asia Policy," 2001, photocopy, p. 4.

15. This argument is developed forcefully in many of Bello's recent papers. See Walden Bello, "U.S. Imperialism in the Asia-Pacific," *Peace Review* 10:3 (1998), 367–373. The quote on "missionary idealism" is drawn from Bello's provocative review of Chalmers Johnson's book *Blowback*. Walden Bello, " 'Blowback': A Review Essay."

16. Quotations cited in Derber, *Corporation Nation*, p. 287.

17. Chalmers Johnson. *Blowback* (New York: Henry Holt, 2001).

18. Ibid., p. 213.

CHAPTER 5

1. For a powerful historical analysis, see Fred L. Block, *The Origins of International Economic Disorder* (Berkeley: University of California Press, 1977).

2. Ibid. Block's is one of the most useful of many accounts of the founding and evolution of Bretton Woods. See also A. L. K. et al. (eds.), *Bretton Woods*

Revisited (Toronto: University of Toronto Press, 1972). See also C. P. Kindleberger, *Balance of Payments Deficits and the International Market for Liquidity* (Princeton: Princeton University Press, 1965).

3. The notion that globalization draws heavily on U.S. constitutional principles is also developed provocatively by Michael Hardt and Antonio Negri. I have been stimulated by their analysis, although I offer a very different constitutional interpretation. See Michael Hardt and Antonio Negri, *Empire* (Cambridge: Harvard University Press, 2000). My thinking about the Constitution has also been influenced by Bruce Ackerman's magisterial three-volume analysis of American constitutional history. See especially Bruce Ackerman, *We the People*, Vol. 1 (Cambridge: Harvard University Press, 1991).

4. The critic who has made this argument most clear to me is Lori Wallach, the tireless leader of Public Citizen, whose works on the WTO have helped shape the global justice movements. See especially Lori Wallach and Michelle Sforza, *Whose Trade Organization?* (Washington, D.C.: Public Citizen, 1999). Concepts of constitutionalism in world affairs have been much discussed by theorists of sovereignty and global constitutionalism. See, for example, Stephen Gill, "Theorizing the Interregnum," which explicitly discusses ideas of constitutionalism in global politics. See Gill in Bjorn Hettne (ed.), *International Political Economy: Understanding Global Disorder* (London: Zed Books, 1995).

5. Max Lerner, "John Marshall and the Campaign of History," in Edward Levy, *American Constitutional Law: Historical Essays* (New York: Harper, 1966), pp. 49–89, 64, 65. Lerner's account of the conflict between Jefferson and Marshall is riveting, as is his focus on Marshall's immense importance in privileging the role of property and contract in the American Constitution.

6. See Richard Falk's many books on the rise of global human rights and constitutionalism expressing a Jeffersonian democratic vision. A recent book is Richard Falk, *Human Rights Horizons* (New York: Routledge, 2000).

7. The 1948 Universal Declaration of Human Rights can be found on the UN's Wet site and in numerous other sources. Adopted by General Assembly Resolution 217A (III) on December 10, 1948, everyone should read the Declaration. For an analysis of the long struggle between conflicting trends in American constitutionalism, see Edward Levy (ed.), *American Constitutional Law Historical Essays*. The essay by Max Lerner is especially useful.

8. See Falk, *Human Rights Horizons*.

9. Block, *The Origins of International Economic Disorder*. See especially Chapter 3.

10. Ibid. The discussion of the views of both Keynes and White is exceptionally valuable here. See especially Chapter 3.

11. Ibid, Chapters 6–8.

12. My discussion of this period—and the role of UNCTAD—has been strongly influenced by the writings of Walden Bello. Some of his most accessible essays can be found in Kevin Danaher and Roger Burbach (eds.) *Globalize This!* (Monroe, Me.: Common Courage Press, 2000). For more detailed, scholarly discussion, see Bello et al., *Global Finance*, especially Chapter 1.

13. Ibid.

14. Susan George, *The Debt Boomerang* (London: Pluto Press, 1999).

15. Jeffrey Sachs, "The IMF and the Asian Flu," *American Prospect*, March/April 1998 (16–21), pp. 17, 21. See also Robert Weissman, "Twenty Questions on the IMF," in Kevin Danaher (ed.), *Democratizing the Global Economy* (Monroe, Me.: Common Courage Press, 2001), pp. 84–99. Danaher's book is a good general source of critical information on the IMF, as is his earlier work, Danaher (ed.) *Fifty Years Is Enough. Op. cit.*

16. Bello et al., *Global Finance*.

17. "How U.S. Wooed Asia to Let Cash Flow In," *New York Times,* February 16, 1999. UNCTAD quote taken from Bello et al., *Global Finance*, p. 5.

18. My discussion on the WTO draws heavily on the work of Lori Wallach. See Wallach and Sforza, *Whose Trade Organization?* For a briefer version, see Lori Wallach and Michelle Sforza, *The WTO* (New York: Seven Stories Press, 1999).

19. See Wallach and Sforza, *The WTO*, for a detailed discussion of the Venezuelan clean-air case.

20. Ibid., p. 21.

21. The discussion on Locke should be qualified by the focus on corporate constitutionalism in the WTO. Locke was focused on property more broadly, especially personal property. The shift from personal to corporate property evolved in American constitutionalism in the late nineteenth century, and this history is useful in understanding WTO constitutionalism. For an analysis of how Lockeanism became a system of corporate contract protection in the revolution of late nineteenth-century American constitutionalism, see Martin

Sklar, *The Corporate Reconstruction of American Capitalism* (Cambridge: Cambridge University Press, 1995).

22. Beard's point about the history of American protectionism is made in Charles Beard, *The Rise of American Civilization* (New York: Macmillan, 1941), pp. 664ff. In virtually all his work on political economy and the world order, Noam Chomsky has stressed the "double standards" governing the global "free-market" discourse, with rich companies supporting "free trade" and "free markets" while often practicing precisely the opposite. See Noam Chomsky, *Rogue States* (Boston: South End Press, 2000), pp. 199ff.

23. On U.S. Gilded Age constitutionalism, see Derber, *Corporation Nation*, Chapter 6, pp. 129ff.

24. Wallach and Sforza, *Whose Trade Organization?*, pp. 112ff.

25. Ibid., pp. 14, 17

26. Ibid., pp. 25ff; pp. 29ff.

27. Ibid., pp. 60–66.

28. Ibid., pp. 161ff.

CHAPTER 6

1. In an editorial opinion, after reviewing early rules imposed by the attorney general after September 11, the *New York Times* raises serious questions about the survival of basic civil liberties in the United States. See "Disappearing in America," *New York Times*, November 10, 2001, p. A22.

2. At the meetings of the 2002 World Economic Forum in New York City, business leaders expressed a strong new commitment to social standards, and they expressed strong concern about the need to solve global poverty as a condition for stable business conditions in poor nations.

3. Melinda Henneberger, "Bishops in Rome Juggle Issues of Poverty and Terror," *New York Times*, October 28, 2001, p. A4.

4. Tony Blair, Labour Party Conference, Brighton, 2001. Bill Clinton, "Clinton at Yale."

5. Jeremy Brecher and Tim Costello have laid out a global alternative reflecting one variant of the "UN camp" in *Globalization from Below* (Boston: South End Press, 2000).

6. The distinguished Princeton scholar Richard Falk has written extensively on the international legal system, the UN tradition of human rights, and its

relevance for globalization and global governance. See Richard Falk, *The Human Rights Horizon* (New York: Routledge, 2000).

7. See Brecher and Costello, *Globalization from Below* and *Global Village or Global Pillage?* See also Amory Starr, *Naming the Enemy* (London: Zed Books, 2000). Starr gives an excellent description of the different global justice movements. For her description of the movements focusing on universal human rights, including labor rights, see especially Chapter 2.

8. See Starr, *Naming the Enemy*, for an outstanding discussion of the localists within the global justice movements. See especially Chapters 4 and 5.

9. For one of the most attractive variants of this perspective, see David Korten, *The Post-Corporate World* (San Francisco: Berrett-Koehler Press, 1999). See also Michael Shuman, *Going Local* (New York: Free Press, 1998).

10. Starr offers a comprehensive discussion of the ideological roots of the antiglobalization localists. See Starr, *Naming the Enemy*.

11. This democratic spirit of the global justice movements has been stressed by Kevin Danaher in a series of books. See especially Danaher and Burbach, *Globalize This!* See also Kevin Danaher (ed.), *Democratizing the Global Economy* (Monroe, Me.: Common Courage Press, 2001).

12. For a discussion of this pluralistic approach to global governance, see Walden Bello, "Reforming the WTO Is the Wrong Agenda," in Kevin Danaher and Roger Burbach (eds.), *Democratize This!*, especially pp. 117ff. See also the essays in John W. Foster and Anita Annand (eds.), *Whose World Is It Anyway?* (Ottawa: United Nations Association in Canada, 1999).

13. See Starr, *Naming the Enemy*, Chapters 4–5.

14. For a discussion of these labor developments, see Brecher and Costello, *Global Pillage or Global Pillage?*, and Brecher and Costello, *Globalization from Below*.

15. For an account of the democratic possibilities of a globalizing civil society, see Benjamin Barber, *Jihad vs. McWorld*. See also Richard Falk and Andrew Strauss, "Toward Global Parliament," *Foreign Affairs*, January/February 2001, vol. 80, no. 1.

16. See Brecher and Costello, *Globalization from Below*, pp. 42–43.

17. Ibid., p. 43.

18. This is the central theme of William Robinson, *Promoting Polyarchy* (Cambridge: Cambridge University Press, 1996).

19. For a detailed discussion of democratizing the economy and corporations in the United States, see Derber, *Corporation Nation.*

CHAPTER 7

1. Most global democrats have emphasized exactly this point. See Jeremy Brecher and Tim Costello, *Globalization from Below* Op. cit., especially pp. 40ff. The same argument is made by Richard Falk, who coined the term "globalization from below." See Falk in his more recent work, *Human Rights Horizons.* Op. cit. Walden Bello has also made this argument about a pluralistic world of international governance authorities, arguing that we need a decentralized system more similar to the pre-WTO era. See Bello's essays, "Reforming the WTO Is the Wrong Agenda" and "UNCTAD" in Danaher and Burbach, *Globalize This!* Op. cit.
2. The International Forum on Globalization (IFG) has drafted a report highlighting the need for "decomission" and replacement of the existing Bretton Woods structure with new UN bodies such as a reformed and refurbished UNCTAD. See International Forum on Globalization, *Economic Alternatives to Globalization* (San Fransisco: Berrett-Koehler Publisher, 2002). See also David Korten, *When Corporations Rule the World* (2nd ed.) San Fransisco: Berrett-Koehler Publishers). On the shift from property to human rights standards, especially in the WTO, see Lori Wallach and Michelle Sforza, *Whose Trade Organization?* Op. cit.
3. Numerous global democrats have made this argument for global regulation. On capital flow regulation, see expecially William Greider, *One World, Ready or Not.* Op. cit., pp. 317ff. See also Brecher and Costello, *Globalization from Below.* Op. cit. The problem of unregulated capital flows—and the need for regulation—are central arguments in analysts of the 1998 Asian crisis. See Walden Bellow, Nicola Bullard, and Kamal Malhotra (eds.) *Global Finance: New Thinking on Regulating Speculative Capital Markets* (London: Zed Books, 2000).
4. Fischer and Stiglitz cited in Louis Uchitelle, "IMF May Be Closer to Lending-Curb Idea," *New York Times,* February 2, 1998, p. D4. Nobelist economist Joseph Stiglitz brings a professional economist's critique to radical financial deregulation and argues for new capital controls. But these cannot

be easily exercised unilaterally, as Malaysia found over the longer term. We thus need international agreements that build regulations on capital flow within the larger system in a way that applies to all nations. The argument for global financial regulation has also been made strongly by George Soros, *George Soros on Globalization* (New York: Public Affairs, 2002). For a summary of Joseph Stiglitz's recommendations, which include deep reforms in the Bretton Woods triumverate and systemic changes in global regulation, see Joseph Stiglitz, *Globalization and Its Discontents* (New York: Norton, 2002).

5. Greider, One World. Op. cit., p. 317.

6. Richard McCormick, "Letter to President Clinton," January 13, 1997. Cited in Derber, *Corporation Nation.* Op. cit., p. 287.

7. Greider, *One World.* Op. cit. See also Greider's columns in the *Nation,* that address this issue on a periodic basis. See also Shannon O'Callaghan, "Healthier Global Competition," unpublished manuscript, Boston, May 6, 1999.

8. Jeremy Brecher, Dennis Brutus, Tim Costello and Brendan Smith, *One, Two, Three Many Argentinas?* (mimeo, 2002).

9. Joseph Kahn, "United States Rejects Bid to Double Foreign Aid to Poor Lands" *New York Times,* January 29, 2002, p. A11.

10. Ibid.

11. Cited in Gerard Coffey, "Argentina," Focus on Trade, 74.

12. Phil Gusson, Jimmy Langman, Mac Margolis, and Alan Zarembo, *Who Lit the Match? Newsweek,* January 14, 2002, pp. 35–37, 36.

13. This discussion and the concrete proprosals for institutional development are drawn from International Forum on Globalization, *Economic Alternatives to Globalization.* Op. cit., Chapter 7.

14. See IFG, *Econonic Alternatives to Globalization.* Ibid.

15. Hazel Henderson, *Beyond Globalization* (West Hartford, Conn.: Kumarian Press, 1999). pp. 24ff.

16. Ibid.

17. Wachtel cited in Derber, *Corporation Nation.* Op. cit., p. 279. For Falk's discussion of the "democratic deficit," see Falk and Andrew Strauss, "Toward Global Parliament," *Foreign Affairs.* Op. cit. For a more detailed account, see Richard Falk and Andrew Strauss, "On the Creation of a Global Peoples Assembly," *Stanford Journal of International Law,* vol. 36, no. 2, 2000.

18. See Derber, *Corporation Nation.* Op. cit., pp. 276–279.

19. Richard Falk and Andrew Strauss, "Toward Global Parliament." Op. cit., pp. 215ff. I draw heavily on the stimulating work of Falk and Strauss in the discussion that follows in the rest of this chapter. For an enlightening discussion that is very critical of the UN partnerships with business and the new Global Compact initiated by Annan, see TRAC: Transational Research and Action Center, "Tangled Up in Blue: Corporate Partnerships at the UN" (pamplet, September 2000).

20. Richard Falk and Andrew Strauss. "On the Creation." Op. cit. pp. 199ff.

21. Ibid. "Toward Global Parliament." Op. cit., p. 214.

22. Falk and Strauss, "On the Creation." Op. cit. p. 208–209

23. Ibid., pp 205fn.

24. Richard Falk and Andrew Strauss, "Toward Global Parliament." Op. cit., p. 220.

25. Terry Collingsworth, "A Proposal for an Enforcement Mechanism for the Social Clause" (Washington D.C.: International Labor Rights Fund, 2002). I want to thank Terry Collingsworth for ideas here in personal conversation as well as his articles about the legal mechanisms of the social clause.

CHAPTER 8

1. Larry Rohter, "Argentina's Crisis: It's Not Just Money," *New York Times,* January 13, 2002, p. 4.

2. Ibid. See Robert D. Kaplan, *The Coming Anarchy* (New York: Vintage, 2000).

3. For a discussion of this democratic crisis, with special focus on the problems created by American foreign policy and the U.S. "democracy" initiatives in the last two decades, see William Robinson, Polyarchy. Op. cit.

4. Peter Katel, Meltdown, *Time* (Latin American edition), January 14, 2002, 12–16, p. 16.

5. Thomas L. Friedman, *The Lexus and the Olive Tree.* Op. cit., p. 106.

6. This is the theme of Charles Derber, *Corporation Nation.* Op. cit.

7. I draw heavily here on the discussion in international Forum on Globalization, *Economic Alternatives to Globalization.* Op. cit., Chapter 5. See also David Korten, *When Corporations Rule the World.* (2nd. ed). Op. cit. and my own work, *Corporation Nation.* Op. cit. Chapter 13.

8. *Economic Alternatives to Globalization.* Op. cit. See *Also Corporation Nation,* Chapter 8.

9. *Corporation Nation.* Ibid., Chapters 5, 12.

10. Korten has written two major works on this subject, both very important. See David Korten, *When Corporations Rule the World* (2nd ed.) (San Fransisco, CA: Berrett-Koehler Publishers, 2001). Op. cit. See also Korten, *The Post-Corporate World.* Op. cit.

11. See Korten, Ibid.

12. See Dean Ritz (ed.) *Defying Corporations, Defining Democracy.* (New York: Program Corporations, Law and Democracy in collaboration with Apex Press, 2001). The book includes both a discussion of charter reform and of current activist projects dedicated to achieving it.

13. Derber, *Corporation Nation.* Op. cit. especially Chapters. 1, 2, 13.

14. For the best recent review of charter reforms, and particularly the pioneering perspectives advanced by Richard Grossman see Dean Ritz (ed.) *Defying Corporations, Defining Democracy.* (New York: Program Corporations, Law and Democracy in collaboration with Apex Press, 2001). See also Lori Wallach and Michelle Sforzo, *The WTO.* Op. cit. See also Korten, *When Corporations Rule the World* (2nd ed.), Ibid.

15. Ralph Nader, Mark Green, and Joel Seligman, *Taming the Giant Corporation.* (New York: Norton, 1976).

16. The UN initiative is deeply flawed by its lack of any UN disclosure or enforcement mechanisms. It has thus rightfully become the object of controversy and anger among many supporters of the UN who fear its capture by global corporate interests.

17. Derber, *Corporation Nation.* Op. cit., Chapter 13.

18. This case was made in the early 1990s by Lester Thurow, *Head to Head* (New York: Morrow, 1992). See also Derber, *Corporation Nation.* Ibid.

19. The posture of the U.S. labor movement is discussed in Jeremy Brecher and Tim Costello, *Globalizing from Below.* Op. cit. See also Derber, Ibid., Chapter 15.

20. Naomi Klein has both inspired and chronicled the activism of anti-consumerist, anticorporate young activists—and older ones too! See her *No Logo.* (New York: St. Martin's Press, 2000).

21. Barber developed his influential perspective initially in *Strong Democracy.* Berkeley, CA: University of California Press, 1984. Barber has put this perspective in a global context in *Jihad vs. McWorld* (New York: Ballantine, 1996).

22. Robert Putnam, *Bowling Alone* (New York: Touchstone, 2001).

23. Barber has already begun this kind of thinking in *Jihad vs. McWorld*. Op. cit. It is one of the important works to conceive the role of civil society and local participation in a globalized world.

24. Nancy DellaMattera and Jennifer Gaudet, "Coming to a Town Near You," Northeast Labor Committee for Global Justice, 2001 (mimeo).

25. See Amory Starr, *Naming the Enemy*. Op. cit. for a detailed elaboration of how localists are actually implementing such strategies. See especially Chapters 4 and 5.

26. This argument is made forcefully and persuasively—with many concrete activist initiatives chronicled—in Stacy Mitchell, *The Home Town Advantage* (Washington D.C.: Institute for Local Self-Reliance, 2000).

27. Daryl McGrath, "Funding Loss Puts Buffalo in Fiscal Crisis," *Globe*, November 24, 2001, p. A10.

28. As always, Lori Wallach is the best guide to these issues. See Lori Wallach and Michelle Sforzo, *Whose Trade Organization?* Op. cit.

29. This kind of argument is being developed by many democracy theorists. Among the most important are Benjamin Barber, *Jihad vs. McWorld*. Op. cit. See also Richard Falk, *Human Rights Horizons*. Op. cit. Also Richard Falk and Andrew Strauss, "Toward Global Parliament," *Foreign Affairs*. Op. cit.

30. Joseph Nye, *The Paradox of American Power* (forthcoming). Nye and Rice cited in H. D. S. Greenway, "The United States Can't Go It Alone" *Boston Globe*, January 25, 2002, p. A22.

31. Thomas Friedman, "Run Osama Run," New York Times, January 23, 2002, p. A23.

32. Among the most powerful and influential arguments for thinking of the United States as Empire, Noam Chomsky's works stand out, although he rarely uses the term. See, most recently, Noam Chomsky, *Rogue States* (Boston: South End Press, 2000). For a powerful argument explicitly making the argument about Empire, see Chalmers Johnson, *Blowback* (New York: Henry Holt, 2000).

33. Thomas L. Friedman, "Run Osama Run." Op. cit.

34. Among the best writers on collective security are Robert Johansen and Richard Falk. See Johansen, "Lessons for Collective Security," Review. (Binghamton, New York: *Journal of the Fernand Braudel Center*, 1992). See Richard Falk, *Human Rights Horizons*. Op. cit.

35. Quotes by Abram and Kirkpatrick cited in Noam Chomsky, *Rogue States.*

Op. cit., p. 134. Chomsky's entire essay here, "The U.S. and the Challenge of Universality" as well as the essay, "Recovering Rights"—Chapters 10 and 9—are both eye-opening.

36. William Blum, *Rogue State* (Monroe, Me.: Common Courage Press, 2000). pp. 184–199.

37. Paul Kennedy, *The Rise and Fall of the Great Powers* (New York: Vintage, 1989).

CHAPTER 9

1. For other firsthand accounts of the Seattle protests, see Danaher and Burbach, *Globalize This!* See, especially, Chapter 1 by Paul Hawken, "Skeleton Woman Visits Seattle."

2. For an excellent discussion of the relationship between labor and environmental groups, see Brecher and Costello, *Globalization from Below*, especially Chapter 4.

3. For a useful history of left dissent in twentieth century, see Flacks, *Making History*. For a discussion of the sixties movements and some of their problems leading to the second wave, see Flacks and also Wini Breines, *Community and Organization in the New Left, 1962–68* (South Hadley, Mass.: Bergin and Garvey, 1982). See also Gitlin, *The Sixties*.

4. The literature on identity movements is vast. See Stanley Aronowitz, *The Politics of Identity* (New York: Routledge, 1992). See also the discussion in Charles Derber, *What's Left?* (Amherst: University of Massachusetts Press, 1995), especially the coauthored chapter with Cassie Schwerner, "Beyond Socialism and Identity Politics," for a discussion of identity politics in the context of the historical evolution discussed here.

5. Naomi Klein has been the most provocative writer on the organization of the Seattle movements. See Klein, "The Vision Thing," *The Nation,* July 10, 2000, 18–21. The idea of the "swarm" has been explicitly and provocatively discussed by Brecher and Costello as part of the "self-organization from below" characterizing the Seattle movements. See Brecher and Costello, *Globalization from Below*, Chapter 7.

6. For a discussion of many of these issues, see Klein, "The Vision Thing." See also Danaher and Burbach, *Globalize This!*, especially the essays by Hawken,

"Skeleton Woman Visits Seattle," and Starhawk, "How We Really Shut Down the WTO."

7. I must reiterate strongly that this is not a call to stop mass protests. They have been stunningly successful, and they need to be sustained. I am simply arguing that they need to be connected to institutionalized actors who can (1) help sustain the protests and (2) help translate their demands into policy.

8. See Walden Bello, "WSF Sets stage for Counteroffensive against Globalization," 2001. www.protoalegre2002.org/publique/cgi/public/cgilua.exe/web/templates/htm/. Bello offers a graphic picture of the alternative "social summit" paralleling the New York World Economic Forum of elites at the end of January 2002.

9. My entire discussion of ATTAC draws heavily on a paper by Marcos Ancelovici, "Organizing against Globalization: The Case of Attac in France" (photocopy, Dept. of Political Science, MIT, draft, June 3, 2001).

10. Cited in Marcos Ancelovici Ancelovici, "Organizing against Globalization."

11. Brecher and Costello, *Globalization from Below*, pp. 104–105. Brecher and Costello have a a useful discussion of the relationship of mass protests to institutionalized parties and NGOs.

12. Naomi Klein, in personal communication, has clarified this interpretation of the meaning of the agreement on pharmaceutical patents reached at Qatar.

13. For other firsthand accounts of the feelings on the streets, and the role of violence by police and protesters, see the essays in Danaher and Burbach, *Globalize This!*

14. This account is based on my own experience in Seattle that day, as well as on successive days.

15. For a discussion of the Genoa police violence, see David Graeber, "Among the Thugs: Genoa and the New Language of Protest," *In These Times*, September 3, 2001, pp. 14–16. In the same edition of *In These Times*, see also Geov Parrish, "One Dead in Genoa: The Movement and Its Martyr," pp. 17–19.

16. I suspect that Marcuse's book would once again be a manifesto of many protesters if it were put into a new edition and made available at the protests. See Herbert Marcuse, *One-Dimensional Man* (Boston: Beacon Press, 1992).

17. This is based on my own personal observation of students and other young people I have worked with or talked to at the protests. They are driven

by spirit and visceral emotions, but they are also hungry to learn and have often read extensively about globalization and foreign policy.

18. See Brecher and Costello, *Globalization from Below*, pp. 93ff, for a discussion of polling data on the U.S. public's attitudes toward globalization. More recent polls, released in January 2002, showed a bare majority of the American public supporting current globalization and far less support in Europe and Third World nations, where more than 50 percent see harmful effects as very significant.

19. The *Business Week* poll was conducted by *Business Week* and the Harris Poll in 2000. See the full data reports in *Business Week*, "Do Corporations Have Too Much Power?" September 11, 2000.

20. See Derber, *Corporation Nation*, Chapters 9 and 13, for a discussion of "positive populism." This seeks to link a radical critique of corporate power with support of the need for business that is democratically accountable.

21. I have learned much on these issues from Mike Prokosch, an artist, thinker, and activist who helped design the Billionaires for Bush skit and related humorous street theater, which helped make the protests a life-affirming process for both participants and spectators.

22. See especially Korten, *When Corporations Rule the World*, and his more recent book, *The Post-Corporate World*. See also Amory Starr, *Naming the Enemy*, for a vivid description of the many localist farm and business strategies being envisioned and practiced in the movements.

23. Mitchell, *The Home Town Advantage*. For skeptics, this is a very persuasive and concrete account of local business alternatives.

24. Many of these initiatives have been deeply flawed, including the FLA and the global compact. Numerous observers have documented the flaws of the FLA, including Charles Kernaghan in reports issued by the National Labor Committee in New York City. Jeff Ballinger, a longtime labor analyst and critic of monitoring and disclosure, is also a fountain of information on the deep flaws at the core of FLA monitoring and disclosure arrangements. Contact him at the Kennedy School of Government at Harvard University. A critique of the UN's global compact—one that is devastating—is found in TRAC, "Tangled Up in Blue."

25. See my discussion of corporate social responsibility in Derber, *Corporation Nation*, Chapter 12.

26. Ibid.

27. See Brecher and Costello, *Globalization from Below*, pp. 53ff, for an important discussion of reconciling North/South perspectives, especially the interests of labor groups in the North and South.

28. All of us are indebted to Charles Kernaghan and Barbara Briggs, who direct the National Labor Committee in New York City, for their tireless effort to bring the voices of Third World worker and labor groups to the United States and elsewhere in the developed world. You can write the NLC for videos, brochures, and papers on the transnational labor campaigns they have successfully promoted over recent years, including the Bangladeshi one in 2001.

29. Jeremey Brecher and Tim Costello have been tireless voices promoting this trend toward international solidarity in the AFL-CIO and its member unions. Evidence of the AFL-CIO shift was a parallel event sponsored by the federation on global labor rights issues while corporate elites were meeting at the WEF in New York City in 2002. Richard Tumpka, second in command to Sweeney in the AFL-CIO, hosted a meeting on global labor conditions with workers from Central America, China, and other parts of the world, including the United States.

30. Evidence for the entire argument in this chapter is provided in an in-depth story in *Business Week* about the shift away from markets toward government activism in the Bush administration, especially after September 11. See the cover story, "Rethinking the Economy," *Business Week*, October 1, 2001, pp. 28–42.

31. Ibid.

32. Ibid.

33. Ibid. See especially, "What Kind of Rescue?," pp. 36–37.

34. For a systematic analysis of this trend, which has dominated American politics well before the Bush administration and the Enron crisis, see Derber, *Corporation Nation*, Chapter 8. See also Ralph Nader, *Cutting Corporate Welfare* (New York: Seven Stories Press, 2000).

35. See Joseph Kahn, "Price of Bush's Trade Powers? Protectionism," *New York Times*, December 8, 2001, p. C1.

CHAPTER 10

1. Charles Derber, *The Wilding of America* (2nd ed.) (New York: Worth Publishers, 2001).

2. Noam Chomsky, Znet Commentary. Internet.Znet Commentary, September 21, 16:11:59, 2001.

3. The best discussion of blowback is in Chalmers Johnson, *Blowback*. Op. cit.

4. Powell cited in Elizabeth Neuffer and Fred Kaplan, "Aid Poor to Beat Terror, Powell, says," *New York Times*, February 2, 2002, p. A6.

5. Arroyo cited in Ibid.

6. Rena Singer, "Feeling at risk, leaders toughen laws," *Boston Globe*, October 15, 2001, p. A6.

7. Serge Schemann, "Leaders Seek to Discern Root Causes of Violence," *New York Times*, November 11, 2001, p. B2.

8. Tim Weiner, "A Bazaar Is Newly Abuzz and the Talk Is of a New Era: After the Taliban, What?" *New York Times*, November 29, 2001, P. B5.

9. Ibid.

10. Yvonne Daley, "The Ugly American (still)," *Boston Globe Magazine*, (December 2, 2001), pp. 12ff, p. 22.

11. Tim Weiner, "A Bazaar Is Newly Abuzz and the Talk Is of a New Era," Op. cit.

12. Shireen Hunter, *The Future of Islam and the West*. Op. cit., p. 166. Benjamin Barber, *Jihad vs. McWorld*. Op. cit., p. 209.

13. Douglas Jehl, "Democracy's Uneasy Steps in Islamic World," *New York Times,* November 23, 2001, pp. A1, 10.

14. Jonathan Wells, Jack Meyers, and Maggie Mulvihill, "U.S. Ties to Saudi Elite May Be Hurting War on Terrorism," *Boston Herald*, December 10, 2001, pp. 1, 6–7.

15. Thomas Friedman, "Today's News Quiz," *New York Times,* November 20, 2001, p. A19.

16. Ibid.

17. Roja Mohan is cited in Friedman, Ibid.

18. For the source of these and following quotes from the Bangladeshi workers, see the Introduction.

19. The overproduction problem and the need for higher demand is made in brilliant detail by William Greider, *One World, Ready or Not* (New York: Simon and Schuster, 1997).

20. All the quotes in this paragraph are taken from Samuel P. Huntington, *The Clash of Civilizations* (New York: Simon and Schuster, 1997), p. 214.

21. Shireen Hunter, *The Future of Islam and the West.* Op. cit., p. 20. Fuller quote cited in Hunter, p. 21.

22. Noam Chomsky, Znet commentary. Op. cit. See also Noam Chomsky, *9–11* (New York: Seven Stories Press, 2001), especially pp. 34ff.

23. Benjamin Barber, *Jihad vs. McWorld.* Op. cit., p. 210.

24. Samuel Huntington, *The Clash of Civilizations.* Op. cit., pp. 217–218.

25. Kara Witalis, personal communication, April 2001. Mitch Albom, *Tuesdays with Morrie.* NY: Doubleday, 1997.

26. Benjamin Barber, *Jihad vs. McWorld,* Op. cit., pp. 287ff.

27. Joseph Lelyvld, "All Suicide Bombers Are Not Alike," *New York Times Sunday Magazine,* October 28, 1901, pp. 48, 52–53, 62, p. 53; Charles A. Radin, "Egypt Launches Crackdown on Islamists, Even Moderates," *Boston Globe,* November 24, 2001, p. A12.

28. Warren Hoge, "A Sense of American Unfairness Erodes Support in Gulf States," *New York Times,* October 2, 2001, p. A6.

29. Joseph Lelyveld, "All Sucide Bombers Are Not Alike" Op. cit., pp. 53, 62.

30. Suzanne Daly, "The War on Terror Finds Wary Support in France," New York Times October 4, 2001, p. A3.

31. Ibid., p. A3.

32. Marion Lloyd, "Mexico musters only tepid expressions of support for US," *Boston Globe,* September 30, 2001, p. A25.

33. Niall Ferguson, "2011" *New York Times Sunday Magazine,* December 2, 2001, pp. 76–79, p. 79.

34. Such accusations are catlogued in excruciating detail by the Washington-based journalist William Blum, *Killing Hope* (New York: Common Courage Press, 1995). See also Chomsky, *9–11.* Op. cit.

INDEX

Adel, Wahidullah, 243, 245
Afghanistan:
  rebuilding of, 244, 266
  U.S. military action in, 7, 23, 129,
    185, 232, 243–44, 250
AFL-CIO, 184, 201, 209, 228
Africa, 156, 229
  AIDS in, 123, 278
  terrorism in, 241–42
African Americans, 251–52
  antiglobalization movements and,
    201, 203–4, 229
Agreement on Technical Barriers to
  Trade, 124
agriculture, 90, 151
  antiglobalization movements and,
    209–10, 214–15, 221, 232
  global constitutionalism and, 108,
    115, 118, 122–24
  global democracy and, 133, 136,
    148, 257
  people power and, 188–89, 196
Ahmad, Jalal Al-e, 255
AIDS, 123, 196, 211–12, 278
Alanezi, Saud, 262
Albom, Mitch, 259
American Friends Service Committee,
  280
American Plan, 223
Amnesty International, 163, 276
Annan, Kofi, 162–64, 181
anthrax, 123, 211–12
antiglobalization, antiglobalization
  movements, 3–6, 8, 16, 19, 155–
    57, 199–233
  activism today and, 271–83

business people in, 221–25
in connecting with mainstream of
  public, 217–21
and creation of new politics, 203–4
in Genoa, 12, 92, 106, 125, 136,
  200–202, 213, 216
global democracy and, 136–37,
  200, 205–6, 209–11, 215, 217–
  20, 224–25, 255, 258–59
global economic crisis and, 230–
  33
globalization of, 225–29
global justice and, 200, 205–7,
  214, 217, 220, 230–33
global New Deal and, 156–57
interesting and valuable qualities
  of, 215–17
members of, 200–203
organization of, 206–9
people power and, 185–86
in Quebec, 48–49, 106, 126, 136,
  200–202, 207, 214
in Seattle, 4, 6, 38, 105–7, 114,
  117, 119, 124, 126, 160, 187,
  199–203, 205, 207, 212–13, 219–
  21, 258, 277
sustainability of, 209–12
violence and, 207, 212–15, 221
in Washington, 4, 80, 126, 136,
  200–202, 207
WTO and, 105–7, 199–200, 211,
  214, 217
AOL Time Warner, 70, 124, 255, 260,
  282
Arabia, al, 263
Arab street, 262–64

Argentina, 170–74
  antiglobalization movement in, 12,
    200, 210–11, 214–15
  economic crisis in, 7, 12, 69, 157,
    173, 230
  people power in, 170–71, 173–74
Arizmendi Esquival, Felipe, 264–65
Armstrong, Karen, 245
Arthur Anderson, 180, 183
Asian financial meltdown, 69–70, 86,
    90–91, 102, 149–50
AT&T, 52, 74
ATTAC, 210–11
auto industry, 75

Bangladesh, 273
  antiglobalization movement in, 227–
    28
  global democracy and, 248, 251–
    54
Banna, Hasan al-, 257
Barber, Benjamin, 186–87, 245–46,
    257–60
barbershoppers, 134–39, 191
Bayer, 123, 211–12
Beard, Charles, 108, 121–22, 199
Bechtel, 159
Bello, Walden, 97–98, 228
Bill of Rights, 54, 64, 107, 110, 146,
    179, 281
bin Laden, Osama, 5, 29–30, 193,
    217
  global democracy and, 236, 238,
    241, 243–44, 246, 248–50, 257–
    58, 263, 266
Black Bloc, 213–14, 221
Blair, Tony, 14, 131, 156
Blowback (Johnson), 101–2
Blum, William, 195
Body Shop, 223–24, 282
Boeing, 178, 201
Boston College, 225, 273
Bove, Jose, 12, 257
Brazil, 209, 211–12
Bretton Woods, Bretton Woods
  Institutions, 98, 253, 279

decommissioning of, 146–49, 151–
    52, 164, 166
  global constitutionalism and, 107–
    15
  global democracy and, 146–49
  global New Deal and, 149–54, 156,
    158–59, 164, 166–68
  people power and, 179, 192
Brisard, Jean Charles, 247
British East India Company, 94–95
Brown, Gordon, 156
Buffalo, N.Y., 189
Bush, George H. W., 37, 118, 266,
    268
Bush, George W., 2, 37, 59, 66, 92,
    95, 149, 176, 212, 279
  antiglobalization movements and,
    220, 229–33
  global democracy and, 49, 54, 262,
    264–68
  people power and, 192–95

campaign finance reform, 175, 277
Canada, 123, 125, 211–12, 227
Canedo, Marion, 189
capital, 60
  democracy and, 51–52
  global constitutionalism and, 112–
    14, 116–17
  global democracy and, 133, 137,
    140
  global New Deal and, 149–52,
    158
  in Popeye economics, 84–85
  in umpire system economics,
    101–2
capitalist, capitalism, 93, 148, 178–
    79, 264
  antiglobalization movements and,
    206, 216, 220
Carnegie, Andrew, 44–46, 74, 251
Carrio, Elisa, 173
Cassen, Bernard, 211
Cellucci, Paul, 48–49
Center for Economic and Policy
  Research, 86–87

Chavez Diaz, Oscar, 47
China, 44, 91, 223
Chomsky, Noam, 236, 256–57
Cipro, 123, 211–12, 269
Citigroup, 70, 124
citizens, citizenship, global citizenship:
  antiglobalization movements and, 222–23, 227
  global democracy and, 138–39, 141–43, 240, 251
  global New Deal and, 164–67
  people power and, 179, 187, 190–91
Citizens' Globalism:
  global constitutionalism and, 107, 109–12, 114, 118
  global New Deal and, 166–67
civil rights movement, 203–4, 251–52
Civil War, 51, 53, 63–64, 121–22, 179
Cleveland, Grover, 50
Clinton, Bill, 5, 37, 69, 131, 152, 174, 193
  antiglobalization movements and, 224, 230–31
  global constitutionalism and, 117–18, 120, 124
CNN, 3, 214, 234, 261
Cold War, 15, 102, 112–13, 184, 193–94, 249–50
collective security, 279
  global democracy and, 143, 239–40, 263–69
  people power and, 170, 191–98
colonialism, 5, 24–26, 31–34, 39–41, 81–85, 88, 154
  antiglobalization movements and, 226–27
  collapse of, 128, 193
  comparisons between globalism and, 25, 32, 39, 92–94
  comparisons between umpire system economics and, 82–85, 93–100, 102

core and periphery relationships in, 40–41
cultural myths in, 55–57
empire system of, 82–85, 93–95, 97–99, 111
  global constitutionalism and, 107, 111, 114, 132
  global democracy and, 243, 257, 265
good and bad sides of, 28–29
politics in, 93–95
rip and ship system of, 83–84
sacrificial, 55–56
Coming Anarchy, The (Kaplan), 172
"Coming to a Town Near You," 187
Commander Esther, 3
Committees of Correspondence, 259–60
communications, 29–30, 74
Communism, 113, 191–92, 249–50, 267
community, communities: activism today and, 272–74, 276, 278, 280–83
  antiglobalization movements and, 199, 201–2, 204–5, 207–8, 218, 221–25
  global democracy and, 134–40, 143, 145, 148, 255, 258–61
  global New Deal and, 160, 168–69
  people power and, 170, 177–78, 182, 184–91, 194
competition, 57, 102, 122, 249, 282
  global New Deal and, 153, 158
  people power and, 178–79, 188
"Confession of Faith" (Rhodes), 56
Congress, U.S., 51, 66, 97, 100, 113, 129, 232
  activism today and, 275–76, 279–80
  global New Deal and, 153, 161
Constitution, U.S., 50, 54, 62–64, 105–8, 276–77
  drafting of, 105–6
  First Amendment to, 175, 180
  Fourteenth Amendment to, 64, 180

and relationship between business and government, 63–64

Constitutional Convention, 105–6

constitutionalism, global
constitutionalism, 61, 103–26, 233
Citizens' Globalism and, 107, 109–12, 114, 118
conflict between developed and poor nations in, 109, 114–17, 122
economic integration and, 113–17, 121–22, 125
Gilded Age and, 54, 122, 125
global democracy and, 106–13, 115–16, 118–20, 122, 126, 132–34, 137, 140–41, 146–47, 261
global New Deal and, 159–60, 162, 166, 168
human rights and, 107–11, 115, 119, 121, 132–33
people power and, 171, 173–75, 179–81, 183, 186
property rights and, 107–8, 112, 114, 117–18, 121–22, 125, 133, 146, 166
umpire system economics and, 100–101, 103–4, 107
United Nations and, 107, 109–12, 114–17, 119–20, 132–33
WTO and, 105–8, 110–12, 117–26, 146, 162, 166

Constitutional Moments, 19–20, 33, 105–10, 173
antiglobalization movements and, 215, 219
faces of U.S. constitutionalism in, 107–9
most recent phase of, 106–10, 119, 128, 132
WTO and, 105–6, 108, 110

consumers, consumerism, 5, 10, 15, 57–58, 124, 139, 152
activism today and, 272–73, 281
antiglobalization movements and, 216, 223, 231

democracy and, 78, 134, 242, 253–55, 257–59
people power and, 178, 182, 186, 188

contemporary sovereignty, 164

core and periphery relationships, 40–43

corpocracy, global, 59–62, 66, 78, 104, 172
in umpire system economics, 93–95, 100

Corporation Nation (Derber), 64

corporations, transnational corporations, 5–8, 12–14, 28, 44–45, 59–79
accountability of, 5, 13, 17, 53, 61, 73, 77, 182–83, 190, 222–25, 250, 253–54, 281
activism today and, 271–78, 281–82
antiglobalization movements and, 199–200, 204–5, 215–25, 230–31
changes in governance of, 181–84
contributions made by, 16–17
corpocracy and, 59–61
democracy and, 50–53, 133–34, 136, 141–43, 146, 170, 176–84, 224–25, 241, 244, 246–47, 250–51, 253–55, 258–59, 261–62, 265, 268, 281
dismantling of, 177–78, 261
exit options of, 52–54, 151–52, 253–54
and fortress model of globalization, 129–30
global constitutionalism and, 108, 118–22, 124–26
global markets and, 59, 67–69, 139
global New Deal and, 149–55, 162–63, 165, 167, 169
layoffs by, 6–8, 177, 188, 232
monitoring and disclosure arrangements of, 76–77
partnering of, 73–75, 77

(corporations, transnational
corporations—continued)
people power and, 170–85, 187–
88, 190
in Popeye economics, 89–90
relationship between government
and, 50–54, 60–67, 72, 76, 78–
79, 94–95, 100, 103, 129, 172,
174–76, 179–80, 185, 225
revising charters of, 179–81, 281
sizes of, 60, 70–71
social mission of, 222–23, 225,
251, 253
in umpire system economics, 94–
95, 98, 100–101, 103
uncoupling of, 71–73, 75
cosmopolitans, 190–91
crony capitalism, 176
Crosby, Ernest H., 55–56
cultural values, cultural beliefs, 55–
58, 75, 77
antiglobalization movements and,
220, 258
global democracy and, 140, 144–
45, 236, 245, 255–62
global New Deal and, 159, 165
people power and, 181, 186–88,
190–91, 196
currency trading, 112, 150

Davos, World Economic Forum
meetings in, 136, 163, 209
debt, debt relief, 69, 116
activism today and, 278, 280
antiglobalization movements and,
209, 221
global New Deal and, 154–58
Declaration of the Right to
Development, 195
decommodification, 148, 159–60
Defense Department, U.S., 113, 237
Delaware, 53
democracy, democratization, global
democrats, global democracy, 5,
8–14, 16–17, 20, 48–54, 72, 76–
79, 128–52, 186

activism today and, 273, 277, 279–
83
aims of, 139, 143–44
as alternative to globalization, 128–
31, 137, 139, 141, 143, 146
as antidote for terrorism, 234–69
antiglobalization movements and,
136–37, 200, 205–6, 209–11,
215, 217–20, 224–25, 255, 258–
59
communities and, 134–40, 143,
145, 148, 255, 258–61
corpocracy and, 59–62
decommissioning process required
by, 146–47
definition of, 12–13
economic, 141–42, 177, 225
federalism in, 140, 145, 148
in Gilded Age, 50–54
global constitutionalism and, 106–
13, 115–16, 118–20, 122, 126,
132–34, 137, 140–41, 146–47,
261
global markets and, 68–69, 78–79,
130–31, 135–36, 138–39, 141–
42, 237
global New Deal and, 149–52, 154–
57, 159–61, 164–68
governing agencies of, 144–49
national, see national democracy
participants in, 9–10
people power and, 170–92, 194,
197–98
powerful movements for, 132–35
reinvention of, 140, 143
and relationship between business
and government, 63, 65–66
subsidiarity in, 139–40, 145
transparency, accessibility, and
accountability in, 146–47
in umpire system economics, 84,
94, 103–4
democratic deficit, 161
deregulation, see regulation
deregulation
development, 195, 278

antiglobalization movements and, 211, 229
global democracy, 237, 244
global New Deal and, 151, 155, 157–58
Diaz, Wendy, 44
Disney, 36, 62, 73, 166, 255, 260, 272
domestic content laws, 123
Douglas, William O., 180
Dow Chemical Company, 72
Duhalde, Eduardo, 157

economic integration, 15–16, 19, 28, 35–49, 70, 92, 97
antiglobalization movements and, 211–12, 218, 226, 232–33
as apple pie, 35–48
colonialism and, 33, 39
cores vs. peripheries in, 40–42
democracy and, 53, 140
flawed assumptions about, 38–39
global constitutionalism and, 113–17, 121–22, 125
global New Deal and, 149, 151, 167
new common sense on, 35–36, 39
power in, 42–43
technology and, 31, 36
as win-win, 36–39, 43, 115
Egypt, 41, 127
global democracy and, 242–43, 246, 248–50, 255–57, 262–63
Einstein, Albert, 234
elections, 218
activism today and, 277, 280
democracy and, 141, 237, 247–48
people power and, 173, 175–76, 186
"Emperor Has No Growth, The," 86–87
employment, see labor
Enron, Enron crisis, 6–7, 60, 66, 69–70, 77, 142, 148, 281
antiglobalization movements and, 218, 222, 224, 230–32

offshore bank havens and, 150, 153–54
people power and, 174–76, 179–80, 182–83
environment, environmental rights, 9, 132–34
activism today and, 273–78
antiglobalization movements and, 201–3, 208, 215–16, 218, 221
global constitutionalism and, 117, 120–23, 125
global democracy and, 133–34, 138–39, 146–48
global New Deal and, 149, 151–53, 156, 159, 161–63, 165–66, 168
people power and, 175, 180–81
equality, inequality, 40–41, 81–83, 93
activism today and, 280, 283
global democracy and, 131, 139, 144, 147, 243
global New Deal and, 148, 155–56
in umpire system economics, 82–83
Esquivel Sanchez, Isidro, 47
Ethyl, 125
Euro Brokers/Maxcor Financial Group, 1–2
European Union (EU), 140, 181
global democracy and, 145, 261
global New Deal and, 165, 167–68
export tax-credit system, 97
Exxon Mobil, 60, 70, 75, 247

Fair Labor Association (FLA), 224
Falk, Richard, 164–65
farmers, see agriculture
federalism, 140, 145, 148
feminists, 202–3, 256, 273
antiglobalization movements and, 203, 208
Ferguson, Niall, 265
Fifty Years Is Enough, 278
financial markets, global, 67–71, 76, 141
antiglobalization movements and, 218, 231
deregulation of, 69–70

(financial markets, global—continued)
  global constitutionalism and, 112,
    117, 119
  global New Deal and, 150–51
  intertwining corporations and, 59,
    67–69
  people power and, 171, 177, 188
  umpire system economics and, 85,
    93, 96, 101
financial services, 149–50, 153–54,
    158
  global constitutionalism and, 113,
    117–18, 124
  regulation of, 100, 113
Fisher, Stanley, 150
Flacks, Richard, 20
food safety, 122, 124
Ford, Henry, 255
Ford Motor Company, 52, 60, 255
foreign aid, 155–56, 262
Foreign Sales Corporation tax-credit
  law, 97
Fox, 34, 261
Fox, Vicente, 3, 264–65
France, 109, 167, 218
  antiglobalization movement in, 12,
    210–11
  global democracy and, 257, 259,
    263–64
Free the Children (FTC), 20–21
free trade, see economic integration
Frick, Henry Clay, 44–45
Friedman, Thomas, 9, 14–15, 193–94
  global democracy and, 248–49
  on global financial markets, 68–69
  on globalization-as-technology, 29–
    30
  on umpire system economics, 85–86
Fuentes, Carlos, 264
Fuji Bank, 1–2, 75
Fuller, Graham, 256

Gap, 52, 186, 251, 253
Gates, Bill, 23, 95, 119
General Agreement on Tariffs and
  Trade (GATT), 98

  global constitutionalism and, 108,
    113, 118
  global New Deal and, 149–50
  Uruguay Round of, 118, 148
General Electric (GE), 60, 72–73, 75,
    201, 261
General Motors (GM), 51–52, 60, 70,
    75, 95, 177
General System of Preferences (GSP),
    115
generic drugs, 123, 211–12
Genoa, antiglobalization protests in,
    12, 92, 106, 125, 136, 200–202,
    213, 216
Germany, 167, 182–83, 267
Ghanoushi, Shiek, 256
Gilded Age, 24–29, 31–34, 43–48,
    57, 74
  constitutionalism and, 54, 122,
    125
  democracy in, 50–54
  gap between rich and poor in, 47–
    48
  good and bad sides of, 28–29
  labor in, 27–28, 43–46
  muckrakers of, 43–44
  see also robber barons
Global Exchange, 223, 279
globalization, global business:
  basic principles of, 2, 139
  as closed affair, 136
  as collective dictatorship, 81–82
  contradictions of, 18, 99
  creation of, 15
  crisis in, 3, 59–60, 185
  dangers of, 24, 104
  definition of, 15–18
  early successes of, 19–20
  emerging rules of, 18
  as end of ideology, 215
  fortress model of, 10, 128–30,
    254
  future of, 5
  history of, 24–34, 39–42, 49–50,
    54–55, 57, 98, 127–28
  instability of, 90–91

legitimacy of, 62
mystique of, 10–11, 63, 65–66, 81, 136, 200, 237, 272
as neocolonialism, 81
public opinion on, 218–19
as race to the bottom, 4–5, 52–54, 149, 177, 260
reinventions of, 19, 21, 25, 127–28, 131, 135–37, 139–40
romance of, 30
statistics on, 86–88
threats to, 1–2, 6
uniqueness of, 29
as work in progress, 77
globalizing projects, 39–42, 51
core and periphery relationships in, 41–42
Global People's Assembly (GPA), 164–66
global warming, 140, 203
activism today and, 275, 277
Kyoto accords on, 152, 163, 194–95, 224, 266, 275
Gorbachev, Mikhail, 131
Gore, Al, 265
Gould, Jay, 31, 50
government, governments, 59–68, 128–31
activism today and, 273, 276–77
antiglobalization movements and, 208, 215, 217, 224–25, 229–33
business elites and, 76–77
corpocracy and, 60–62
democracy and, 51–54, 63, 65–66, 130–31, 133–34, 137–38, 140, 142–48, 235, 237–40, 246–47, 252–53, 255, 259–61
global constitutionalism and, 107, 112, 116, 119, 121–26
global New Deal and, 152, 157, 159–62, 164–65, 168
people power and, 170–76, 178–80, 183, 185–86, 189–90, 193, 197
reinvention of, 174–75

relationship between business and, 50–54, 60–67, 72, 76, 78–79, 94–95, 100, 103, 129, 172, 174–76, 179–80, 185, 225
in umpire system economics, 83, 94, 97, 100–103
Granny D., 277
Great Britain, 40, 69, 82, 98, 116, 156, 197, 265
colonialism of, 26, 32–33
global constitutionalism and, 107, 109, 122
Great Depression, 131, 151, 156, 184, 243–44
Greenpeace, 163, 275
Greenspan, Alan, 70
Greider, William, 150, 152–53
Grossman, Richard, 179
Group of 77, 25, 81, 115–17
Gulf War, 103, 268

Hammoud, Sheik, 30
Hanna, Mark, 50
Harkin, Tom, 37
Hartmann, Thom, 179–80
Henderson, Hazel, 159
high-tech markets, 157, 188
history, making life vs. making, 20
Hoffman, Abbie, 35
Home Depot, 185, 221
Homestead Steel strike, 44–45, 251
Hope for Africa, 229
hormone-treated beef, 122, 124
human rights, 9, 77, 104
activism today and, 276–77, 280
antiglobalization movements and, 206, 208, 218, 220, 223–24, 227–28
democracy and, 54, 133–34, 140, 142, 144–48
global constitutionalism and, 107–11, 115, 119, 121, 132–33
global New Deal and, 149, 153, 159, 165–69
people power and, 181, 195–96

(human rights—continued)
   and treatment of workers, 44, 46–47
Hunter, Shireen, 245, 256
Huntington, Samuel, 58, 257–59

identity politics, 204–5
India, 123, 238, 249
inequality, see equality, inequality
Intel, 178
intellectual property rights, 137, 166, 196
   antiglobalization movements and, 211–12
   global constitutionalism and, 118, 122–23
International Chamber of Commerce, 77
International Criminal Court, 163, 195, 266–68, 276
International Forum on Globalization (IFG), 157–58, 228
international law, 18, 66, 104
   global constitutionalism and, 120, 146
   global democracy and, 146, 239–40, 259–60, 267
   global New Deal and, 149, 166
   people power and, 193–94
   in umpire system economics, 93, 97
International Monetary Fund (IMF), 4, 7, 11–12, 59, 69, 76, 80–81, 86, 90, 145–52
   activism today and, 274, 276, 278–79
   antiglobalization movements and, 199–200, 211, 217, 219, 229
   decommissioning of, 146–49, 157–58
   global constitutionalism and, 107–8, 110–12, 114–17, 119–20, 122, 162
   global democracy and, 146–49, 237, 241–43, 265
   global New Deal and, 149–52, 154, 156–63, 166

people power and, 171, 174, 179, 188–89, 196–97
   powers of, 119–20
   Structural Adjustment Programs of, 242–43
   targeted by Third World nations, 116–17
   in umpire system economics, 93, 96, 98–99, 102
International Trade Organization (ITO), 108, 113
Internet, 97, 159, 185, 260
   activism today and, 272, 278–81
   antiglobalization movements and, 206, 208, 210, 226–27
   and globalization-as-technology, 29–31
Interstate Commerce Commission, 64
investment, investors, 5–6, 19, 25, 37, 43, 130, 271
   antiglobalization movements and, 218, 231–32
   democracy and, 51, 78, 138, 142
   global constitutionalism and, 108, 114, 118–19, 124–25
   global financial markets and, 67–69
   global New Deal and, 149–51, 154, 161–62, 167
   people power and, 172, 175, 177–78, 180–83
   in Popeye economics, 84–85, 88–90, 92
   in umpire system economics, 95–96
Islam, 26, 30, 58, 193, 203, 220
   global democracy and, 236–38, 241, 244–51, 253–60, 262–63
Israel, 235–36, 238, 256, 262–63, 266

Jackson, Jesse, Jr., 229
Japan, 113–14, 116, 121
Jazeera, Al, 261
Jefferson, Thomas, 13, 54, 199, 276
   Constitutional Moments and, 107–9, 121, 126

Johnson, Chalmers, 101–2
Johnson, Lyndon, 222
Jubilee South, 154
Jubilee 2000, 278
Jungle, The (Sinclair), 43–44
justice, global justice, global justice
    movements, 4, 8, 16, 29, 89, 128
    activism today and, 275, 277, 282
    antiglobalization movements and,
        200, 205–7, 214, 217, 220, 230–
        33
    author's role in, 18–19
    global constitutionalism and, 112,
        132–33
    global democracy and, 130–32,
        235, 255, 259
    global New Deal and, 160, 168
    people power and, 183, 187–88,
        195

Kahn, Abdurahman, 241
Kaplan, Robert, 172
Karimov, Islam, 250
Kashmir, 238
Kennedy, Paul, 197
Kernaghan, Charles, 44
Keynes, John Maynard:
    global constitutionalism and, 112–
        14
    global New Deal and, 151, 158
Khan, Aimel, 243–44
Kielburger, Craig, 20–21
Kipling, Rudyard, 26, 55, 265
Kirkpatrick, Jeane, 195
Kolko, Gabriel, 63
Korten, David, 177–78
Krugman, Paul, 37, 157
Kuwait, 262
Kyoto accords, 152, 163, 194–95,
    224, 266, 275

labor, 4, 6, 8–9, 23–25, 50–52, 64,
    73, 85, 110–13, 130–33
    activism today and, 271–76, 278,
        280–83
    antiglobalization movements and,

        200–204, 206, 208–11, 214–15,
        217–19, 221, 223–33
    business elites and, 76–77
    in core and periphery relationships,
        41–42
    democracy and, 13–14, 51–52,
        131, 133, 136, 138, 140–44, 146–
        48, 240, 248, 250–54
    economic integration and, 36–37
    FTC on, 20–21
    in Gilded Age, 27–28, 43–46
    global constitutionalism and, 108,
        110, 112–13, 117–19, 121, 123,
        125, 132–33
    global markets and, 67, 139
    global New Deal and, 149–53, 157–
        58, 162, 165–69
    people power and, 173–78, 180–
        85, 187–90, 195
    in Popeye economics, 90–91
    working conditions for, 14, 24, 27,
        36, 43–48, 153, 251, 254, 275
    see also sweatshop abolition
        movement
Lease, Mary Elizabeth, 50
Lederer, William, 245
Leforestier, Alain, 263–64
Lerner, Max, 108–9
Levi Strauss, 177, 223
Lexus and the Olive Tree, The
    (Friedman), 85–86
Lieberman, Joseph, 66
living standards, 86, 110, 168
    in core and periphery relationships,
        41–42
localists, localism:
    activism today and, 273–76, 280–
        81
    antiglobalization movements and,
        205–6, 220–22, 258
    global democracy and, 134–41,
        145, 255–56, 258–62
    global New Deal and, 160, 168–
        69
    people power and, 170, 174, 177–
        78, 184–91

(localists, localism—continued)
  see also community, communities
Locke, John, 108, 110, 121–25

Maastricht Treaty, 165
Macapagal Arroyo, Gloria, 240–41
McCormick, Richard, 100, 152
McDonald's, 73, 272
  antiglobalization movements and,
    12, 210, 212
  global democracy and, 256–57,
    264
  people power and, 186, 188, 191
McDonnell Douglas, 191
McKinley, William, 50
McKinnon, Cynthia, 153
Makokoba M'kambo market, 32
Marcuse, Herbert, 216
Marianne, 264
markets, global markets, 117, 139,
  159, 274
  antiglobalization movements and,
    205–6, 210–11, 215, 230–33
  democracy and, 68–69, 78–79, 130–
    31, 135–36, 138–39, 141–42, 237
  financial, see financial markets,
    global
  people power and, 171, 174, 179,
    185, 191
  2002 crisis in, 130–31
Marshall, John, 108–10, 121–22
Marshall Plan, 113, 156
Massachusetts Bay Company, 94
Maugham, Somerset, 80
Mbanefo, Arthur, 25, 81
Mbecki, Thabo, 25, 81, 242
media:
  activism today and, 281–82
  global democracy and, 260–61
Mernissi, Fatima, 256
Mesopotamia, 40, 127
Mexico, 7
  antiglobalization movement in,
    3–4
  global democracy and, 138, 264–
    65

labor in, 46–47, 184
Microsoft, 23, 47, 70, 73, 75, 77, 95,
  119, 124, 178, 281
middle classes, 72
  global democracy and, 13, 130
  people power and, 171, 173
Middle East, 235–39, 241–43, 245–
  49, 251, 255–56, 258, 262–63,
  266
military, military power, militarism,
  59, 62, 66
  activism today and, 277, 279
  antiglobalization movements and,
    230, 232
  in fortress model of globalization,
    128–29
  global constitutionalism and, 107,
    112–13, 119, 132
  global democracy and, 235–37,
    240–41, 243, 247–49, 256, 262–
    68
  people power and, 191–94, 196–97
  in umpire system economics, 82,
    93–94, 101–3
Millennium NGO Forum, 164–65
Mitsubishi, 70, 75
Mohan, Raja, 249
Monsanto, 123
Morgan, J. P., 54, 74, 100
Multilateral Agreement on Investment
  (MAI), 161–62
Murdoch, Rupert, 34, 59, 257
Murrow, Edward R., 170
Musa, Said, 81

Nader, Ralph, 53, 179, 273–74
National Conference of State
  Legislatures, 125
national democracy:
  as antidote for terrorism, 245–50
  people power and, 170–76
National Labor Committee, 275
National League of Cities, 125
Netanyahu, Bibi, 235–36
new common sense, 35–36, 39, 85
New Deal, 77, 112, 131, 148

New Deal, global, 144, 148–69, 243
  decommodification in, 148, 159–60
  human rights and, 149, 153, 159,
    165–69
  participation in, 148, 160–66
  redistribution in, 148, 154–59
  regulation in, 148–54
new economy boom, 6
New International Economic Order
  (NEIO), 115–17
New Jersey, 52
News Corp., 34, 75, 255, 260, 282
new social movements, 204–5
New York City, 137, 155, 202
New York Times, 3, 37, 47, 55, 92,
  117, 157, 216, 243
Nike, 46, 62, 76–77, 166, 176
  activism today and, 272–73, 281
  antiglobalization movements and,
    212, 226
  global democracy and, 251, 253–
    55
Nixon, Richard, 193, 230
nongovernment organizations
  (NGOs):
  antiglobalization movements and,
    223–24
  global New Deal and, 163–65
nontariff barriers, 123
North American Free Trade
  Agreement (NAFTA), 124–25,
  168, 175, 180
Northeast Labor Committee for
  Global Justice, 187, 189
Nye, Joseph, 192

offshore bank havens, 150, 153–54,
  158
oil, 62, 71, 74–75, 84, 103, 193,
  217
  global constitutionalism and, 113–
    14, 120
  global democracy and, 49, 243,
    246–47, 250
One-Dimensional Man (Marcuse),
  216

Oslo ban on landmines, 163
Oxfam International, 37, 163, 278

Paine, Tom, 170
Pakistan, 238, 242–44, 248–50, 254,
  263
Palestinians, 235–36, 238, 241, 262,
  266
participation, 148, 160–66
Patriots bill, 129
Pennsylvania, 180
people power, 170–98
  collective security and, 170, 191–
    98
  democratizing global business and,
    170, 176–84
  national democracy and, 170–76
  reviving local democratic
    communities and, 170, 184–91
people's Davos, 136–37, 155, 209
personal authenticity, 216
pharmaceuticals, pharmaceutical
  companies, 122–23, 196, 211–12
Philip Morris, 60, 281
Popeye economics, 84–85, 88–92,
  104
  reason for failure of, 89–91
Pôrto Alegre, antiglobalization
  protests in, 136–37, 155, 209
positive rights, 107, 110–13, 120,
  122
postmodernism, 204, 206
poverty, 24–26, 37, 40, 42, 57–59,
  72, 81, 129–32
  activism today and, 272, 277–80,
    283
  antiglobalization movements and,
    203, 206, 215, 217, 219–20, 225–
    27, 229, 232
  and cultural beliefs and values, 57–
    58
  and gap between rich and poor, 5,
    10, 13, 47–48, 78, 87–88, 92–93,
    131, 154, 158, 237, 243, 280
  global constitutionalism and, 113,
    115, 133

(poverty—continued)
global democracy and, 13, 130–32, 141–42, 146, 235–37, 240–45, 248–49
global New Deal and, 148, 154–60
people power and, 171, 174, 176–77, 188, 190
Powell, Colin, 13–14, 240, 266, 268
power, 9, 11–12, 15, 18, 34, 45, 59–63, 73–74, 129–31, 273
antiglobalization movements and, 200, 202, 204, 206, 209–11, 218, 221–24, 227
of business elites, 76–77
democracy and, 51–53, 78, 130–31, 138, 140–42, 144–45, 235, 238, 240, 246, 252–53, 255–56, 258, 260, 262–65, 267–68
in economic integration, 42–43
global constitutionalism and, 106–8, 111–13, 115–22, 126
global markets and, 68, 78, 139
global New Deal and, 150–52, 154–55, 159, 161–65, 167, 169
and relationship between business and government, 60–63, 65, 67
in umpire system economics, 82–83, 93–97, 99–104
see also people power
Prebisch, Raul, 115
privatization, 118
antiglobalization movements and, 211–12, 224
global New Deal and, 159–60
people power and, 187, 189
Progressive Era, 48, 63, 77, 100, 148
property rights, 3–4
antiglobalization movements and, 206, 211
global constitutionalism and, 107–8, 112, 114, 117–18, 121–22, 125, 133, 146, 166
global democracy and, 146–47
global New Deal and, 149, 152, 166
intellectual, see intellectual property rights

protectionism, 18, 196
antiglobalization movements and, 228–29, 232–33
global constitutionalism and, 121–22
global New Deal and, 151, 153
Public Citizen, 279
Putnam, Robert, 186–87

Quebec:
antiglobalization protests in, 48–49, 106, 126, 136, 200–202, 207, 214
International Forum on Globalization teach-ins in, 228

Reagan, Ronald, 37, 157, 204, 230, 232
global constitutionalism and, 118, 125
"Real 'White Man's Burden,' The" (Crosby), 55–56
recessions, global recessions, 6–8, 11, 128, 130–31
antiglobalization movements and, 206, 217, 229–33
global democracy and, 131, 142, 254–55
global New Deal and, 148–49, 156–57
people power and, 184, 188
redistribution, 148, 154–59
Reebok, 76–77
regionalism, 142, 145, 261
regulation, deregulation, 64, 118, 261
antiglobalization movements and, 218, 225, 232
of financial markets, 69–70
of financial services, 100, 113
in global New Deal, 148–54
relative deprivation, 242–43
Renaissance Mediterranean economy, 40–41, 127
Revolutionary War, 108, 121–22, 260
Rhodes, Cecil, 26, 32–34, 40, 56–57

Ricardo, David, 38–39
Rice, Condoleeza, 192, 194
robber barons, 26–28, 31, 44–45, 48–54, 57, 77, 98, 148, 223, 250–51
people power and, 175, 179
and relationship between business and government, 63–64
Rockefeller, John D., 26, 33, 48, 54, 57, 74, 223
Roddick, Anita, 224, 282
Roman Empire, 40, 43, 127, 197
Roosevelt, Franklin D., 112–13, 132–33, 157, 243
Rosenbaum, Ruth, 47
Royal Dutch/Shell, 60, 70, 75, 172, 177
Rubin, Robert, 117
Russian Federation, 65, 266

Sachs, Jeffrey, 47, 116, 149–50, 156
Sadat, Anwar, 246
St. Simon's Island meeting, 166, 168
Sangano Munhumatapa, 32
Sanger, David, 92
Sanitary and Phytosanitary Standards Agreement (SPS), 124
Santa Clara Act, 64
Saudi Arabia, 243, 246–47, 250, 256–57, 263
Savio, Mario, 216
Schwartz, Morrie, 259
scientific management, 45
Scott, Bruce, 87
Seattle, Wash.:
antiglobalization protests in, 4, 6, 38, 105–7, 114, 117, 119, 124, 126, 160, 187, 199–203, 205, 207, 212–13, 219–21, 258, 277
International Forum on Globalization teach-ins in, 228
Serra, José, 211
service industries, 148, 151
global constitutionalism and, 118, 122, 124
see also financial services
Sharon, Ariel, 235–36

Shaw, George Bernard, 1, 23, 59
Shelbaya, Omar, 262
shrimps, 124
Siemens, 70, 75
Sierra Club, 201, 209, 275
Sinclair, Upton, 43–44
Sklair, Leslie, 72
Smith, Adam, 38
Social Charter and Generalized System of Preferences, 167–68
social Darwinism, 57–58
social services, social welfare services:
antiglobalization movements and, 211, 218–19, 224, 229–30
global constitutionalism and, 107, 111–13, 116, 133
global democracy and, 131, 248
global New Deal and, 151, 158–59
people power and, 171, 177, 183, 188–89, 195, 197
socioeconomic rights, 107, 110–13, 120, 122
Socrates, 127
Sony, 34, 51, 70, 177
Soros, George, 149–50
South Africa, 26, 81, 211–12
South-South Summit Declaration, 154
Soviet Union, 267
collapse of, 102, 193
containment policy on, 112–13
speculation, 150, 158, 221
stakeholder laws, 182
Standard Oil, 50, 52
Stiglitz, Joseph, 149–50, 156
stock market bubble, 188, 231
Strauss, Andrew, 164–65
Subcomandante Marcos, 4
subsidiarity, 139–40, 145
Sultan, Gamal, 262
Supreme Court, U.S., 51, 64, 108, 189
sweatshop abolition movement, 21, 166, 168, 184
activism today and, 272–73, 275, 278

(sweatshop abolition movement—
continued)
antiglobalization movements and,
200, 214–15, 224–28
Sweeney, John, 184, 201, 228

Taliban, 241, 243–44, 248, 250, 266
taxes, 63–64, 97
antiglobalization movements and,
210, 221, 230, 232
global New Deal and, 150, 153–55
people power and, 175–76, 178
technology, 41, 51, 123
associating globalization with, 29–
33
economic integration and, 31, 36
telecommunications, 74
terrorists, terrorism, 5–8, 10–11, 23,
54
activism today and, 276, 279
antiglobalization movements and,
203, 208–9, 211–14, 217, 220,
222–25, 230–32
causes of, 240–44, 256
difficulty in defining of, 238–39
and fortress model of globalization,
129–30
global democracy and, 131–32,
142, 234–69
and globalization-as-technology,
29–30
global New Deal and, 148–49, 156–
57
people power and, 190–94, 196–97
on September 11, 2001, 1–3, 5–7,
13, 17–18, 25–26, 28–29, 37, 49,
58, 61–62, 67, 128–31, 148–49,
156–57, 191–92, 196–97, 199–
200, 208–9, 211–13, 217, 220,
225, 227, 230–31, 234–35, 239,
241–42, 256, 260–64, 266, 268,
276, 279
U.S. war on, 6–7, 13–14, 103, 129–
31, 192, 231, 235, 239, 263,
265, 267–68
Texaco, 75, 247

Thoreau, Henry David, 143
Tobin tax, 210
Tocqueville, Alexis de, 138–39, 186
town meetings, 142, 184–85
Toyota, 34, 60, 75
trade, 4–7, 16, 31, 33, 68–69, 73,
81, 130
activism today and, 273–74, 280
antiglobalization movements and,
208, 217, 229
global constitutionalism and, 107–
8, 112, 114–15, 118–20, 123–25
global democracy and, 146–48
global New Deal and, 149, 151–53,
155–58, 160–61, 167
people power and, 188, 196
in Popeye economics, 90–92
protectionism and, see
protectionism
in umpire system economics, 96–
100
see also economic integration
Trade-Related Intellectual Property
Agreement (TRIPS), 122–23
Treasury, U.S., 113, 119
Tuesdays with Morrie (Albom), 259
Turner, Ted, 34

umpire system economics, 82–88, 93–
104
baseball analogy on, 82–83, 95–96,
101
comparisons between colonialism
and, 82–85, 93–100, 102
economic slowdown under, 86–87
global constitutionalism and, 100–
101, 103–4, 107
goals of U.S. in, 99–104
politics in, 93–96, 99–103
Popeye economics and, 84–85, 88
special role of U.S. in, 18, 82–83,
107, 193, 197
uncoupling, 71–73, 75
Unilever, 73
United for a Fair Economy (UFE),
280

United Nations, 7, 20, 87, 94
activism today and, 276, 279
Charter of, 159–60, 194
Commission on Human Rights of, 195
Conference on Trade and Development (UNCTAD) of, 114–17, 145–48, 153
Framework Convention on Climate Control of, 163
and gap between rich and poor, 47–48
General Assembly of, 111, 159, 164–65, 195–96
Global Compact of, 181
global constitutionalism and, 107, 109–12, 114–17, 119–20, 132–33
global democracy and, 132–39, 142, 144–49, 194, 239–40, 242, 244, 252, 260, 265–68
global New Deal and, 152–53, 155–60, 162–68
International Insolvency Court for, 157–58
International Labor Organization (ILO) of, 45, 111, 145, 147, 152–53, 166–68, 252
people power and, 179, 181, 193, 194–96, 198
popular participation in, 162–66
powers of, 111, 120
relations between global business and, 162–63, 165, 181
Security Council of, 111, 120, 162, 164, 195, 240, 266, 268
United States:
expansionism of, 264–65
unilateralism of, 192–93, 196–98, 264, 266–68, 279
United States Council for International Business, 100, 152, 162
Universal Declaration of Human Rights, 181, 195
global constitutionalism and, 107, 110–11

global democracy and, 132–33, 146, 252
global New Deal and, 159, 166
Uzbekistan, 250

Vaughan, Diane, 71–72
Vietnam War, 80, 202–4, 222
Vinson, Carl, 113
violence, 40, 42, 47, 60, 67, 80, 82
antiglobalization movements and, 207, 212–15, 221
and fortress model of globalization, 129–30
global democracy and, 132, 135, 234–69
global New Deal and, 149, 156
people power and, 190–91, 193
see also terrorists, terrorism
Voltaire, 35

Wachtel, Howard, 160
Wahabbism, 247
Wallerstein, Immanuel, 39
Wall Street Journal, 256–57
Wal-Mart, 7, 37, 44, 60, 169, 226
global democracy and, 251, 253, 255
people power and, 178, 185, 188
Washington, D.C.:
antiglobalization protests in, 4, 80, 126, 136, 200–202, 207
September 11, 2001 terrorist attack in, 227
Washington Consensus, 36–37
wealth, 92–94, 126, 197
activism today and, 276–80
in core and periphery relationships, 41–42
democracy and, 13, 78, 131, 133, 141, 237, 241–44, 246, 256, 265
and gap between rich and poor, 5, 10, 13, 47–48, 78, 87–88, 92–93, 131, 154, 158, 237, 243, 280
of global corporations, 70–71

(wealth—continued)
   global New Deal and, 154–59
   and intertwining global financial
      markets and corporations, 67–68
Welch, Jack, 72–73, 261
westoxication, 255
White, Harry Dexter, 112–13
"White Man's Burden, The" (Kipling),
   55
Wilding of America, The (Derber),
   234
Worker Rights Authority (WRA), 167
World Bank, 4, 20, 59, 80–81, 145–
   49
   activism today and, 278–79
   antiglobalization movements and,
      200, 211
   decommissioning of, 146–49, 157–
      58
   on economic growth, 86–88
   global constitutionalism and, 107–
      8, 111–12, 114, 116, 120, 162
   global democracy and, 142, 146–
      49
   global New Deal and, 151–52, 155,
      157–59, 162, 166
   people power and, 179, 189
   in umpire system economics, 93,
      96, 99
WorldCom, 66, 183
World Economic Forum, 13–14, 136–
   37, 163, 209, 240–41
World Social Forum, 209
world system theorists, 39

World Trade Center, September 11,
   2001 terrorist attack on, 1–3, 5,
   17–18, 59, 67, 71, 148–49, 193,
   227, 231, 234–36, 256, 263,
   266, 268
World Trade Organization (WTO), 3–
   4, 11, 15, 54, 59, 62, 69, 90,
   132, 145–52
   activism today and, 274, 276, 278–
      79
   antiglobalization movements and,
      105–7, 199–200, 211, 214, 217
   Constitutional Moments and, 105–
      6, 108, 110
   creation of, 117–19
   decommissioning of, 146–50, 157
   global constitutionalism and, 105–8,
      110–12, 117–26, 146, 162, 166
   global democracy and, 146–49,
      260–61
   global New Deal and, 149–52, 154,
      157–63, 166–67
   judicial tribunals of, 125, 160–62
   Lockean vision of, 121–25
   mission of, 118–19, 122
   participation crisis in, 160–62
   people power and, 174–75, 179–
      80, 189–90, 196–97
   powers of, 119–21
   in umpire system economics, 93–
      94, 96–99, 104

Zapatistas, 3–4, 135, 200
Zimbabwe, 26, 32